@BLK_PEEPSTOP

PREFACE:

One night, Nov 9, 2012 4:00 AM, while expunging excrement from my body after having eaten a whole bag of Chips AHoy chocolate chip cookies and four bowls of Honey Nut Cheerios, all with milk, while also high on an Ice Coffee (I usually do not drink coffee) I had purchased earlier from "The Pantry" on Decatur and Lewis Ave in Brooklyn, NY after my two mile run around the Bedford Stuyvesant block of Decatur and Chauncey Street between Lewis and Stuyvesant Avenues; I was reading a book, "Men Women and Children" by Chad Kultgen. I thought the book to be true to average American middle class White life; it was a dramedy and I was enjoying the read. It hit me – that while I already had a book in production which would take me years to finish, and just after hearing that I would make a good writer from my girlfriend I'd been involved with for 11 years (currently my fiancé as of this writing in 2013; 2015 we broke-up) through an emotional tumultuous relationship which had not culminated into marriage just yet - a project which I thought I could finish very quickly as a book and maybe even a series of books came to mind.

I had been searching for a new employment position and dealing with covert (so they thought) discrimination of recruiting agencies as well as from individual company HR recruiters who all would call me at this time due to a great background and resume, but the moment they heard my voice - which

- 1 -

I was not doing my job to disguise it to sound like Brian Gumble, defunct of any natural bass and/or Black inflections in speech – and heard that I was a Black American man, it seems they quickly lost interest in speaking with me regarding Accounting Manager positions paying $85,000 - $110,000 even though I had 10 solid years of work experience, 5 at the last company I was employed. I had recently passed my Certified Public Accountant (CPA) examination, which I thought would boost my credentials as a job candidate, but recruiters and companies all seemed to have no interest in finding me positions or hiring me.

A deep enmity for Corporate/White America and in tandem Black America began to brew inside me. I began to despise my own race of people because I thought, due to their ignorant ethos, cultural shibboleths and ways of living, it was reflecting badly on me in the eyes of recruiting agencies and employers who took the chance to invite me in for a personal interview, but I was not receiving any offers. On this night in October is when I came up with the Twitter name @BLK_PEEPSTOP (since then deleted) to expunge all of my thoughts about things Black American people do, don't do, say, don't say, think and don't think which are either beneficial or detrimental to Black American people's survival on American soil.

- 2 -

MICHAEL IRVIN WALKER

For it seemed to me White Americans and Corporate America had and have been discriminating against Black Americans blatantly in the early 60s and 70s and covertly during the 80s, 90s, 2000s and beyond; you'd think we'd get it by now and wean ourselves off of their placating, assuaging and coddling us, to become our own independent society who covertly (just as they do us) does not deal with or need them to survive. This charge was further exacerbated on Sun Nov 4, 2012 when I got my hands on a book called "Jerusalem 1913", a story of how Zionist Russian and German Jews infiltrated Palestine in the early 1900s and took over the land to brew the boiling pot that cooks to this very day of Arabs having been pushed out of Jerusalem, fighting and bombing Israelites.

As I began to read my tweets, I thought that while some needed no further explanation, many others were not inexplicable and needed further analysis. So, I started to write a book of my interpretations of the tweets. At the start of this book, there were 494 tweets directed at Black American people to infuriate them, educate them and hopefully get some discourse going of how we can become a better people. A few people started following me on twitter, but I quickly blocked them because I did not want any people of any kind, any organization following me; eventually, I came to the conclusion, I DID NOT WANT ANYONE FOLLOWING THIS TWITTER PAGE.

I addressed most of my tweets starting with: #blackpeople, hoping that would reach a number of them out in the tweet-o-sphere, but that did not seem to be doing anything. I wondered if my tweets were getting blocked because they were too political or of a strong seditious nature. The first few days the tweets came to mind in rapid succession but quickly began to slow down. I surmised in my mind I was not doing this for followers, but to get this info out of my head and consciousness as I was talking to myself rather constantly on these particular issues because one cannot readily verbalize these type of phrases or thoughts to Black American people without them getting very defensive or upset: as I tried many of times to disseminate some of these thoughts on my girlfriend and got into fervent discussions, she called them arguments, which left her uneasy and losing sleep.

My point to this whole project is that Black American people do not speak of such ills. We sit silent while everything goes wrong in our culture, and we are used and abused by White American people of all backgrounds: Italians, Irish, Jewish, WASP, Germans, Russians, etc. Everyone seems scared to address particular issues. But these are things I've reasoned with myself that need to be said directly to Black American people by Black American people.

There is a dichotomy of feeling in my writing, I'm a little jarred when other races of people talk about Black American people in this context, but

MICHAEL IRVIN WALKER

when I speak on them myself, it seems I harbor many of the same ill feelings. I think the difference is, I'm expressing these feelings hoping they will be erased and get better, or as I recently read in The Gene Keys by Richard Rudd; "these people want their entire community to thrive in order that they can draw more and more people up the hierarchy away from the self-destructive patterns of the lower frequencies." When other people of other races express these feelings, my thought is they are laughing at us with no hope that things will get better.

My layout will be simple. I will post the tweet as written on twitter. I will then proceed to explain and articulate, as to what caused the thought behind the tweet and expound upon my direct reasoning and interpretation since twitter does not allow you to do such with just 140 characters.

CONCLUSION

On December 5, 2013, the death date of Nelson Mandela or rather a week or so afterwards; hearing of his valor and valiant willingness to forgive, forget and move on past the ills and injustice the nation of South Africa had brought upon him and Black African people during apartheid; reading excerpts from Bill Clinton's book "My Life" in conversations with Mandela, Bill Clinton: "I know you did a great thing in inviting your jailers to your inauguration, but didn't you really hate those who imprisoned you? Mandela: "Of course I did for many years. They took the best years of my life. They abused me physically and mentally. I didn't get to see my children grow up. I hated them. Then one day I realized that they had already taken everything from me except my mind and my heart. Those they could not take without my permission. I decided not to give them away." Bill Clinton: "When you were walking out of prison for the last time, didn't you feel the hatred rise up in you again?" Mandela: "Yes, for a moment I did. Then I thought to myself, they have had me for twenty-seven years. If I keep hating them, they will still have me. I wanted to be free, and so I let it go.". Upon reflecting upon Mandela, I once again equivocated regarding the meaning and importance of this book, and decided THIS BOOK IS VERY NECESSARY! With the senseless murders of Black American males Mike Brown in

MICHAEL IRVIN WALKER

Furguson Missouri and Eric Garner in Staten
Island, NY, and many more that have taken place
since then; everyone, both Black and White
Americans needs a social and moral
readjustment.

Even still with the above caveat, most of the
book is unjustified complaining about things that
with hard work and time can be overcome; more
importantly it revealed an inner lethargy and lack
of will and courage to fulfill my own personal
greatest ambitions throughout my lifetime.

My charge for example, that many Black
American celebrities do not use Black American
lawyers for their legal representation is baseless.
Nina Shaw is a very prominent Black American
attorney who has represented or currently
represents many Black American super
celebrities in Hollywood in contract negotiations
and protection of intellectual property rights. She
still has the omnipresent Jewish American partner
and many other partners who are not Black
American; maybe there aren't enough Black
Americans who practice entertainment law well
and/or that wish to practice in the great sunshine
state of California. Or, maybe like Mandela, she is
forgiving, forgetting and bucking the system
coming out on top, bringing in most of the Black
American talent and power base to her partners
who also contribute with their own client base.
Maybe someday, Nina will break off and take all of
her Black American super clients with her,

proselytize young Black American entertainment lawyers, bring them under her wing and together monopolize the entire Black American Hollywood acting client pool, just as it seems Jewish Americans monopolized New York Broadway musical writing, Hollywood studio production and the media/advertising industry.

My criticism of Black American people is a solipsistic lack of empathy, at best, of a people who have, willingly or subconsciously allowed ourselves to be swooped up within a system and made moribund through philistine consumerism, racial rejection and government coddling which has acerbated our slothful condition of "trying just a little or not at all" to educate and uplift ourselves into a healthy, spiritually, socially and economically better state of being. Reading Malcolm Gladwell's "Outliers" I also gained an educational perspective as to the social and economic ills which are so pervasive within the Black American community; my conclusion is this:

1. I'm Black

2. I'm dark skinned Black

3. Since arriving in this land Black people were slaves and have been discriminated against in every facet of life.

MICHAEL IRVIN WALKER

4. Once we were freed from slavery, we didn't have valuable skills to transfer to a profitable living (such as the Jews who were merchants, garment factory workers, etc).
Even if we did, White American people discriminated and broke us down to rape and offal (i.e. Black Wall Street).

5. Even when we ran our own towns with some dignity and respect on a political and economic front, White American men often came in and destroyed them for fun or for recrimination of a false and egregious charge of a Black boy/man smiling (Emmet Till) at or raping a White American woman.

6. Even if the towns survived through intimidation and destruction, once desegregation hit, ALL THE BLACK PEOPLE THOUGHT IT BETTER TO STOP USING OUR OWN SERVICES AND USE THOSE OF WHITE AMERICAN MEN.

7. In the face of giving away all of our economic business and resources during desegregation to White American men who would not hire us or if so, not at a decent - save and send your children to medical and law school - wage, we were driven down into the crucible of poverty and despair.

8. Even if our families did have the resources to send a child to a university, they were segregated or very hostile environments for learning

participation and educational advancement.

9. Then comes along FDR with his NEW DEAL and EVERYBODY GETS ON WELFARE, becomes sedentary, unimaginative and let the government take care of them.

10. Even if Blacks had imagination, or thoughts of ingenuity and/or artifice to get ahead, such as that of the Jewish Borgenicht family in Malcolm Gladwell's "Outliers"; to grow the apron and clothing making business; went to a White American "Yankee" (as they called them) materials wholesaler Mr. Bingham and ask that could he sale the material directly to Mr. Borgeicht to eliminate the middleman. Mr Bingham thought this bold of a Jew to make such a request, but yet in still, granted the request. With a Black man who would've thought of making the same request, the known steel wall of racism would have kept it just a thought never taking the step to make such an overture and if he did, more likely than not the request would have been quickly eradicated, evil words spurn and request vehemently denied.

11. Most children like me, did not see prodigious overnight work ethic, entrepreneurship and/or the award to come from it when we were growing up, which would have given us the impetus to strive for something much greater.

MICHAEL IRVIN WALKER

12. Even when our ancestors did graduate college, their ambitions upon graduation were palliated without legacy and recommendations, or relegated to abysmal sisyphean nominal unimportant task (actually happened to me on my last job); therefore, not able to practice what they learned in the real world.

13. Many professionals, if they stepped out on their own path, without real world experience, they often faltered in getting the details correct (not necessarily my case); therefore, gained the reputation, "NIGGERS DON'T KNOW WHAT THEY'RE DOING" chiefly among other Black people (which is the unspoken attitude I get when trying to proselytize future NBA/NFL high school and college students parents, as future clients of mine) which fosters a distrust, EVEN TODAY, in our educated professionals: lawyers, cpas, etc.

14. According to Malcolm Gladwell, what is now taking place in Sports and particularly entertainment with Will Smith, Jay Z, Tyler Perry, Sean "Diddy" Combs, Shonda Rimes, Master Pee, Baby "Birdman" and a few others, they were all born at the right time "1969".

15. I was born too late to be in the peer group of the upper echelon of rappers and producers (which I did have dreams of being) who are now multi-millionaire moguls. While many in my peer group, particularly women have gotten college

educations, our numbers aren't significant enough to cause a paradigm shift such as that of the Jewish Lawyers born in 1930 or the Silicon Valley Billionaire Boys Club of 1955; therefore, I guess the only thing I can do is: WORK 16-24 HOURS EVERYDAY UNTILL MY DEATH, to create a better situation for me and the future generations of my family to come after me.

Will Black American people ever coalesce into something greater within America? YES, one day a grand epiphany will occur and WE WILL STICK TOGETHER as a better American people. Till then, I'LL BE THE BEST AMERICAN I CAN BE!

MICHAEL IRVIN WALKER

MANUSCRIPT:

#blackpeople, what I'm about? I would like 4 u 2 realize how no 1 really likes us how we do not support each other how undereducated we r

#blackpeople u may think I'm promoting a race war, gross prejudice, etc. no, go about it n the same stealth manner as they do, with a smile

Reading this book, you may think, "this guy is a self-hating race trader." When in all actuality, I love my race so much, I've looked around and analyzed what goes on in our community or "hoods" as we like to call them. First observation, yes, we have been subject to racism and preclusion from opportunity. Second observation, yes, we have allowed ourselves to be beat down, seemingly without a fight, without much organization; NOT ACCEPTABLE! We seem to have settled for the table scraps we have been given by the government and programs of racial equality which came along with the Civil Right Movement; acquiesced and ceded all power and control of our lives: social, economic and yes political to other races of people: Irish, Italian, Jewish, WASP etc.

We seem to take each other for granted. We take each other's education for granted. We take getting an education for granted. We take hard, long farmer's-hours (5AM – 9PM NOT 9AM TO 5PM) work ethic for granted. All of the things we take for granted are things that have gotten other races, which were pariahs in America, respect in many different areas of life and economic industries in which they prosper in this nation.

Do I hate Black American people, NO! I just wish we would realize that we could be a better people and make our future history in this country so much greater and richer with the use of civilized manners, education, articulation of the English language and self-appreciation of all the talents we do and can possess, not just football, basketball, singing, dancing and acting; which we do not have full and total control of these talents we seem to be so great at.

For, it seems to me that every other outside culture to these United States of America has complete or majority economic, political and inter-working control of an industry or a few industries: Jews (media, film, real estate), Irish (fire and police departments), Italians (mob, construction and unions), Arabs (corner stores in the hood). These people have complete and total control over these industries with very little interference and questions regarding their operations practices. Black American people make music, but Clive Davis and Jimmy Iovine controls/controlled the industry. Black American

- 14 -

MICHAEL IRVIN WALKER

people play basketball, but David Stern (who has retired/died and now bequeath his position to one of his brothers of Jewish ethnicity, Adam Silver) is the commissioner interpreting rules and regulations of the NBA, and there has been one maybe two, majority control Black American owners, of any NBA franchise.

Black American people have been freed from slavery much longer than Jewish people have suffered from the Holocaust and racial discrimination in Germany and in America. How is it that Black American people have been held down by racism and preclusion from opportunity for such a long stint of time? Even in this day and age when Jim Crow is over, we have a great number of persons within a generation who have graduated from college; many Black American people are on a tract and/or have already started their own successful companies. My question or longing to know, is, when do we start to replicate success, entrepreneurship and long standing company enterprises and legacy building as a culture; not necessarily racism, but rather racial nepotism, because a rich White American billionaire may invite you into their home as a friend, but may not invite you into the board room as a participating decision making board member and/or share secrets to his/her success, or even much less, give you a decent gainful employment job (the kind that allow you to save and buy a nice home, drive a decent car, save for your children's college education and your retirement), but they'll train their son or daughter or even the sons and daughters of their White American friends into a management level employee, COO, CFO or successor CEO. Of course, no one admits this or says it out loud, it just is, and as it seems, FOREVER WILL BE!

> stop walking slowly around a track
> thinking u r exercising. Ur only
> working out ur ankles, not ur fat ass
> & stomach #blackpeople

> #steveharvey #blackwomen always
> have excuse of y they can't get 2 the
> gym or running. get ur ass n the gym
> & on the treadmill. no excuses

> #blackpeople y do most think it's so
> hard to run for exercise? "Wow, is
> you runnin around the whole block?"
> A black man asked me after my 4th
> lap round

One morning while running 8 laps around the Boys and Girls High School track in Bedford Stutvesant Brooklyn, NY, a distance of approximately two miles, I saw all Black American people on the track doing some sort of workout, which was good, but was it really? I saw a middle age couple probably in their early 50s walking very casually around the track in their workout clothes and sneakers. The woman was not particularly fat or out of shape and

- 16 -

MICHAEL IRVIN WALKER

she looked nice for her age. The man had a round gut and looked very out of shape. After they walked around the track three or four times, they proceeded to the bleachers and she began stretching as if she had done some strenuous muscle and joint straining exercise which could later leave her sore.

I saw other older people in their early to late 50s walking around the track as well. I also saw two fat younger women in their 30s sauntering casually and having conversation while calling themselves exercising. There were two gentlemen there who looked maybe like prior cell mates or just unemployed neighborhood guys, or they could have had jobs of some sort (who knows, but given the high unemployment rate among Black American males ???); they had sun-burned, dehydrated, caked up dark skin; had on baggy clothing so I could not tell if they were fat and out of shape or not. They were doing push-ups and sit-ups together, and they'd walk casually around the track twice - which during the walk I saw one of the guys smoking a cigarette - before retreating to do more stretching, push-ups and sit-ups.

There was one woman in between the ages 35 – 41 running a little and walking a lot. While another lady in her 40s, whom I could tell was fine in her younger day; maybe she had a kid or two, maybe not. While she was not walking casually, she was walking at a speed a little less than what it takes to move a person's heart rate up for sufficient fat burning exercise. In her tight workout outfit, you could tell she used to have a nice ass and big perky breast in her former years, but due to bad eating habits and lack of exercise, her roundness expanded and had become shapeless and unattractive. As I passed her on the same spot of the track every two laps I ran, I thought, "if she ate better and actually did a more strenuous workout, she could retrieve her nice body for a woman her age." She was already out on the track every morning, which meant she was dedicated to her workout of walking, but seeing little results. Another woman in her 40s would always stick close to the bleachers. Her workout consisted of jumping rope a bit and running up and down the bleachers at a rapid rate until she got tired, which was a pretty good work out, speeding up her heart rate. But looking at her, as she was also out there every morning, you could tell she ate all the wrong foods which only made her current exercise regimen help to maintain her current out of shape look.

Seeing these individuals doing this mediocre exercise only gave me motivation to run past them during my 8 laps with pride in the fact I had built up my wind to run such a distance; sure, I know many people run much longer. But as a petite guy, running a triumvirate of 5 miles during the week would cause me to lose weight which was not my goal. As I was passing these individuals, I'd think to myself, "**Black American people are so lazy and do not like to exercise**"

MICHAEL IRVIN WALKER

When I was 29 I started running in an effort, I believed, to keep my weight down as I'd heard a person starts gaining significant weight in their 30s. When I first went to the track in Astoria Park, Astoria, Queens, NY I forced myself to run 1 whole lap around the track non-stop. Of course, not having run regularly, this left me winded. I'd stop at the 1 lap mark and walk to the next curve of the track, where I'd then proceed to run another lap back to that point. I'd then walk to the next curve of the track and then began another lap back to that point. I'd do this four times then I'd go home. I'd repeat this regiment at least 4 days a week. As the laps began to get easier, I then progressed to a lap and a quarter, and so on. I'd do that routine four days a week until I built myself up to 2 laps at a time, 4 laps, 6 laps then to 8 laps. I had started in April and was up to 8 laps by June. In August I was running 8 to 12 laps around the track 5 or 6 days a week, until my pants in a certain belt loop started falling off of me, which was when I realized I was running too much and/or eating too little so I cut back.

My point is, though I did not know the young woman's routine of her laps and how she was going to go about building up her tolerance to run longer, something told me she would not keep up a routine because Black American people running for long stretches is not what I see many of us do on a regular basis. And the walking casually around the track without any rise in heart rate, which I saw many people doing, especially the younger fat Black

American women, literally disgusted me in its perpetuation of lethargy. Walking in a non-rapid pace only exercises your ankles and more likely than not, walking at any rate, it takes a person twice as many miles/laps to walk as it does to run. Fat Black American women who were probably eating a diet high in pasta, fried foods, salt and sugar; walking around the track gossiping was doing totally nothing for them. They seemed to think just because they got out there, they were doing something good, when in all actuality, they were doing next to nothing.

Walking is better than sitting, but you merely get your blood to flow at best, and strengthen your ankles, doing nothing for your fat stomach, which a running, change in diet and sit-ups work-out would help tremendously; nor does walking do anything for fat thighs or waist which requires other strenuous exercise. Just because you go to the gym does not mean you are working out. To gain muscle or lose weight, you must work out properly and eat properly as well; eating is a totally separate subject to be discussed later.

#blackpeople stop eating friend chicken and mac & cheese every other night, it is killing u with high blood pressure and diabetes

MICHAEL IRVIN WALKER

#blackpeople u do realize u can survive on less than a full course meal everyday & that jogging helps you live longer. eat more fruits and vegs

Let's start with health facts. When you eat pasta/carbohydrates they provide the body with fuel/energy to operate. The night before every New York City marathon, there is a big pasta dinner party for the runners. Why, you may ask? The purpose is to sustain their energy for running 26 miles the next day. If you eat pasta and do not exercise to burn off the energy, what was not used for energy purposes turns into sugar, which then is stored as fat causing weight gain. Add cheese into the mix and a spare tire, muffin top, large thighs and expanded waist are inevitable.

Growing up, my immediate family of my grandmother, two aunts, my mother and one cousin, we ate pasta about three to four days a week in the form of Kraft boxed macaroni and cheese, which we later switched to Velveeta boxed macaroni and cheese shells; we'd eat that with either fried pork chops or fried chicken. Later in the week, maybe Saturday, we'd have spaghetti and ground beef which was cooked in such a large portion it lasted two to three days. In talking with my friends, their family meals consisted of the same foods.

Have you ever noticed a young Black American woman in her 20s who has a fine body, but as she approaches her 30s, she's constantly gaining weight and starts saying she needs to lose weight? She never does and as the years pass, she gets fatter and fatter. This is due to her diet and lack of exercise. Her diet more than likely consists of many carbs, fried foods, bread and sugary and/or alcoholic drinks. Even if she starts to work out, her shape does not change much due to her difficulty changing her eating and drinking habits. I have a nice frame for a man my age. My diet consists of baked chicken and vegetables, chips-a-hoy cookies, honey nut cheerios with milk, and water in my home refrigerator to drink with my meals or to quench my thirst. If I eat pasta and drink sugary beverages, it's usually at someone else's house, a party or the holidays. I also purchase fried chicken and pizza approximately once a month.

You do not have to give up all of the foods you love, but the problem comes in when you're frying chicken in your home three times a week, frying cheese burgers and fries in your home every Saturday, cooking or even ordering out pasta/cheese/alfredo dishes three times a week. Even combined with exercise, you will not see much results unless your exercise regimen is often and rigorous or raises your heart rate for a significant amount of time.

I met a woman when she was 49 years old, going on 50. She had a better body than many 26 – 33 year olds I'd see in New York City. In talking with her, we quickly hit it off because she's a proponent of

- 22 -

MICHAEL IRVIN WALKER

exercise, eating healthy and keeping up a beautiful image. In fact, she is semi-famous around her neighborhood of Crown Heights Brooklyn, NY (they call her Panama) for being virtually the only woman her age who looks as well as she does. She dresses with a younger flavor, which does not look bad or ridiculous at all because she has a younger body which compliments the clothes she wears. She let me know her exercise regimen, which is really quite simple and non-strenuous, but the trick is she does it every morning without fail and does some things at night without fail and she also does not eat a fatty fried meat, pasta cheese and bread filled diet every night of the week.

Her exercise regimen consisted of 150 crunches (not sit-ups, but crunches), 90 squats assisted by grabbing on to the sink, 120 push-ups standing at a 45-degree angle from the sink or wall, 100 arm curls with a 10lb weight for each arm and 100 (50 to each side) waist twist with a kitchen broom. Her diet consisted of an apple for breakfast with tea on the weekdays, two boiled eggs with a slice of toast and tea on the weekends. She has a light lunch during the weekdays, which consist of (not all in one day) a variety of vegetables and fruits or tuna salad with wheat bread, half a bottle of orange juice, or sardines and crackers or a salad. Her dinners consist of salt fish, potatoes and other vegetables, baked chicken or fish, rice and vegetables, beef stew with potatoes and vegetables, spaghetti. She has a late night light sweet snack of a slice of cake or sweet crackers, or cookies and Ice Cream. SHE DOES NOT

- 23 -

COOK WITH ANY SALT, but rather uses other substitutes for flavor. One thing I noticed regarding her diet, is she eats cereal for dinner on Tuesday; hence, the "you do not have to eat a full course meal every night to survive". SHE DOES NOT EAT FRIED ANYTHING! SHE DOES NOT EAT MACARONI AND CHEESE! If you notice, she eats all of the food groups, not just vegetarian or vegan or atkins. She does not overeat and stuff herself; maintains a regular exercise routine and consistent diet. She was married 25 years, had two kids and has always maintained a fine-looking body for years continuing into her 50s; men, 20-something try and talk to her all day when she walks the streets going to work or during a weekend stroll.

#blackwomen stop going outside in head rags looking like u r walking out on a slave plantation. u look ridiculous, ignorant & pusillanimous

On the streets of New York City, especially Brooklyn and probably other cities as well, Black American women walk outside with these scarves wrapped around their heads and tied into a knot at the front. It looks so Aunt Jemima and servant like. Black American women wear these scarves as if they are a fashion statement; like they are sexy. In actuality, and I do not know how they are impervious to the fact, they make these women look poor, sloppy, unintelligent and spineless. And these are probably women who complain they cannot find a good enough man in their lives.

- 24 -

MICHAEL IRVIN WALKER

First of all, if a guy approaches you with this type of scarf tied on your head, he only cares about coitus with you and he, more likely than not, is not all together himself. With the scarf on your head, no man who approaches you has any type of respect for you and probably doesn't have respect for himself. He's not prone to satisfy you sexually, probably has low self-esteem and may even beat on you. These scarves make a woman look lifeless. If you do not mind looking as if you have no courage and no respect for yourself, by all means, continue to go outside with these head rags tied around your hair.

y do u think u c white people always jogging in winter spring summer fall? It helps u live longer & the oxygen n take makes u smarter

The "oxygen intake from running makes u smarter" is me being facetious, but the fact may be true. I started running at age 29 and while it may not make you smarter, there are some added benefits to it: healthy heart, added life span, weight control, energy boost, solace and peace of mind you experience while pushing yourself through the breathlessness (which eases after 1/2 a mile), ease of stress, added to a sense of accomplishment for running in the first place. In the aspects of solace, piece of mind and accomplishment I would say those are qualities that go along with a person being smarter and thinking clearer.

But back to White American people now; on any given day, at any given time, take a trip to Central Park, the parks along West End/West Side Highway in Manhattan, or along certain sections of the FDR Drive or even walk across the Brooklyn Bridge and there will not be a time that you take one of those trips you will not see White American people running: Winter, Spring, Summer, Fall. There may be a majority of White American people in America who do not run for exercise or sport, but when you take a look around, the majority of the runners anywhere, especially in winter are White American people. My fiancé recently remarked to me, day after Thanksgiving, "you goin' running? It's cold as hell out here." To which, I remarked, "people run in the cold"; her response, "yeah, crazy people!" As I continued to walk to the track, I thought to myself, "so Black American of her to say something like that."

I'm a proponent of running, exercise, good health, good mind and body. I have yet to run a marathon and probably never will, but never-say-never. Maybe if Black American people took the extra effort to do some exercise which is somewhat arduous and challenging, maybe most of our great grandparents, great aunts/uncles, grandparents, parents, aunts/uncles would not have died from or currently have diabetes. Or should I say, "most of my......." And definitely my current generation will not fall victim to the same fate of high blood pressure, heart disease and diabetes complications. As to the smart White American people thing, I'd be willing to bet, take any middle manager, middle or senior

- 26 -

MICHAEL IRVIN WALKER

executive of any Fortune 500 company and for the majority of them, running or some other form of semi-strenuous workout activity will be in their exercise regimen. Being a part of company management and making 6 figure salaries seems smart to me, especially in a capitalistic, materialistic society such as America.

stop treating other black people, when they approach u as if they r incompetent. stop ignoring other black people who say they want to work for you

black people u must go about running ur small business with an initiative for future black social change

black people if u own a small business u can find a black cpa through NABA & if u type in black lawyers association on the web, many pop up

some1 said to me "i'll never switch from my russian guy he saves me money." Black slaves saved america money, but america isn't loyal 2 us. hmmm!

This tweet was born out of my fantasy that when I passed the CPA Exam, as a Black American CPA, I'd be able to walk up to any Black American business owner, Black American celebrity, Black

American NBA/NFL player, Black American rapper and have a brief conversation with them bestowing the knowledge that I was a Black American CPA, pass them my card, we'd exchange information and the person would automatically become a client. My line of thinking was that individual Black American professionals would be delighted to work with other competent, affable, congenial and convivial Black American professional individuals to handle their business matters.

Once I moved to New York, I found a Black American doctor and a Black American dentist. I think of Chris Rock's comedy skit: "The only Black people who live in my neighborhood are Jay Z, Mary J. Blige and me. Across the street lives a dentist. You know what a Black American dentist would have to do to live in my neighborhood? HE WOULD HAVE HAD TO CREATE TEETH!" This wouldn't be necessarily true if all of the Black American elite music and movie celebrities, as well as sports stars who live in New York or pass through on assignment would go visit Catrisse Williams, VIP Smiles for their 6-month cleaning or cosmetic dental work. It should be automatic. But Black American people do not think like this.

When I first passed my CPA Exam it was NFL Draft night 2011. I had printed up some make shift cards with the name of my CPA firm and phone number on them. I went and snuck into GreenHouse night club on the corner of Vandam and Varrick Street

MICHAEL IRVIN WALKER

NYC. As soon as I hit the entrance door to the club, I was looking Shaunie O'neal and Evelyn Lazoda right smack in the face. I had seen Shaunie O'neal earlier in the day at the Converse store on Broadway in SoHo on my lunch break from work.
I thought to approach her in the store, as I felt pretty confident in my outfit, intelligence and articulation, but didn't have a speech exactly prepared for her to speak about the subject of becoming her CPA, and plus she had a friend with her so I let the opportunity pass.

In the club I was armed with cards to pass them out to people in VIP and I was trying to make commission/finders fee deals with the pretty ladies in VIP to connect me with the guys with money; with the music blaring, they either could not hear me or had no clue what I was talking about. I approached a few guys who appeared to have money or were brawny enough to be new NFL draftees or current players in the league standing directly inside the - sectioned off - VIP area; they nodded their heads, took my card and went about their way. I made my way over to speak briefly with Shaunie, as I was too afraid to tell her I was a CPA who'd like to work for her, I simply asked her had she noticed me in the Converse store earlier that day. She said something back to me which I could not hear, we smiled at each other and that was that. I had also passed a card to Evelyn Lazoda and said something to the effect of, "I'm a CPA, take my card. I want to make sure you and Ochocinco don't go broke." She looked at me in stupefaction, took the card, I bid her a nice night and that was that. Shaunie's boyfriend at the time was a light skinned young model. She was in the Converse store earlier that day purchasing black Chuck Taylor sneakers for him that he had on his feet that night. I talked with him in the hallway leading to the entrance/exit about being his CPA. He sold me the story that his agency takes care of that business for him. I next bumped right into and gave a card to the boxer Zab Juda, he looked at me as if I was stupid or he didn't know what I was talking about. At one point, I was standing next to a guy who had on a diamond necklace, I think his name was Pierre. He was in ear shot of me and we could hear each other very well, he said to me, "I have about three CPAs who work for me." He took my card. I saw him later at the diner on 23rd St. driving a metallic blue S550 Benz AMG, getting out of the car clearly inebriated. I spoke with him once more and showed concern for his safety, which Pierre assured me, he would be OK. He was the guy I had most contact with that night in passing inside the club and at the diner. I never heard from him.

It seems as if on the surface, Black American people take other Black American professionals (CPAs, Lawyers) for granted as not knowing how to handle business. I have asked many Black American business owners in Bed-Stuy the, "who's your CPA?" question. A partner of the Therapy Wine Bar, told me someone they've used for 16 years whom I found out was some guy out in Benson Hurst Brooklyn, NY of all places; a place where in the late 80s early 90s, a

MICHAEL IRVIN WALKER

Black American man couldn't – even mistakenly - be caught in the neighborhood or he would be beat, occasionally to death, as was Yusef Hawkins in 1989. One partner of the Voudou Bar said they use some Russian guy who specialized in bars and that he saved them so much money in setting up the POS system, etc, and went into how they wouldn't have time for me to learn their business and/or make mistakes; therefore, they would never hire me as the main CPA of the bar that I'd supported with my dollars as a patron, as did many other Black American persons in the neighborhood, simply because it was Black American owned. They would not grant a Black American CPA the same courtesy their business was thriving on. Of course, this conversation was taking place on a Saturday night, with me being full of liquid courage (though, I do not think the person knew that) and I have not had a chance to initiate a formal meeting; I'll let you know how that goes. (never had that meeting; Voudou Bar subsequently closed).

I recently read a book called "how to get anyone to SAY YES, in 8 minutes". What I learned is that when persons are approached by someone they are not familiar with or do not have a prior relationship, their automatic unconscious response to any offer you make to them is repulsion. People do not know they behave in this fashion; this, on the surface explains why when approaching celebrities or sports players in a club, they are befuddled by my approach and I never hear from them; the NBA/NFL trains athletes to be on guard for people who try and sell them on business investments or financial advisement services, (not absolutely sure if they train them to be leery of Black American people; but looking at how adamantly they tried to convince LeBron James to not let his close, past high school state championship bound, team mates/friends handle his business affairs, I wouldn't doubt it). Even with the club scenery and training of freshly minted millionaires to be on guard, I have read of many financial advisors, CEOs of hedge funds and stock brokers meeting clients sitting next to a pool on vacation or in a country club, being handed brochures out the trunk of a persons' car and later following up to do significant business with that person. So while it's understood about the unconscious response, shouldn't there also be an override to get to a positive response - when approached by someone from your own race, whom you know is limited in opportunity and resources, whom you share many cultural traits and shibboleths, seemingly intelligent and articulate with enough nerve and chutzpah and ingenuity to approach you; at the very least, a hustler, grinding to make his/her life legally better - at least to exchange telephone numbers and let the person work to set up a proper meeting?

I have tried to get persons I've been associated with all my teenage years and the bulk of my adult life, from my hometown where I grew up to get me a meeting with NFL players they were directly related to in reference to being their CPA or having the NFL player give me a reference to another rookie player or

MICHAEL IRVIN WALKER

just giving me tips as to what they expect out of their professional CPA who handles their tax filings or financial management. I was granted no such meetings nor spoke with the players to receive no such advice or references. No other race behaves in this manner and it is a PURE SHAME and lack of intelligence and non-support on our part; the Black American race, a race perpetually discriminated against by every other race within America.

As the population continues to grow within America, as immigrants legal and illegal enter the country with their hunger for survival - find a needle in a haystack work ethic - and government relief (Welfare and Affirmative Action) roles continue to get smaller and/or non-existent, it is imperative we as Black American people, especially those of us who are entrepreneurs, do business with one another, establish scholarships to put our children (especially young men) through universities, teach them through interning, apprenticeship and hire them into long-term gainful employment positions.

For Black American people and Black American men to survive, going forward, there must be an effort to trust in the education and work ethic of ourselves; even switching out the professional services that were sought upon persons of other races and replacing them with future growing professionals of our own race and culture. It is not a matter of reverse discrimination, but a matter of survival and a reprove to a system that has always treated us unfairly and will continue to do so. An interpolation of a lyric by Phife from A Tribe Called Quest in which he said, "Ego, I'm on my own jock still / cause if I don't say I'm the best / tell me who the hell will" ("Word Play" Beats Rhymes and Life album) I say "BLACK AMERICAN PEOPLE / we must be on our own jock still / cause If we don't say we the best, tell me who the hell will?" NO ONE!

institutionalized racism restricts #blackmen from getting jobs but it's also true #blackpeople r sometimes loath & lethargic on the job

#blackpeople n corporate america notice the white women & Asians working late n2 the night, u go home at 5:30PM then complain about a raise

#blackpeople corporate america will never tell us this but they think we r lazy, inarticulate & ineffective which is sometimes true

      This tweet explanation came to mind thinking about my last 5 year stint working a job in which I was motivated to stay and work late, take on more responsibility at the job in an effort to get promoted. When my girlfriend would call me at 7 PM and I told her I was still at work, she'd quickly rebuff, "why are you still at work?" And when I'd have conversations with the few Black American people on the job about

MICHAEL IRVIN WALKER

how late I stayed a particular night or was going to stay, as we chatted while I was going to get something to eat on their way home at 5PM/5:30PM, they'd all spit out a well-known dictum within the Black American community, "they ain't workin' me like a slave."

I began to think of my CFO and how he'd be on the job 9PM/10PM at night walking around jovially speaking with his executive peers, also working late. I thought of the articles I'd read where Congressman were called to meetings 11:30PM – 3:00AM in the morning to get some bill pushed through to the Senate. I thought of stories I read about CEOs working 16 hour days, 80 to 100 hours a week or CPAs working for the Big 4 accounting firms who reported working the same amount of hours during busy tax and quarterly income statement preparation and audit season for clients. I thought of the question, "how is it possible to work that many hours in a 5 day week?" I summed it up that they work on weekends and/or from home to come up with these ridiculous hour counts. I thought of how much these individuals got paid; some $1Mill a year, other $250K-$500K a year. CPAs often work 2 to 4 years at a CPA firm making $40K - $65K, then go to a corporate company as a senior accountant or accounting manager and are put on a track to make $85K - $125K in 5 to 6 years.

When I walked around the office during my latest time of working at 9PM, I'd rarely see any Black Americans working at that hour. But I would see many of the Black Americans gathered at the elevator between 5PM/5:30PM. I spoke with one young woman and asked does she ever work late. She quickly replied no and that, "it's not about working longer or harder but about working smarter." I asked her where she wanted to be in 5 years, she said to have her MBA and be within a management position in her current field. I then asked her, "don't you think that is going to require you to work longer hours?" She said, "yes, I'll cross that bridge when I get to it." I also asked, "do you hope to get a nice raise at the end of this year of working for our current company?" She quickly blurted out an emphatic yes. While some of the younger Caucasian individuals went home at the sound of the clock striking 5PM as well, there were also quite a few who were around at 7PM - 9PM.

Apres 2007/2008 when thinking about hard work, I often think of Barack Obama and that he, a Black American man (though he's half White American) was not supposed to win the Democratic Presidential nomination in 2008, especially over a White American woman candidate, Hillary Clinton whose husband Bill Clinton was already a proven great Democratic American President. But yet, not only did Obama win the nomination, he won the presidency by a landslide over John McCain in November 2008. I think it took tremendous emotional

- 36 -

MICHAEL IRVIN WALKER

fortitude to stay the course and move forward to become The United States of America's first, so-called, Black American president; he is, after all, half White American.

Once I saw this feat being accomplished by Barack Obama of being the democratic representative to run for office, is when I decided to study to take my CPA Exam, an exam which only 40% of candidates who sign up to take it, pass; the numbers are even more abysmal among the Black American candidates who sign up and take the exam. Every road block I came to in studying for the CPA Exam I thought of Barack Obama and the adversity he overcame to become the presidential nominee and eventually president; he and Michael Phelps. The tireless work ethic it took to accomplish what those two individuals accomplished that year of 2008 was a mammoth and colossal aberration from the status quo. Passing the CPA Exam was the hardest I'd ever worked in my entire life.

As I studied, passing and failing parts of the CPA Exam, and reflected upon my life and future career which I saw as being on its death bed if I didn't pass the exam (actually passing the CPA Exam WAS THE DEATH BED OF MY CAREER; go figure), I took a look back at my career and the careers of many White American or other Americans in Corporate America. The arduous preparation for that exam made me realize that either Black Americans are less intelligent and/or put in less work ethic than other ethnicities; a primary reason for the low passing rates among us, of not just the CPA Exam, but and seemingly (as reported in the media) any entrance type/prerequisite exam. Most CEOs of companies and those in management positions in Corporate America have their Masters In Business Administration, CPA, JD etc; Some do not have this educational training, but many do. Many Black Americans have not put in the hours of hard studying and work ethic to obtain the educational and on the job training, i.e. Malcolm Gladwell's "Outliers" 10,000 hours, but complain about non-promotions and advancement.

I started to delve into the aspects of my career. The most of a raise I'd ever received on my professional jobs was 3%. I began to ponder why that was. I knew exactly why. It was because at the onset of my first job out of college, I wanted to be a Hip Hop producer of musical songs to rap lyrics. I left my jobs every day at 5PM, rarely staying past 6:30PM to complete or get extra work done or ask for more responsibility on the jobs and was often times goofing off e-mailing my cousin or girlfriend all day or writing journals in Microsoft Word on my work computer. Add to that the fact I am a Black American male and there you get the lowest raise a job would offer an individual as a simple cost of living inflation raise. On my first job, I was angry about it and quickly made steps to leave. My second job, my manager gave me warning that he knew I was jerking off and that I was not carrying as much work as the rest of the team and that I should step it up and contribute more. But I

MICHAEL IRVIN WALKER

really didn't care, I was living in New York, closer to my dream of becoming a Hip Hop producer than one could get. I was leaving the job every night by 5:30PM going to my apartment to produce a beat on my ASR10 Keyboard beat machine sequencer.

I got fired from my first job in New York due to my lack of enthusiasm. I found another job 6 months later, which after my first 6 months there, I was working under a new Accounting Manager who quickly noticed my weaknesses in lacking attention to detail and was on me like white on rice. She reprimanded me for minor mistakes and tardiness. I'd get to work at 9:20AM – 9:30AM every morning as opposed to 9AM because no one ever said anything. When she did say something, from that point on I was there every morning at 8:30AM – 8:45AM and making sure during the day I covered every inch of detail of my work to doting my "I"s and crossing my "T"s. But she eventually ended up firing me anyway, on a day no less, when she checked my work, there were no mistakes and I turned it in two days early and asked her for more work to do or if she needed help on any special assignments.

After that termination, I could not find another solid job for 3 years, literally 2003 – 2006 I was unemployed. Employers would not touch me. One thing I noticed is that I was not articulating my experience well to seem very knowledgeable about accounting. I also noticed that I had a lazy drawl to my speech pattern and delivery which my current live-

- 39 -

in girlfriend would point out to me as well. I immediately began to work on my accounting, speech and vocabulary skills; finally, 3 years later I guess I perfected it and someone agreed to hire me.

To address another matter regarding why Black Americans leave at 5:30PM; after a 3 year break from work, on this new job which I was glad to receive; ready and willing to work prodigious overtime hours, I noticed that I quickly learned my job to every last detail by the first year. My supervisor did not offer me any raise, which I didn't want or feel I needed because I was getting paid $20K more than 3 years ago. Shortly after the first year, I told the CFO that he was underutilizing my skills and I could take on more responsibility. During the same period, the company shifted part of the accounting responsibilities to a shared services group and this severely cut into my work; with not much more responsibility, I began to hang around work less frequently and leave at 5:30PM with the rest of the Black Americans and other co-workers who felt that to be an appropriate hour of egress.

When the second year on the job rolled around; I noticed a 3% increase in my paycheck. I was livid, especially after making a great contribution to the team the first year and being told so through various e-mails by the manager who hired me. I quickly requested a meeting with the CFO and Director of Accounting. In that meeting I laid out my contribution, how I had saved the company money by

- 40 -

MICHAEL IRVIN WALKER

filing the excise tax returns in a timely manner, which they had not filed timely a few times prior, to the tune of late penalties of $15,000. I presented all the things you read in magazine articles and blogs they tell you to do and enumerate to your superior at raise negotiation time. The meeting boiled down to the CFO telling me no, I would not receive more than 3% due to certain mistakes which he could not properly detail and recapitulate to me; I'd receive another 3% in Sept, which this was now June. I tried to propose a compromise to give me the extra 3% now as a retro-pay; mind you this only added up to $1,800, which was currently less than they were paying employees for job candidate referral bonuses. Also, unbeknownst to him, I was in his office listening while he was on the phone with a department manager giving little resistance and ultimately approving of more than a 20% raise to an employee. I made up my mind at that moment I was leaving the company and started going home every day at 5:00PM. The problem with leaving the company, it was 2008 and during the time of the housing crisis economic fall-out - Mr Hank Paulson "Mr. Bailout" - and there was not a job to be found.

I tell that story because often times it is the case, even if Black Americans do play an integral part on the team and make major contributions they still get overlooked for raises and/or promotions they can economically feel. To add to the story, I was seeing White American young women and men getting promoted to supervisor of their position every three to six months which I know a raise came along with as well; some of whom I did not see working late nightly hours. A Black American sees this and can quickly become prostrated, but, It is often the case that Black Americans are the ones who leave at 5:30PM every day, are talking loudly to friends on the company phone or their private cell phones during work hours, they get into work late and leave a little early. After putting 1 to 2 years on the jobs they are walking around talking about how much smarter they are and should have gotten promoted or given the opportunity. While that behavior could fly for many White American men and women, Black Americans you must stop the aphorism of lethargy and stick to the saying, "we must work twice as hard to get to the same place."

stop being lazy n ur work ethic, especially when working 4 other black people. It's a new day. Lethargy has no place n a post obamas nation

#blackpeople complain that other #blackpeople do bad business. Did u tell them about it & give those people a chance to correct their mistakes

#blackpeople everybody makes mistakes. If u do not or are not allowed to learn from ur mistakes is where the problem comes in

MICHAEL IRVIN WALKER

#blackpeople n other communities, a person is assigned a job & is the go 2 person 4 that job even if a fuck up, they're reprimanded & keep job

#blackpeople after so many fuck ups, the person learns from mistakes & becomes a better professional till they no longer make mistakes

#blackpeople this is how the lawyer becomes great, the doctor becomes great, they r supported by their community untill they r great #support

There is a dark cloud over Black American people when it comes to doing business for one another; we tend to take one or the other for granted as customer, employer or employee. We tend to approach the business matter as if we are friends with the other Black American and they understand our personal problems which hinder us from doing the job in a timely manner or properly and vice versa. THIS IS AN IMPROPER APPROACH, especially as it relates to the new millennium. Though I do not perform my work with clients in that manner, I do feel it is a road block to me obtaining the type of clients I want, i.e. The Therapy Wine Bar and Voudou Bar, as well as Bed-Vyne wine; all within Bedford-Stuyvesant Brooklyn, NY.

I've spoken with the partners of each of these establishments and they each kindly blew me off as if I was not a real CPA, or that I must have been joking when inquiring to them about that type of business and they quickly argued me down when trying to push them on the matter; or placated me in face-to-face conversation, but never returned e-mails or calls.

Friends of mine who purchased a nice 3 bedroom home in Greensboro, NC told me a story of trying to give a Black American woman real estate agent a chance to show them homes in the area, which they described to her where they wanted to live, the type of home, school system for their child etc. They told a story that she showed them nothing of what they informed her to; and the last straw that broke the camel's back, she showed up late to an appointment with rollers in her hair. They quickly took their business to a White American male real estate agent who quickly showed them exactly what they wanted, where they wanted and they closed the deal in 30 days. I've heard other stories of details not being taken care of in other matters. THIS MUST STOP! BUSINESS IS BUSINESS, and in business, the person you're doing business with IS NOT YOUR FRIEND! They are your customer, to be treated with the utmost respect and professional care to seal all of the details of the job to complete it with the best of your absolute ability.

MICHAEL IRVIN WALKER

But on the part of Black American consumers of Black American services and products, in an effort to heal and progress in the process, I asked my friends from Greensboro, North Carolina these questions: did you tell the lady her first mistake, after the first showing, of not showing property in the preferred area? Did you tell her after the second disappointing showing? When she showed up late with the rollers in her hair, did you properly reprimand her for her behavior, fire her and tell her why she was being fired? To each of the questions they replied NO! They, with their properly justifiable frustrations took their business to the most-mighty of all business dealings, A WHITE AMERICAN MAN!

It is understandable that Black American people would naturally think if a person is in legitimate business as a professional, they should know how to conduct themselves as such. Many minority Black American business owners do conduct themselves with the utmost ethical and professional standard in all dealings, but many others also tend to relax their professional presentation when dealing with other Black American people. It is a natural sense of commonality that is ingrained within the Black American diaspora and struggle within the United States of America that brings this about; seemingly saying, you should understand, overlook and/or excuse my behavior as between family not to be disclosed to outsiders. Maybe in the 1960s, - 1990s, but in the new millennium, this attitude is not excusable and though still very prevalent, it is also the duty of those insulted by inferior service from their

- 45 -

Black American brothers and sisters to make known the indiscretion, give a warning and chance for correction and upon final termination of service outline the reason for termination.

In every learned subject, there is a process: talking, learning another language, potty training, criminal court. The process is there to help those going through it to learn from it, its inter-workings: pull your pants down, sit on or stand in front of the toilet, release; if you release on or in your clothes, you've done it wrong, receive your reprimand and try to do better the next time. Without the process of reprimand and explanation of the wrong course of action taken, there is no learning. And though many Black American people may say, "that is not my job to teach other Black American people, I can just go to someone better", more likely than not, a White American person; this, in the long-term does not help our race of people become better people, better business persons to build better companies for our future children to gain skills and employment.

If we do not start thinking macro instead of micro, the same complaints that were had 20 years ago, the same complaints we have today will be the same complaints we have 20 years from now: high unemployment among Black American people especially males; takes twice or three times as long for a Black American man to get a job than any other person; Black American people not doing great professional detailed work.

MICHAEL IRVIN WALKER

Our children especially the males aren't going for college education in greater numbers; probably because you did not have patience to work with and/or hire a Black American real estate agent, Black American lawyer, Black American CPA/Accountant and if you felt they needed it, in reference to improper service that was given you, reprimand them and tell them to correct their mistakes.

do u ever notice how hard it is 2 get hired for a job. even after multiple calls from many employers, u can not seem to close the deal. why?

do u recognize potential employers & recruiters call based upon ur resume, but upon speaking 2 u, ur suddenly missing a qualification. why?

White Americans are majority racist. They are uncomfortable being around Black American people; for all of their education and so-called intelligence and open minds, they have not quite figured out the protocol to working with Black Americans. The reason you get so many calls is you have a very American sounding name: Christopher Smith. Your background is even on par with that of White Americans: MBA, CPA, 7 Years work experience. But once they get you on that telephone and you start talking, they quickly notice the speech inflections and/or deep voice; a dead tale you are Black American. I think most have a

- 47 -

clandestine edict from the superiors of the company to either hire a Black American or not to. If it's a green light for a Black American in that particular position for the company, you may get an interview.

Sometimes you'll notice on the interview the White American person's discomfort in speaking with you; as much as they try to hide it, it's saliently in their eyes. I recall in two separate interviews with White American males, each rolled his eyes as if what I was saying to him was completely irrelevant, even though when it was their turn to speak, they each seemed like affable guys whom I could have easily gotten along with as my superior; the interviewers thought otherwise. In one particular interview, the interviewer began riddling off to me regarding things I should say in subsequent interviews with other companies and suggested I could be a CPA on a music tour of recording artist or as a business manager of artist, and he rushed me out of his office before I could finish my closing statement. I never heard back from him since that interview, though I followed up twice with him regarding the position.

Another reason for the apprehension of White Americans hiring Black Americans is often times self-experienced tales of lethargy and lack of details in performing the job. They do not believe regardless of what our degrees may be or how long we've been on a previous job or how arduous a state examination we've passed, that we will do the job efficiently and thoroughly, and they do not want to take the chance.

- 48 -

MICHAEL IRVIN WALKER

Even if you look them dead in the eye and say, "I've made past mistakes, I've learned from those mistakes and I am ready to roll up my sleeves and dedicate myself to the service of learning and performing the challenges of this job". Due to past experience with other Black American hires, THEY DO NOT BELIEVE YOU! Black Americans receive no second chances.

As opposed to divulging how they really feel about us in an effort to come to rapprochement and that we may correct the problems we have, they'd rather ignore it and try to hire around us, etc. In addition to that, in the spirit of nationalism, nepotism and racism, they'd also rather give the salary and position to a White American woman or man. They do not feel you, as a Black American person deserves it, no matter how well you're dressed, how articulate you are in speaking about your experience, they do not want you past a certain level. In accounting, that level seems to be Senior Accountant, while the $90K - $120K Accounting Manager and/or $150K-$250K Controller/Director of Accounting roles go to a White American or any other ethnicity than Black American who is younger than you.

A Certified Public Accountant Examination, passing all four parts, is supposed to spell attention to detail, work ethic, integrity, dedication and passion to move forward in the profession; for a Black American male like me, employers did not get the memo. But according to Malcolm Gladwell's "Outliers", this was the same discrimination process which created all of the great Jewish New York City lawyers born in the years approximate to 1930; in the late 1950s to 1960s, prestigious downtown Wall Street law firms would not touch them (Jewish American Lawyers), even told them so to their faces after putting them through rigorous interview processes (illegal today; these days they call you on the phone, listen to nothing but your elocution to determine if you are Black American as they ask you questions for 10 minutes, cordially and properly end the call and never call you ever again, ignore your follow-up e-mails unless you press them, in which case they say, "we've moved on with another candidate who's a better fit); therefore, the Jewish lawyers started their own firms (as I have, but subsequently closed)), took the legal profession squalid work the top firms rejected, in turn helping greatly to hone skills in particular areas of law such as corporate mergers and acquisitions which later redounded into torrential money rain makers; thus today, the prominent Jewish law firms with 1000 lawyers and the 80 year old Jewish partners.

#blackpeople it's documented fact throughout corp america we r last hired & 1st fired. so y amongst ourselves aren't we 1st hired & last fired

I have been hearing the saying, "Black Americans are the last hired and first fired" since I have had an active human memory. It would seem if that was the case, we would turn that around and deal

MICHAEL IRVIN WALKER

mainly in our own labor pool when we open businesses and/or hire someone to perform a service. If you're a hiring manager in Corporate America, it may not be your ultimate choice of whom to hire and whom to fire. You could very well have interviewed a qualified, intelligent and articulate Black American and wanted very much to work with them, but an edict and/or popular (false) democratic vote came down to choose another candidate who was not Black American.

A famous story of the Jewish Rothchild family follows: *The Rothchild banking family had humble beginnings in the Jewish ghetto of Frankfurt, Germany. The city's harsh laws made it impossible for Jews to mingle outside the ghetto, but the Jews had turned this into a virtue - it made them SELF-RELIANT, and zealous to preserve their culture AT ALL COST!*

Mayor Amschel Rothchild well understood the power that comes from this kind of concentration and cohesion. He entrusted none of his business to outsiders, using only his children and close relatives. THE MORE UNIFIED AND TIGHT-KNIT THE FAMILY, THE MORE POWERFUL IT WOULD BECOME! Soon, his five sons were running the business. They established themselves as the most powerful force in European finance and politics, by resorting to the strategy of the ghetto - EXCLUDING OUTSIDERS, concentrating their forces. One son decided it was time to get married. This PRESENTED A PROBLEM FOR THE ROTHCHILDS, since it meant incorporating an outsider in the Rothchild clan, an outsider who could betray its secrets. JAMES THEREFORE DECIDED TO MARRY WITHIN THE FAMILY, and chose the daughter of his BROTHER Solomon. The brothers were ecstatic - this was THE PERFECT SOLUTION TO THEIR MARRIAGE PROBLEMS. James choice now BECAME FAMILY POLICY! While other rich and powerful families suffered irrecoverable downturns during tumultuous times in history, the tight-knit Rothchilds managed not only to preserve BUT TO EXPAND THEIR UNPRECEDENTED WEALTH! ("48 Laws of Power" Robert Green)

Take a well-known shop such as B&H, a camera photography shop in Manhattan NYC. If you google camera shop NYC, it is sure to be in the top of the list. The place is owned, operated and employs 100% Yarmulke wearing, Hasidic Jewish; no Black American people, no Irish or German White American people, no Italian American people, no Asian American people, no Latino American people. It is a very reputable - high traffic customer base of all nationalities - legitimate business. No one protests or says it's a racist store because it only hires Jewish people; the owners and operators do not feel any pressure or need to hire anyone outside of their Jewish race.

Black American people on the other hand somehow feel they are practicing reverse racism if they do not hire a White American person. Black American people try to preach and promulgate equal

MICHAEL IRVIN WALKER

opportunity/diversity more than government mandated Fortune 500 companies who hire a very limited number of Black American people even though they have vast resources to hire more into gainfully employed positions. I think (though I could seriously be wrong) if all of the billion dollar sales, hundred million dollar earnings Fortune 500 companies were to hire every qualified, college educated Black American candidate who came through their door, there would still be plenty of high paying jobs and positions for the majority of White American people they favor as well as other minority groups (White American women, Latinos, Asians, etc). Do you see them taking such an initiative, NO! On Fortune 500 company websites are hundreds of unfilled jobs that they simply will not fill while many Americans, not to mention the disproportionate numbers of Black Americans with education and job skills are unemployed and/or underemployed.

So why is it, I ask, that the majority of high-net worth individuals within the Black American population do not actively seek out educated Black Americans to carry out important business dealings. We all know Black Americans need an economic galvanization within our communities; need jobs of importance and stature to support the efforts of our college educated youth. For every position a Black American person gives to a person of another race, a person of the Black American race is being pushed down further into poverty, despondence and eventual crime and prison.

Fortune 500 companies seem to go above and beyond to remain majority White American; with the next push being that of women (majority White American) executives pushed into the forefront of those companies. Why is it that Black American people do not go above and beyond to hire their own people in their quest to start small businesses and economic growth among their first and second-generation college graduate population? Every other culture has so often, covertly and tacitly practiced these tactics against us; it is standard accepted practice. What are we doing? Sitting back not doing anything, asking why are our youth walking around with their pants down, asking why aren't Black American men getting married and/or being fathers, asking why Black American men are in prison in greater numbers than any other race in this free nation. The answer is, without a shift in our behavior, political participation and an unspoken grassroots nation within our nation, WE WILL FOREVER CONTINUE TO PARISH AND ASK WHY?

have u as a black doctor lawyer cpa dentist told a black celeb what u do & that u'd like them as a client & totally ignored u. why?

In the summer of 2011 still high off of the passing of my CPA Exam, I paid $1,500 to attend Rush Art For Life at Russell Simmon's home in the Hamptons, Long Island, NY. I did not go with a big

MICHAEL IRVIN WALKER

intention of talking to every celebrity there, but just to be chill and if the opportunity arose, I'd speak with a celebrity and kindly ask them whom their CPA was. I spoke with: Russell Simmons, Taraji P. Henson, Kevin Liles, Andre Herrell, Gale King (though I just introduced myself to her and passed her my card, saying "my company is going to one day be your CPA company and manage you and Oprah's money" and SHE LOOKED AT ME LIKE I WAS NUTS! LOL!) and La La Vasquez.

It was like talking to a wall speaking with these celebrities about that type of business. I guess they are not used to it. They are used to everyone clamoring for a picture or an autograph or hug, etc, which I did get a picture with La La. But on the CPA matter, Andre Herrel quickly blew me off with no consideration what so ever; Russell Simmons listened and quickly told me, "this is not the place to talk about that", and took my card; La La was kind in saying that she and Carmello Anthony had a CPA but that she'd take my card. When I sat down next to Taraji she was polite in telling me she'd been working with someone in that capacity for a long while and she took my card when I suggested to her if there was anyone she knew who needed a CPA, refer me.

When I looked back in hindsight, I didn't have a plan or speech for anyone to try and request a meeting or anything, or any type of rebuttals to their frozen answers to my questions or conversation techniques to find out who their current CPA was, and why they had chosen that person, etc. I just assumed these individuals would recognize a handsome guy as a Black American CPA and show me some type of love. To their credit, I understand at times they've heard of their peers, in working with Black Americans, being robbed or mistakes being made mishandling their fortune. With the barrage of request they receive daily, it's hard for them to decipher a serious conversation such as "Who's your CPA and may I talk about that person becoming me."

I have come to understand that some celebrities already have Black American representation through BESLA, Black Entertainment Sports Lawyers Association. I do not know how much the National Association of Black Accountants (NABA) is associated with sports figures and entertainers.

On my part, as a professional CPA dedicated to detailed professional service, I have a dichotomy of feelings on the matter. If I was a sports figure or entertainer, I'd personally seek out Black American law and financial representation. I'd listen to Black Americans (as Muhammad Wilkerson of the New York Jets did to me) trying to sale me professional services and give them tips or try to connect them to my CPA to possibly work for them or get advice and/or mentorship. But I do feel celebs' pain of dealing with many innocuous requests regarding their attention and time. Then again, how many Black American men and women are coming into their space trying to be their lawyer, doctor or CPA? Know

MICHAEL IRVIN WALKER

the difference between ground beef and filet minion, champaign and dom perignon.

as a #black doctor lawyer cpa dentist, #black celebs ignore u, 6 mths later u find out they r n tax trouble, had a stroke or teeth missing?

    I read about Lauryn Hill being in tax trouble. Here is my other problem with the germane nomenclature of celebrities such as: Method Man, Lauryn Hill, Young Buc and Mike Tyson. Method Man for example, a cool sangfroid down to earth type of guy; you, as a regular person would probably believe you could walk up to Method Man and talk to him, smoke a blunt with him, etc; maybe you could, I've never personally met him. But if I met him these days, I'd be inclined to try and talk him into becoming a client of mine, which I'd be honored to have him both as a Black American man and a fan of his music. Method Man might not be so inclined to speak with me about accounting and tax matters and becoming a client of mine. But yet, I heard that Method Mans' SUV had gotten repossessed by the IRS for non-payment of taxes. Young Buck, the IRS ran into his home in "Tenn-e-key"/Tennessee due to non-payment of taxes. Lauryn Hill, at the time I heard about her situation, owed $3Mil to the IRS.

    While I have never met any of these individuals; if I had, if I was their CPA/Financial Advisor, I'd be on top of all details and have open

- 57 -

@BLK_PEEPSTOP

communication with them to be sure we as client/CPA are sending in checks to get their tax bills paid.
These individuals obviously do not have that type of representation who cares about them, their careers or their culture, probably much less their image as Black Americans. As I've previously mentioned, I've talked with celebrities about becoming their CPA.
They all blew me off, either politely or not so politely. But yet, when thinking about the situations of Lauryn Hill, it's hard for me to believe that no one ever approached her, either White American or Black American regarding overseeing her financial and tax situation; the outcome of which ended with her in the news for tax evasion. If she was approached by a White American individual whom she may have thought was competent and professional enough to take away that financial worry, she must have been sadly mistaken. If she was working with a Black American individual whom she felt the same way about to take care of that particular business for her and they didn't, I'd assume that would make her double skeptical of Black American persons working for her in that capacity.

There should be extra consideration given Black American individuals to serve the persons in that professional capacity. Jewish individuals are known to keep outsiders out, but Black American individuals let anyone into our circle, and it's usually those apocryphal "anyone's" who screw up our business. We have no loyalty within our culture.

MICHAEL IRVIN WALKER

stop ignoring the professionals in ur
family and not paying 4 their services or
wanting the service for free. #blackpeople

It started to happen. I passed my CPA Exam in
April 2011. November 2011, I'd gotten two calls from
family members regarding financial advice and tax
matters. No one had mentioned money in the least or
paying me for my time. It was just assumed I was
supposed to serve them for free. And when –
because I definitely will – ask them for compensation,
they will probably bristle.

If a family member or friend of yours is in a
profession that you would normally have to pay
someone else in the same capacity, offer to pay your
family member. Professionals go through blood sweat
and tears to become the savants they are. Perhaps if
family, friends and Black American people in general
fully supported Black American professionals and
businesses, we could have a better economic
situation in our community: jobs, property ownership,
culturally supported (with our own dollars) schools,
etc.

ever notice as a #black person u know the
names jake gyllenhaal & anne hathaway.
ask white people who is taraji p henson &
they shrug. why?

I wrote a long extensive piece on this subject called, "an eye for an eye does not leave everybody blind". The premise of which, take the names: Tom Cruise, Steven Speilberg, Brad Pitt, Angelina Jolie, George Clooney, Julia Roberts, Demi Moore, Bruce Willis; all White American individuals that many Black American people recognize and can call out these names off the top of our head. But take Black American movie stars or talented actors/actresses: Viola Davis, Taraji P. Henson, Idris Elba, Don Cheadle, Kimberly Elise, Terrance Howard, Tyler Perry, Nia Long, Jamie Foxx; ask a few White American people at work have they ever heard of these individuals and the majority of the answers will be, no!

While everyone knows the names Denzel Washington and/or Will Smith, many/most of our Black American movie stars, White American people choose to ignore them. It is blatant ethnocentric, ignorance and/or racism and cultural disrespect. Even the most celebrated movies of old and present within the Black American community, White American people have not even taken the time to rent them on video or DVD, such as: Boyz N' The Hood, Menace II Society, Coming To America, Friday, Ray, Just Wright, Obsessed, Why Did I Get Married, etc. It's like White American people make it known: you are a second class citizen; your entertainment/movies is second class, your actors are second class; a point made acerbically clear by the dearth of academy award nominations of Black Americans throughout the entire 85 year history of the program; though a recent

MICHAEL IRVIN WALKER

new changing of the guard seems to be ushering in with the Academy of Motion Pictures nominations and Oscars won, less than 50 years apart, by Denzel Washington, Forrest Witaker, Jamie Foxx, Octavia Spencer, Lupita Nyong'o and Daniel Kaluuya.

ever notice ur always hanging around white people at work & after work but ask them to come hang out with #blackpeople and they decline

When working in Corporate America, you meet many White American people who claim or act as if they are so open minded and cool. They talk with you at work, go out to lunch with you, etc; regular common folk.

At some point a White American person on the job is going to have a party during the weekend and invite a few Black American people from the job. What you'll notice happens is nearly all of the Black American people invited to the White American persons party will show up. They arrive at the party and greet the host and commence to drinking, eating and socializing with the rest of the party; not only that, they stay a long while before leaving, maybe till the majority of the party is making an exodus.

The same situation occurs when co-workers decide to go out for drinks after work; the scene is always some bar filled with people other than Black American people, but the Black American people who are there with their co-workers seem to get along just fine, drinking, talking, dancing with the rest of the crowd.

When the shoe is placed on the other foot; say a Black American woman on the job decides she is going to invite co-workers, mainly White American co-workers out to a local bar around her neighborhood to meet up with some of her friends after work, the White American people are always busy, or the destination is too far a commute for them to make it, etc. Or, if they do decide to show up, they will say hello to everyone, get a drink, maybe some food, or they blatantly disrespect the cultural food and will not even try to eat it as a show of non-provincial open mindedness. The White American people will usually stay in one spot, closest to the person or persons they know best, away from the general crowd and not mingle too much with the other party/bar guest. They'll arrive really early to a house party when there is virtually no one else at the party; after maybe an hour, hour and a half, when the party still has yet to really kick off, they start saying goodbyes, nice to meet you and head for the door; often with contrite excuses: "we have to get up really early in the morning." "we have another party we have to stop by and we don't want to get home too late, we have to get up really early."

White American people, for all the education and civilization and family values they have, are very culturally biased and down-right ignorant when it comes to being open to other cultural experiences

MICHAEL IRVIN WALKER

and people. It's as if, "if the crowd is not all or majority White American people", they cannot seem to get socially comfortable. You can almost see this as the reason for animus and the obstinate refusal to abdicate their position on racism, segregation and civil rights after slavery all the way up until the 60s when they were forced by law to do so. Their very nature is to treat other cultures as anathema to normalcy that they feel comfortable being around.

Many Black American people, especially those who are non-savants and/or adverse to education i.e. "hood rats", act in the same manner, but they are quicker to integrate and make themselves comfortable and express themselves than most educated, quote unquote civilized White American people are; or maybe not.

@jayz says all black everything n his song, yet his body guard is white his accountant is probably jewish & only his hangers on r all black

@jayz said 2 much black and 2 much love = 4ever, yet an intelligent black person who may have things 2 say can't get close 2 him & say hello

@BLK_PEEPSTOP

@therealswizzbeats & @aliciakeys claim 2 b so cool and down 4 the hood. is having bert padell as their accountant doing anything 4 the hood?

JAY Z, here is a prime example of someone who puts up a smoke screen as if, "I come from the hood, so I'm down with ya'll, we're the same, I love Black American people, etc." Granted, he employs many Black American people and/or takes care of many Black American people: his family, sister, nieces, nephews, Tah-Tah, Bleek, etc. Sheldin and Sherwin who manage his 40/40 Clubs are beautiful intelligent Black American men, etc. That is all well and good.

Who is on Jay Z's lawyer squad, does he employ Black American lawyers through BESLA? Who is on his Accountant, CPA and Financial Advisor squad? John McNeilly! I spoke with one individual who claimed he worked in a prominent position at Club 40/40 in New York City, "Jay got us fucking with them Jewish Niggaz" is what he told me when I inquired about who does his (not Jay Z's) tax returns.

My research I've done has shown that nearly every well-known Black American rapper from 1988 on up, used Bert Padell as their tax accountant. Bert being a prominent figure in the music business for doing that type of work, I'd expect that back in the 80s. But in 2013, especially as Bert is in his 80s, there is no excuse for many Black American entertainers who defer to a Black American audience for their

- 64 -

MICHAEL IRVIN WALKER

livelihood (even though, especially rappers, it has been shown they are heavily supported by White American suburban kids), to be affiliated with anyone outside of their race for all business dealings.

Think of it this way, how did Bert Padell become such a well-known and famous tax accountant, with NOTORIOUS B.I.G. rapping his name in song? (112 Only You Remix) "Stash more cash than Bert Padell / Inhale / Make you feel good like Tony, Toni. Tone" - Bert Padell didn't even know who Biggie was or hear the line until Clive Davis told him about it - How disrespectful is that? Yet, many Black American music entertainers still opt to use him and not seek out competent Black American CPAs to do the same job.

Bert Padell became that prominent accountant because White American people deferred to him long ago to perform those services for them. As he performed the service more and more, he got better and better and was referred to more and more people in the industry, till he is now the full-fledged, competent, professional go-to guy for that service. In the previous 25 years, he has worked with nearly every New York prominent entertainer, musician, comedian that has had a name for themselves.

A guy like Jay Z, Russel Simmons, etc could start the same chain reaction for a Black American CPA firm or CPA Accountant. These guys have so much power to galvanize the community in so many positive directions: "A small part of the reason the

President is Black / I told him I got em when he hit me on the jack" (Jay Z "What We Talkin' Bout). Jay Z has wielded this power so many times, it's ridiculous, but never have I seen it done stealthily, like every other race does, or publicly done so to benefit a Black American business or blow out a Black American brand except his own.

In addition to that, on his 2nd album, on the song "Imaginary Player" Jay Z puts out an edict to people, not to speak to him or talk to him like they know/knew him before rap; that he doesn't owe them anything. In fact, I knew a guy who used to be in private rooms with Jay Z at the Cleveland Cavs stadium during LeBron's high school games, who was a hustler just like Jay Z, as was his claim to fame; Jay Z would only ignore him in the food line or when he tried to spark up general conversation about music and/or advice for his friend who was trying to start a Hip Hop music company. I, myself, saw Jay Z on a Wednesday night in Club 40/40 (prior to the remodeling) upstairs coming out of one of the private rooms, no one was up in that particular hallway; because of the song, I didn't acknowledge him or try to speak to him, which at the time I was trying to be a Hip Hop producer myself. And yes, I know you cannot speak to every clown at every moment or give attention to every person saying, "please listen to my demo", but you'd think in a more private setting, which I have described (he probably should have spoken to me), Jay Z would be a little more cordial to persons who've supported his career and have respect and adulation for him; of course, I wouldn't know, I DIDN'T

- 66 -

MICHAEL IRVIN WALKER

SAY ANYTHING. And, can not a Black American guy do a good job as a bodyguard? ALL BLACK EVERYTHING! YEAH RIGHT!

As it pertains to Alicia Keys and Swiss Beats, I have never met them, but on Bert Padell's website, it clearly states they are both clients of his. They are a beautiful Black American (though she's half White American) music couple, with power and recognition. They should be giving some of that power back in the form of their professional team being majority Black American. Just as every other race of people adheres to mainly their kind in their circle, so should Black American people.

We complain about our communities and the children being hopeless, and failing in school, etc. Maybe if Black American children could dream of being the CPA or Lawyer to Beyonce or Rick Ross; Mr. Ross - who raps so proudly of being down with Jewish accountants/lawyers - Black American children would have something concrete to chase after besides the dream of becoming an artist who would also let every race of people except their own handle the most important business of law, tax and financial planning of their career.

as a #blackpeopl it is our duty to seek out black professionals to handle our business besla, naba, etc. black doctors dentists, etc

There are only but so many prominent Black Americans and the degrees of separation between them is minimal, 2 degrees at best, so it should be rather simple, just as it is to get them to attend BET Awards, to metastasize their billions of dollars in net worth and spending power into a culture where all Black American NBA/NFL players use a Black American Accounting Firm or Black American CPAs found through NABA and Black American lawyers/sports agents found through BESLA. If Rappers, R&B Singers, Tiger Woods, Serena & Venus Williams, Black Actors along with all the other Black Americans, blue and white collar workers within America did this, as well as used Black American Doctor's and Dentist, etc. we could have Fortune 1000 to 500, maybe even Fortune 100 companies of our own, with great asset values and goodwill.

We are the greatest creators of the intangible asset goodwill: Nikki Manaj: "Couldn't get MICHAEL KORS if you was fuckin' MICHAEL KORS"; Jay Z: "Big things, thick chains, ain't shit changed get brain in the four dot six range" "You bought a 4.0 you better get ya change . Ain't no platinum in those Cartiers switch ya frames." Heavy D: "NIKE I'm for em, out the store I bought em and on the ba ba ba basketball court is where I sport em" "I got all flavored NIKEs with the fat colored socks". RUN DMC "MY ADIDAS".

Within Sports and Entertainment there has to be hundreds of millions of dollars being spent using the resources of other cultures for financial and law services as well as doctor, physical therapy and

MICHAEL IRVIN WALKER

dental needs; money going out of Black American people's pockets, not coming back into our communities for educational and scholarship purposes, company and employment purposes or any other purpose.

I think the argument regarding clothing brands is a non-starter because Black American people, all people really, have been BRAND MIND FUCKED and predisposed to nike, louis vutton, gucci, christian louboutin, balenciaga; then again, Under Armor was making a strong splash against the market share of NIKE, so it could have been possible for a ROC-A-WEAR or SEAN JEAN - both which seem to have experienced a declivity in popularity after the first decade of the new millennium - to be world renown, high fashion, top quality international brands promulgated by Kanye West "The Louis Vutton Don (who can't get a meeting with Louis Vutton executives.) But in reference to CPA, Law, Medical and Dental services; these are services people need, not services people want. Imagine if all Black American people acquired services they needed from other professional Black American people, it could make for some powerful professionals upon which our children can build their educational aspirations, hopes and dreams.

#blackmen u do realize as u r watching latinos and mexicans build houses n ur neighborhood, they will replace u living there n 5 to 10 yrs

The way the nation is going at this point in time, Black American men, even the educated ones are the last on the totem pole to receive work. Take a look at renovation projects in any neighborhood, particularly urban neighborhoods, all you see are Mexicans and Latinos working. The Black American guys are standing around doing nothing, even if they want to work, they cannot get the work. The pecking order is, throughout all job offering: White American men, White American women, Asian men & women, Latino men & women, Black American woman, BLACK AMERICAN MAN last and begrudgingly.

What I am saying to Black American men is they need to get up and do something to put themselves in a better economic place in America. The Latino immigrants, legal and/or illegal are making hard working and hard-earned strides and will be in a better place in the economy in the years to come because of their work ethic. The very neighborhoods that they are working in - say in the Bedford-Stuyvesant Brooklyn, NY gentrification process - they will be living in those very homes in 10 to 20 years, maintaining a comfortable working class to middle class life.

MICHAEL IRVIN WALKER

The Black American man will be pushed out into jail/prison or far out, poorer dilapidated neighborhoods. The dichotomy of the whole situation is that Black American men, having been those same minority workers years ago, who were underpaid and overworked, do not even see what is happening before their very eyes; they may even be proponents of the Latinos, legal and/or illegal immigrants receiving work, as long as it is not White American men who have profited from almost every profession: policemen to firemen; over the last couple hundreds of years. But the flip side to that coin is Black American men will be left to the proletariat crucible of the societal social and economic order in America.

blackpeople u do realize beating & screaming @ ur children, only makes them violent future chris brown & ron artest. talk 2 em & b patient

This was an analysis I came up with approximately 12 years ago. At that point, my daughter was 4 years old. To that point, I could never recall whipping her and/or yelling at her out of frustration such as you see many Black American mothers doing; screaming at their children in the grocery store, train or walking down the street when their children are talking and being inquisitive as a child should be.

- 71 -

I sat and analyzed my own violent outrage toward one particular young woman in my life. I can remember always saying to myself, "if I ever catch my girlfriend cheating on me, I'm going to beat her ass". I had done just that at age 16 when I caught my girlfriend in her aunts' apartment with another guy. I had also done just that after evesdropping on my girlfriend's phone conversation with another guy discussing he and she continuing to convince me that the baby she was pregnant with, was mine, when it was really his. Begrudgingly, she ended up pressing charges against me a month later; had me arrested while visiting her apartment because she assumed I stole her credit card; which I'd never ever stolen anything from her in the past. I was prosecuted guilty in court six months later and spent two weeks in the city jail starting Jan 2, 1997.

My analysis brought me to the conclusion that due to whippings I had received during child hood from my aunts, grandmother, father and mother and one from my step father; It brewed an anger inside me that was waiting to be released. I had angry fights with men and women in my life. I came to the conclusion whippings teach children a lesson, "when someone does something wrong that you do not agree with, strike out in violence to fix the problem." That simple sentence is the cause of children fighting in school; fighting, arguing and engaging in domestic violence as adults.

MICHAEL IRVIN WALKER

When dealing with children, they are going to do things the parents do not agree with. The simple reason for this is they are learning; everything is new to them. When I hear many parents screaming at their children "you know better", they do not actually know better nor have the mental capacity to learn all that is right and wrong, especially after you telling them a mere one time; therefore, parents must be patient with children, talk to them about what you perceive is a problem or recurring behavior. If the children are doing something repeatedly wrong and/or heinous, you may need to get a doctor involved. Many single parents cannot afford a psych doctor, their health plans or welfare do not cover one, which gets to another point to be discussed maybe later, DO NOT HAVE CHILDREN OUT OF WED-LOCK AND BEFORE YOU ARE FINANCIALLY READY!

blackwomen stop walking around looking like u r 3 months pregnant at age 22 & don't even have a boyfriend & r no where near pregnant!

blackwomen age 30 walking around looking like they've had 3 kids, but haven't had 1 & wonder y they can't find a man to marry them.

Granted women have an easier time gaining weight and a harder time than men keeping it off. But, to the contrary, while I see many White American men

- 73 -

and women in the gym and running miles outside the gym every day, even in winter, I rarely see Black American women running.

I can recall a situation when I worked for a media agency, I'd always see the 20 something year old White American women eating weight watchers at lunch time and regularly going to the gym after work. When the agency hired a beautiful Black American young woman in her 20s, she looked like she was 2 months pregnant, yet hadn't had a baby, or her look was such that she recently had a baby within the last year and just hadn't quite worked off the baby fat and stomach pouch. She'd often comment that she needed to go to the gym, or that she'd planned on going a particular night, but never made it. As I watched her over two to three years her stomach kept getting worse and worse.

When thinking about marriage, I am trying to hold true to my ancestry and marry a Black American woman, but the weight short coming is affecting the process. I will not marry a fat woman or even one I perceive who will let herself go completely in 10 years and get fat and sloppy.

This is my problem with Black American women, they do not seem to care about working out and maintaining their sexy. They seem to think just because they may have a protruding sexy ass in the back which is sexy to many Black American men, their stomach, arms and thighs do not matter. I can even reference a famous Black American female

MICHAEL IRVIN WALKER

comic Simmore, who conveyed the same exact sentiments in her onstage comedy, "men don't give a fuck about a little bit of gut." But, this is not the truth, especially in reference to many educated men.

Men are very visual, and we imagine if a young Black American woman is already slowly getting fat and is not doing much about it, and she plans on having a baby, she more likely than not, definitely is not going to do anything about it in the future. The future is what some are looking at, and if all things remain consistent, I see a bleak picture in the future due to self-loathing and slacking, I will not set myself up for failure.

And even looking, comparing and contrasting White American against Black American women in New York across all age ranges, White American women seem slimmer on average. Even if they are married with children, they still seem to manage to keep a nice somewhat sexy body; after all, a baby is going to cause most women some body damage that is irreparable. In addition to them taking precaution, running and exercising, they watch their diet.

I know this 24 year old Black American young lady, very cute, has a nice job and a great personality. She has the budding growing gut, which is a sign she does not run or work out much. I can recall introducing her to one of my friends whom she asked me for the introduction. Later, he said he would not consider anything serious with her; "very cute", he said, "but the gut among other little things cancels her

- 75 -

@BLK_PEEPSTOP

out of the running to be Mrs.....". This particular guy has his MBA, is tall and handsome and works out regularly himself; why would he, as a man, consider anything less attractive and more out of shape than he.

Black American women wonder why many of their relationships fuse out and never make it to marriage. Marriage is about more than love, it's a package of goods, most of which must be grade "A" top quality before you'll see a man on his one knee with a ring in hand.

#blackactor can not get a job on a main stream movie to save their life, but somehow believe dating only whites will make it better

Halle Berry, Zoe Saldana: While Halle Berry has an impressive resume as an actress and so does Zoe Saldana, Hollywood is a racist town and revolves on split of color lines: roles specifically for Black American men, Black American women, White American men, White American women when in all actuality they could just cast the actor who could come across giving the best performance without regard to color or race. These actors seem to think dating only White American men boost their potential for continued success in Hollywood. And maybe it does: Halle Berry, top actress; Zoe Saldana, stars in top grossing big budget films, but notice her self-

- 76 -

MICHAEL IRVIN WALKER

starring role Columbiana, though it covered budget, and might I add, was a very excellent movie, still was not exactly a block buster.

Kerry Washington whom I've seen mostly in movies made by Black American directors/executive producers or had a cast consisting mainly of Black American people; For Colored Girls, She Hate Me, Little Man, Lakeview Terrace, I think I Love My Wife, Peeples. Yet, I have never spotted her in a relationship with a Black American man. She was supposedly engaged to some White American guy but they never made it to the alter. Though as of this writing, she attended all of the 2014 awards season shows pregnant by a Black American male.

Zoe Saldana seems to have it in her contract that she must date, have love scenes, walk onstage at awards shows to present awards with a White American guy only: Columbiana, Death At A Funeral, Out of the Furnace. I've never seen Star Trek and Avatar but they don't count since there was heavy make-up/animation and color was not relevant. But look at her personal life, with a White American guy for 11 years before splitting up.

Halle Berry; her attraction went from light skinned Black American men to only White American men and/or Latin Americans: She split with her current baby daddy whom she was married to, rumored or maybe fact, he was a billionaire. She then went into another relationship with a White American guy whom she split up with. As of this writing, she

- 77 -

was with a guy who appears to be Latin American (I do not wish to verify), but fact, HE IS NOT BLACK AMERICAN, especially brown or dark skinned Black American. As of last edit, she's with some light/half white/latino music star. NO BROWN TO DARK BLACK MEN ALLOWED!

For the record I loathe famous Black American men entertainers and sports players (too many to name) who promulgate the same behavior in the women they choose for their mates; self-loathing sad souls is how I view them all, spitting in their own mother's faces by not so much as bringing a woman home who looks anything similar to her what so ever, her sisters or her own mother; complete antipathy to brown skin!

To add some defense to the situation, I was completely head over heels in love with a White American woman in my senior year of high school, and in a few highly sexual relationships with others afterwards. Kim Kardashian is damn beautiful and sexy. And if a Black American celebrity is going to be with a White American guy, I'd prefer it be in the ilk of Tom Cruise, Jake Jyllenhaal, Mathew McConaghey; someone with some flair and/or natural swagg. Caveat: thinking about it, Halle Berry's child's fathers looked like cool guys as well. It's not particularly the look at all, but rather the pattern.

My problem comes in with obvious patterns that shun one particular thing over another, especially within the spectrum of your own race. If you

- 78 -

MICHAEL IRVIN WALKER

discriminate in such a manner, you may as well say slavery, Jim Crow and the current murders of Black American teenagers in Florida by White American men, is justifiably correct.

Myself, from my senior year high school relationship, everybody had me pegged to marry a White American woman. Since her, I have dated two very dark skinned Black American women, various brown skinned women, one Jamaican who at first glance appeared to be Half Black/White American or Puerto Rican, my fiancé is brown skinned with a bald head. There is not a pattern there in my dating and ultimately who I plan to marry is an ordinary easily identifiable Black American woman.

@unclerush is color struck, he only dates white, mulatto and asian. have u ever seen him with a #blackwoman as beautiful as naomi cambell?

#blackmen u must stop being color stuck & only dating light/mixed women, u realize ur practicing self hate that the media has pushed upon u.

This extends the argument of Kerry Washington, Halle Berry and Zoe Saldana only dating White American men to Black American men practicing the same behavior. Russell Simmons for example has made his fortune promoting music and culture of Black American men and women and being down for the cause all the while only dating White American, Asian or light-skinned Black American women. And granted Russel is light himself so maybe he prefers someone a little closer to his hue of Black American to date and/or marry.

There is always the argument that whom you fall in love with is out of your emotional control. Then there is my argument, if you are a Black American woman or Black American man, being that there are so many beautiful shades of us, you have an "apocryphal" duty to at least date two different shades and not just one shade in 3 consecutive relationships.

Let's do some numbers; how many White American men do you see dating only Black American women and completely treating their White American women, no matter their nationality, as anathema when it comes to even the most debauchery of salacious satisfaction and/or love? And I'm not saying women of other races are not attractive and should not be indulged in.

#blackwomen who will not suck & swallow or toss salad, but wonder y the football & basketball player n college r having fun with white girls

MICHAEL IRVIN WALKER

#blackwomen I had 2 girlfriends. the 1 who tossed my salad took back shots, sucked and swallowed became a wife. the other a 4gotten memory

#blackwomen there were other factors which made her a wife, but those sexual pleasantries were not a small factor n the decision process

I recently started looking up images of the wives of rich celebrity and professional sports player Black American men: Reggie Bush, Michael Jordan, Robert "RGIII" Griffin III; what did I find, you already know, WHITE AMERICAN WOMEN or women that were not the complexion of Michelle Obama or darker.

When I was in college, I noticed the athletes were all mainly having sex or in relationships with White American women students. I pulled one guy aside and asked him why. He said, man after we win a game, they are there serving us in every way imaginable: food, drink, sex (fellatio and swallow, scrotum licked, salad tossed, hand jobs and intercourse, as well as anal, with little effort). He said at first, he viewed it as an anomie, but it all switched to him seeking out White American women to be in friendly, sexual and companion relationships with. He said he tried to date a few Black American women and the experience with them just wasn't the same; either they wanted to wait too long to perform sexual intercourse and/or when they did do it, they would not

- 81 -

touch his penis during foreplay and getting them to perform fellatio took too much time and/or coaching. He said his experience and every encounter with the White American girls on campus or the sports player groupies was that they were ladies in the street, BUT TOTAL UNINHIBITED FREAKS IN THE BED!

If you as a Black American woman want the attention of a star basketball player at UCLA, you have some major competition to fight through: public attitude/perception (that White American women are more amiable in relationships), looks and sexual favors go a long way for a young inexperienced man. You have to learn with him, but keep on top of him and keep him whipped, because it seems many White American girls take secret sexual and fellatio classes to keep on top of and to stay in the game.

Even I myself, when I was in college, dated this Caucasian female I had met in high school. From the time I had met her in high school to the time of our relationship in college, our sexual escapades advanced to dramatic levels: from her wearing cotton or lace French cut panties to her only wearing thongs; from her reluctantly performing fellatio to her loving it and taking the full protein blast in her mouth and swallowing it, particularly when she was on her period. She learned or developed a technique whereby she claimed she used certain muscles in her mouth and tongue that definitely got the job done; from the dichotomy of me not willingly giving nor cowering to giving cunnilingus, to her actually teaching me how to do it to bring her to the highest

- 82 -

MICHAEL IRVIN WALKER

apogee; from our try and fail performances at anal sex to her eventually requesting it and me completing full stroke ejaculation; from, we never had a discussion about it, but rather she - by shear vicissitude of kinky satisfying sexual activity - began to lick my scrotum and toss my salad.

You may ask, so what is the moral to the story? The moral is, Black American women, over the last few decades or so, have been marketed as, "WHY ARE BLACK WOMEN SINGLE?" I have tried to answer the question as candidly and from an educational observational and analytical standpoint as I could.

While I was in college, I was a totally pussy whipped, cuckold, mandingo love slave to this White American woman. Even when I tried to have sex with Black American women, I could never reach erection because they never took the steps at satisfying me the way she did. And I cannot count on both hands the number of Black American women I've met and had sex with that would not touch my penis during foreplay, and getting them to perform fellatio took too much coaxing. With White American women that I have been with in the past, there was never a nay say discussion about fellatio.

It has been said that White American women would rather suck a man off than kiss him; and take this quote from a female student out of Penn State University, from an article in the New York Times regarding females adapting/preferring a hook-up culture in college and early career life; "by the time she got back to a guy's room, she was starting to sober up and didn't want to be there anymore, and giving the guy oral sex was an easy way to wrap things up and leave." Of course, that could be twisted into a conversation about why would she feel she was obligated to do anything but say, "I've had a great time tonight. I'm getting ready to go. We'll talk and maybe hook-up later." But that's another book/topic, not this book and a book which I will not be writing. Back on topic, rather it's casual or in a relationship, a blow job can ingratiate a woman to a man; Black American women better learn how to "USE WHAT WE GOT TO GET WHAT WE WANT!" (Lyn Collins "Think {About It}")

I can recall this beautiful dark skinned young lady I dated: she had a nice body, wore her own hair, was a Howard University graduate and we'd have very scintillating conversation; problem, she did not like to perform fellatio and her rhythm was off during sex, particularly when she was on top. She had everything I wanted in a woman, but the sex was banal to say the least; needless to say, it was a very ephemeral relationship.

A guy whom I became good friends with was married 10 years to a Black American woman whom he said never sucked his penis; she found the act demeaning and to be of the lowest level of female degradation. I told him, I WOULD NOT MARRY A WOMAN WHO DID NOT SUCK MY DICK, NO WAY!

MICHAEL IRVIN WALKER

While down and dirty sex is not everything (*yes it is, lol*), it is a big part of what gets the ball rolling in any relationship between a woman and man; it is a large portion of what bonds them together; though men may cheat, it is a large portion of what BRINGS THEM BACK HOME! Though the Black American college basketball and football players may be cool with the Black American girls on campus, what the White American girls do behind closed doors, is a large portion of why they get taken along to the NBA and NFL to become wives and/or are the main party girls in the sports and entertainment world among Black American men.

Another part of the problem is Black American men, especially the dark skinned ones from the southern region of the United States are slave-brain-washed to the point of self-hatred and think light/White American complexion is better. But that's for another section/tweet. My motto to young girls who hope to find themselves married (not only to professional sports Black American men or celebrities, but to any man) is: KEEP HIS DICK IN YOUR MOUTH/HAND AND A THONG ON YOUR ASS!

i can not get a job in corporate america, i can not get a job working 4 #blackpeople, I can not get an acting job on a ron howard movie #wtf

as a #black lawyer i can't represent queen
latifah jayz common snoop tyler perry
oprah anthony davis d.rose chris rock.
who can i represent

Once I passed the CPA Exam, I quit my
fulltime job, thinking I would quickly be able to find
another one. I had 6 years of experience on my
previous job and a CPA Exam passing verification
letter; that should have been a jewel for any
employer. But once recruiters started calling me,
they'd say I needed public accounting experience or
that I was not familiar with the particular industry of
the job.

Speaking of employers requiring industry
experience; it is just a discriminatory and candidate
elimination tactic. A prime example of three
individuals without direct industry experience who
were considered highly successful at their jobs: John
F. Kennedy as President of the United States, his
brother Robert F. Kennedy as U.S. Attorney general
(NY TIMES called him inexperienced and
unqualified), Clive Davis receiving an offer to work for
Columbia Records with no music or entertainment
experience to speak of.

I know White American individuals more
recent in time, who have been appointed titles or
granted jobs in industries which they were a novice;
an older lady who went from retail convenience food
store chains to vice president of a bank; industry
doesn't get any more disparate than that.

- 86 -

MICHAEL IRVIN WALKER

I can recall when many jobs only said you need 5-7 years of experience and CPA/MBA preferred, public experience, "PREFERRED". All of a sudden, all recruiters were telling me, public experience was required once they got me on the telephone; nowhere on my resume did it ever say I had public experience, so why did they call me in the first place?

As my tweet infers, what is a Black American man to do? Black American people cannot seem to coalesce around each other and support much but a slave or Jim Crow movie promoted by Oprah, music or clothing. As I've mentioned before, I'm trying to build this accounting firm (no longer the case) through Black American friends and family and none of them will become clients of mine. I've tried talking with celebrities about any work I could possibly do for them as a professional, not a retinue, and they've all ignored me or no consideration was given after our introduction/meeting.

Think of all the great Ron Howard movies which grossed top dollar and also paid the stars a significant salary: Splash, Cocoon, A Beautiful Mind, Cinderella Man, NONE OF THEM HAVE STARRED OR FEATURED AS SUPPORTING ACTOR A BLACK AMERICAN MAN! NEVER!

I do not get people's racial ethnocentricity. Even Tyler Perry who makes most of his money from films starring mainly a Black American cast, has made a movie with a plot involving White American people, but those big Hollywood honchos like Brian Grazier

- 87 -

@BLK_PEEPSTOP

and Ron Howard they do not seem to cross the color line very often; the closest is Ron Howard directing Jay Z's "Made In America" documentary in 2012/2013.

In 2015 Brian Grazier produced of the hit show "EMPIRE" So maybe things are and will change; I'm not an actor (actually as of 2022 I am) so I don't really know. And, also as of 2022 Ron Howard has even gotten into the game of working with Black American actors; wonder if this book had gotten into their (Ron Howard and Brian Grazier) hands post 2013? Hmmm?

Once again I ask, what is a Black American man to do? If he does crime, he goes to jail, if he goes to Corporate America, he's given lack luster responsibility and pay; then railroaded and fired. If he wants a part in a major film release, Hollywood directors and film execs only give that spot to one guy every 10 or so years: Sidney Poitier, Denzel Washington, Samuel Jackson, Don Cheadle, Will Smith, Anthony Mackie and now Yahya Abdul-Mateen II.

IT'S LIKE BLACK AMERICAN MEN HAVE NO WHERE TO TURN FOR REAL STEADY PREVALENT SUCCESS! And society cringes when we do get a little success and act like avaricious peasants; when in poverty and despair, we become despondent to society at large and wear our pants on our knees with our ass showing as a poignant FUCK YOU! Because down all roads and avenues in some

MICHAEL IRVIN WALKER

fashion or another, we are led to a HUGH YELLOW SIGN! "FUCK YOU BLACK MAN!

#blackpeople notice how underarmor has burst on the sports scene n a major way? do #blackpeople know how 2 build a brand 4/by black people

Under Armour burst on the scene out of nowhere. One day the brand appeared to consist of cheap sportswear apparel, the next day the brand was everywhere; appearing on high school as well as college sports uniforms; professional sports personalities Kemba Walker (NBA), Stephen Curry (NBA), Cam Newton (NFL), Sloane Stevens (Tennis), Saul Canelo Alverez (Boxing) have/had endorsement deals with Under Armour.

Upon doing a little research on the brand, a guy made up a logo and started the business out of his grandmother's garage in Washington, DC in 1996. Here it is, a mere 16 years later, not that 16 years is a short amount of time, but it seems relatively short for a little-known brand to be grabbing market share and stealing NBA and NFL Players away from NIKE to endorse its products. Under Armours' most daring move was an effort to lure NBA All Star and MVP Kevin Durant from NIKE with a - $285Mil cash and equity - 10 year deal.

Under Armour went public on the stock market and has greatly increased in value. The brand seems to be ubiquitous within American culture. Every time I go outside, I cannot escape the presence of the Under Armour Logo, which is a very clever logo for the brand; a loop of the U, with the loop of an A intertwining with the bottom of the U to make for the line that crosses the A, both in unique curve shapes to make for an original, noticeable and indelible logo.

How did this happen for Under Armour? The owner said he started out selling sweat wicking branded shirts from the trunk of his car; I'm assuming to his friends and family first, which included former University of Maryland football player Alumni who went on to play in the NFL, then off to other strangers and schools and local/regional amateur sports teams. As the story goes, somewhere along the way Warner Bros contacted him to outfit the sports players of the movie Any Given Sunday, directed by Oliver Stone, starring Lawrence Taylor, Jamie Foxx and LLCOOLJ. From that revenue, he placed ads in ESPN Magazine and it all started to grow rapaciously from there. I'll also assume along the way he had his own financing or got financing from his family and/or friends; as he grew and orders could no longer be filled from the trunk of his car or production from his grandmother's garage, he began to get other financing, venture capitalist partners to finance a factory and brand expansion. The rest is history.

MICHAEL IRVIN WALKER

My point about Black American people is, many people have great ideas for brands, to take them to high heights of multi-million dollar companies, but they never seem to get off the ground. Take me for example, who has an idea for a national accounting firm to service Black American sports players and entertainers, to be the go-to brand for Black Americans, nationally with multi-offices to service the various clients in many states and expand overseas even. As I've mentioned before, my friends and family, which I thought would be my start and support system are not supporting me. When Black American people start the process of creating what they would like to be the impetus for a major brand, to take and hire other Black Americans and build our culture around something other than music, entertainment and sports, and they get little initial support, the idea dies in its incipient ephemeral stages (as mine did).

When a White American man wants to start a national brand: Under Armor, McDonalds, Groupon, Twitter, Facebook, Amazon, Google, THE INTERNET; the list goes on and on and on; many fizzle out, i.e. govWorks, but many succeed. A Black American man: Tyler Perry Studios (can only seem to brake significant ground through entertainment).

Black American people need to show more support of cultural brands and hold them accountable for quality. That is the complaint I hear the most; Black American peoples' businesses lack quality. Everybody says this, but no one tells the actual

- 91 -

business men and women their quality faux pas, which doesn't correct the problem, which leaves us right where we started, NO WHERE!

#blackpeople notice every online article, tv person, news & media station show twitter names? its called #white corporate support of brand

black people y r twitter feeds shown on every news/talk/entertainment show? it's called white corporate boosting of the brand 4 future ipo

black people how do u think the breast cancer org gets the nfl to wear pink. idea, execution, support of idea among 2 white people run orgs

To take the Under Armor example one step further. Take a brand like Facebook and/or Twitter. Everyone in America and abroad starts to use it, which is fine, but notice how in a short 6 years, all the media outlets are allowed to post their Twitter @ names on their news broadcast. Every live show on TV has a Twitter # hashtag for people to tweet about it and late- night show comedians create Twitter # hashtags on their shows for people to tweet about.

Usually for heavy brand promotion and advertising by TV shows, news broadcasters, commercials; the type of views and press Twitter is getting would cost hundreds of millions even billions

MICHAEL IRVIN WALKER

of dollars. I do not know the cost to Twitter but something tells me entertainment and news people are either doing this at their own volition and the media outlets are allowing it for free; even if Twitter is paying full price for ad service, no other brand in history has ever been advertised across all television channels, illimitably, perpetually and perennially.

What is the answer to the Twitter permeation and perennial presence? It's White American people, (Jewish owned entertainment and media outlets) # hashtags promoted ubiquitously by media industry insiders, tastemakers and celebrities; White American corporations, (News Corp, Walt Disney Company, CBS, etc.) allowing # hashtags to be promoted on television shows, news broadcast, entertainment news outlets.

The constant # hashtags have raised consciousness of the Twitter brand as well as raised value for its initial public offering which took place on Nov 7, 2013 at $26 per share, which opened to trading at nearly double that, $42 a share to the tune of raising $1Bil plus in funds for the company operations; quickly making its founders $100Millionaires and $1Billionaires.

This support, which Twitter received, constantly creates behemoth, multimillion to billion dollar brands which in turn creates power and jobs for many White American people with approximately 1% or less than the total of those jobs being employed by Black American people, usually in positions of low level to supervisor, non-executive ranks.

This same type of support can be duplicated amongst Black American people. But people need to conglomerate their brands (i.e., there are thousands of stylist brands and PR brands which all want the celebrity clientele) and create something that people need, not what they want.

My point, without support and people knowing how to even show support and company creators unable to get financing to garner and advance the cause of support, Black American people will never see prominent brands for the masses, which are started, owned and operated by and employ Black American people.

Beyonce can't get a role n a cohen brothers film, but I bet jayz has worked with alchemist, scott storch, bert padell & owns justin bua art

The Cohen brothers, who made their biggest splash in Hollywood with the film "No Country For Old Men" which had no Black American people in it at all; they also directed "O' Brother Where Art Thou", which I remember only having one Black American man in it as an old wise blind sooth-sayer. They are big name directors in Hollywood the same as Ron Howard, who typically do not cast Black American men in their films nor Black American women. (As of 2021, Denzel Washington is being directed by The Cohen Brothers in Macbeth); wonder if this book had gotten into their (The Cohen Brothers) hands post 2013? Hmmm?

MICHAEL IRVIN WALKER

Beyonce's been in a few films and would like to consider herself an alluring serious actress. She was in "Dream Girls", a part which she egocentrically promoted as a role that made her a real actress; she also executive produced "Cadillac Records" and "Obsessed" both which she starred in. But a beautiful woman, even if not such a beautiful actress, such as she, is not on The Cohen Brothers Radar or many other prominent Hollywood directors.

Take a guy like Jay Z, Beyonce's husband, this guy is a mega-powerful Hip Hop star. All sorts of people probably clamor to work with him in any capacity: from beat producers to CPAs to artist who may want to sell him their art or at least hope that he buys it through an art gallery.

CAVEAT: Upon further research, I did not find any evidence that Jay Z has ever worked with Alchemist, a Jewish Hip Hop producer who has worked with: Mob Deep, The Lox, Nas and other notable Hip Hop acts of the 2000 decade era. Also, neither has he worked with Scott Storch who has produced records for: Fat Joe, Chris Brown, The Roots; just to name a few. I cannot honestly say Jay Z has any Justin Bua art in his collection.

My problem is it always seems as if a White American boy makes the most significant money from Hip Hop Culture: producers (Scott Storch), independent record label owners of Profile Records, Tommy Boy and Duck Down Records (Cory Robbins, Tom Silverman and Drew Ha respectively). And, it seems that if a Black American man or woman would dare to take complete control of a process from creativity to distribution of an art form created by Black American people, it is thwarted by the larger White American power system or self-destructs due to in-fighting upon the Black American individuals.

Berry Gordy for example; heralded as the greatest Black American icon within the music industry, both, for what he did and the time period in which he did it. I'd like to imagine his legacy reworked to have had total control of his entire enterprise; just as he created a Black American family to create what has become known as some of the greatest music in American history, imagine if he had taken it a step further to hire many Black American men who were unemployed living within Detroit, Michigan and other major cities and created an entire distribution network: truck drivers, rack-jobbers, etc. When you think about it, he had to pay those cost to a distributor to begin with; why not arm himself with the power of distribution.

In hind-sight, this could have easily been done because from the time I was 5 years old to age 17 growing up in Warren, OH, I only knew of one record store, a mom-and-pop shop, RBGs, owned and operated by a Black American man Doc Pugh, his son Jimmy Pugh and later operated by a good friend of mine Adriel Peabody Lampley. The entire Black American population of the small town bought 45s, albums and cassette tapes from that one record shop. I'm sure there were many more like it throughout

MICHAEL IRVIN WALKER

Mississippi, Tennessee, Los Angeles, New York, Texas, Philadelphia, Washington D.C. etc.

The Motown sound was so unstoppable, that even White American mom and pop and/or major record shops had to carry the music. Berry Gordy should have had his own distribution system. I'd be willing to bet if I asked him why he didn't, the answer would be, "the White American power structure, the mafia and other factions would not allow for such a powerful, total control process to be owned and operated by a Black American man."

I support @bevysmith 4 wanting 2 promote an image of a brown girl with real hair on her head so brown girls will know the xtra ain't needed

One day Bevy Smith tweeted something to the effect, she's proud of who she is and it would be good for a little brown girl to see her on TV and think to herself, "that could be me." The media and Black American people amongst themselves discriminate against regular everyday brown to dark skinned Black American women in movie rolls, R&B singers, girlfriends of sports player's and Black American celebrities and GAP ads.

The company GAP seemingly only promotes mulatto Black American kids and young adults in their ads. If there is a dark skinned individual in their ads, it

- 97 -

is an established celebrity such as Don Cheadle or Denzel Washington, etc.

Dark skinned Black American women wear ridiculous weaves in their hair, trying to look something other than their natural selves; long hair and/or permed hair is not the problem, but rather fake extra-long hair on Black American women IS THE PROBLEM; trying to uphold a standard of beauty that apparently the media promulgates and thinks main stream American society has an affinity for.

i support moves will smith makes to take care of his own people like duane martin & practices nepotism like everyone else with his children

If you take a look at most movies that Will Smith has starred in that were major box office hits, - I Robot, I AM LEDGEND, Hancock, The Pursuit of Happyness, 7 Pounds - and view the executive production credits, you see two names: Will Smith and James Lasiter; on the surface, there is nothing to that right? Will Smith invest his money, just as George Clooney, Brad Pitt and others do and produce movies to make more money.

But if you are a Hip Hop fan as far back as 1988, and listened to the DJ Jazzy Jeff and Fresh Prince 2nd album titled, "He's The DJ, I'm The Rapper", on the LP (Vynl Record) version, there is an interlude called "Too Damn Hype". In it, Will "The

- 98 -

MICHAEL IRVIN WALKER

Fresh Prince" Smith starts rattling off names of people in his entourage; this was 20 or more years prior to Will Smith executive producing movies. He's talking about how he and his crew are "TOO DAMN HYPE" and you'll clearly hear him say two names in particular, "JAMES JL Lasiter" "CHARLIE MACK is in effect"!

So, when I take notice of the executive production credits on Will Smith movies and I see James Lasiter; the same guy he was friends with from his teenage years as an upcoming and eventually established rapper; what that says to me is Will kept it real with his friends from his neighborhood and took them along for the ride of fame with him as a rapper, but also for those who wanted to take it a step further and follow him to Hollywood, he has made it worth their while. He is living by the ethos I believe in, that friends should progress from a friendship, joking and gallivanting to actually putting money together to support one another's business ventures and getting paid together. Every race of people practices these ethos except Black American people. There is always something that gets in our way, that stops the process or the process never gets mentioned to get started in the first place.

All powerful men have practiced nepotism with respect to employing their family members, even if their family members were not qualified for the job. John F. Kennedy appointed his brother Bobby Kennedy to Attorney General of the United States, with both, little law experience and no judgeship in any court.

Nepotism, cronyism is especially prominent in Hollywood. Talia Shire, the only female character of the Corleone Family in the movie The God Father is the sister of the movie's director, Francis Ford Coppola. Sophia Coppola, who acted (not very good acting to say the least) as Al Pacino's daughter in The God Father III is Francis Ford Coppola's daughter. Drew Barrymore comes from a long lineage of professional thespians. Martin Sheen is the dad of Emilio Estevez and Charlie Sheen; there are many other parent and sibling family combo stars in television and film.

So, when Will Smith's son Jayden Smith made his acting debut with Will in the movie Pursuit of Happyness and people made a fuss, what was the big deal? When Jayden once again was chosen as the lead actor for the remake of The Karate Kid, a movie executive produced by Will Smith, James Lasiter, and Jada Pinkett-Smith, there were also some harangues from critics. But nepotism has been going on from the beginning of time and the Rothchild's really took it serious to mate first cousins so they could really keep it all within the family. A powerful Black American man does it in regards to his children and there is a big fuss?

MICHAEL IRVIN WALKER

#black celebs work with & respect other races of people who, if they didn't have money, would despise them, & never work with them n return

@BeRealBlack4Me trying 2 find the words 2 say just that. black people love & support this system which has repeatedly stabbed us n the chest

I have applied to Jewish law firms that had open accounting positions. I've applied to the Yeshiva University in upper Manhattan to an accounting position and actually had an interview. I have approached Jewish men in their Yarmulkes hanging out with NFL football and NBA basketball players on draft night regarding how I could get on their accounting team to possibly work on some of the Black American athletes' (most of the athletes they surround themselves with are Black American) accounts of taxes and financial management. I was met at every turn with a blank stare and/or the statement, "someone in my family office takes care of that business already" Not, "let me take your card and I'll give you a call and we'll work something out, or talk about it, etc."

A famous NFL agent Drew Rosenhaus, his brother Jason Rosenhaus is the CPA whom I'd "assume" takes care of the tax filings for what I'd "assume" would be all of the famous pro Black American and Non-Black American football players with multi-million dollar contracts signed to his

- 101 -

agency. Jewish guys are prominently known for keeping their employment within their own family or an, all Jewish circle. They only work with/for Black American people who have a lot of sports and entertainment money, which they can then allocate upon their Jewish peers, to make commissions and fee revenue as well.

Take for example, Drew Rosenhaus NFL Agent and Jeff Rubin Financial Advisor, who established a relationship within two years and were making millions together. Drew Rosenhaus (Jewish) works/worked in tandem with Jeff Rubin (Jewish) to sign players to Jeff's Pro Sports Financial advisement company, which Jeff was making a reported $500,000 a year from clients which included 26 clients referred to him by Drew Rosenhaus. In September 2012, both Drew and Jeff were being investigated by the NFLPA because a group of notable Drew Rosenhaus players had given Jeff $43,000,000 all in total to invest in an Alabama Casino which subsequently was raided and filed for bankruptcy.

Black American celebrities need to start seeking out and building the same kind of relationships and referral systems for Black American lawyers, Black American CPAs, Black American financial advisors, etc to keep some of that money within our community. Black Enterprise Magazine, Ebony Magazine and Essence Magazine need to report these relationships and careers to Black American children and adults as something to aspire to; instead of a circle of poverty and dreams, the

MICHAEL IRVIN WALKER

Black American community could start building a circle of prosperity and real highly compensated jobs amongst ourselves and wealthy realities for regular individuals to accomplish.

The way the system is designed today, Black American youth and educated Black American men and women have limited places to turn for avarice hopes and dreams because other cultures of people who control most corporate establishments are turning us away at an alarming rate. IT SEEMS NO ONE WILL WORK WITH US, SO WE MUST WORK WITH OURSELVES!

do u know i have been interviewed @ 2 yeshiva universities, called back with n 2 yrs apart, met the same guy (he must have 4got) but no job

#racism i experience n searching 4 job n #corporateamerica, i feel all #blackpeople should practice this non-sense n dealing with #whitepeople

First of all let me say, I applaud Jewish individuals for making it out of persecution when they were considered the pariahs of society, using Jewish nepotism to get themselves ahead in America; i.e. after David Stern, a Jewish man retired as commissioner of the NBA, his named successor was

Adam Silver another Jewish man. I'm all about adroit business moves for prosperity of people as a whole.

Being that it is different cultures seem to stick together to give one another a leg up, is it totally niggardly of me to promulgate Black American people hoarding their resources for the benefit of other Black American people, the same as the Mafia Italians did, Irish and most notably Jewish people? Jewish people have legally arisen in this society more prominently than any other racial/cultural group in history.

When I was searching for a staff accountant job during the years 2003 – 2006, I had an interview at the Yeshiva University in upper Manhattan, near 172nd street. The guy interviewing me had on a yarmulke and we had a pretty decent conversation. I could not tell if he was prejudice against Black American people in the least. When my live-in girlfriend at the time came home and I told her about the interview with a Jewish man, strangely to me, she said, "oh, you ain't gettin' that job, Jewish people do not fuck witt niggaz." This is the first I'd ever heard of that type of racism amongst Jewish and Black American people. At this particular time, I hadn't heard the story of the Crown Heights incident where a Jewish man and two little Black American children had been hit by a car at an intersection, a local Jewish hospital ambulance came, took the Jewish man away and left the two Black American children there to be picked up by a regular ambulance and they were either dead on arrival of the ambulance, or they died shortly afterwards.

MICHAEL IRVIN WALKER

I'm a Black American man, I'm expecting racism and prejudice to some degree in my life, so no big deal. About a year later, I was called in to another interview at the same school (a Yeshiva University) and talked with the same guy who did not recognize me. Guess what? NO JOB! The fact I had two interviews means the company or even this particular hiring manager liked my resume. The fact I did not receive an offer, means they did not like my appearance, that of a BLACK AMERICAN MAN!

If everyone practices adroit, covert racism against Black American people, why don't we practice it in recrimination? White men and women blatantly tell their daughters they are not allowed to date Black American men. As you see, from a previously tweeted issue, Black American people seem to want to date every other shade of Black American besides dark brown and/or go totally opposite of their own race for a mate.

Black American people need to practice COVERT RACISM / NATIONALISM against other races of people, just as it has been both overtly and clandestinely practiced against us. "Smack me / and I'll smack you back" (EPMD "You're a Customer" from Strictly Business album). Because even though we are in a post-civil rights, post Black American (even though he's half White American) President of the United States, Black Americans are still subject to harsh cold unstated discrimination, preclusion from opportunities: just because the hiring manager doesn't tell you, "I can't hire a Nigger", doesn't mean that is not the interpretation to be taken from, "we've decided to go with a more qualified candidate."

i have a black dentist a black doctor i drink at a local black owned bar in my neighborhood i eat at b.smiths in ny and hamptons #support

My dentist is Catrisse Austin of VIP Smiles in NYC, my doctor is Mike Jones on 34th St in NYC. I eat at Peaches restaurant in Bed-Stuy, Brooklyn, NY and drink at Therapy Wine Bar, Voudou Bar and The Heights Bar also all in Bed-Stuy, Brooklyn, NY. When I was out visiting my distant cousin in Bridge-Hamptons, Long Island, she took me to eat at B. Smiths restaurant off of the water.

I honestly do not see how Black American people will not go out of their way to support Black American owned business establishments. I'm talking about a legitimate business establishment, not the mom and pop, white paper taped signs in the window bullshit soul food/BBQ hood restaurants; but restaurants and bars that are operated by intelligent folks who saved their money, had the place nicely, modernly decorated, employs young Black American men and women, and also provide good service to their customers.

It is my belief that in the past, Black American establishments conducted their business in a churlish, parsimonious fashion and did not provide their

MICHAEL IRVIN WALKER

customers with good service. But currently, we have people who have done their research on customer service and are on top of the details of their businesses to provide the customer with the best possible experience just as they would receive from any other haunt they might frequent, which is owned by other ethnicities of people. I call these newly educated entrepreneurs, the generation of the Obamas' Nation. The generation that no one thought would, BUT CAN AND WILL!

the majority of our race is ignorant. only 20% of us have college degrees. that's y the rachet entertainment survives & the intelligent dies

I wish some black people would stop acting ignorant making the rest of us look bad. 😳

Complaints have been rampant within the Black American community for better entertainment, television shows, movies, etc. But yet, the biggest movies to take hold of the majority Black American population have been Tyler Perry's Madea movies, where Madea is the main character with a wealth of wisdom and knowledge as to the dramatic matters of love and life. She is not the most articulate of persons, speaking an uneducated down-home southern dialect often using the word "ain't, never using the word "are" in between the words "what" and "you"; the word "yo" instead of "your" and replacing consonants in words such as "throat" to say "throak" is also very prevalent in Medea's lexicon. The most popular of television shows are reality television shows: Housewives of Atlanta, Love & Hip Hop Atlanta, where the content is far less stellar than the greatest Black American television show of all time, "The Cosby Show".

While movie directors such as Spike Lee decry Tyler Perry's Madea movies and many people often say how wretched reality television shows are, the audience and ad sales numbers and ratings are often through the roof. The reason for this is, a personal estimate of mine, is that of the total Black American population, only 20% of us are educated, articulate, renaissance people; another 10% never made it to or graduated college but have good common sense; that leaves 70% of persons who are uneducated, inarticulate, ghetto, wretched or whatever other euphemism you might want to use in describing them.

The population that complains about Madea and Love & Hip Hop Atlanta are far out-numbered by those who identify with the characters of the movies and reality shows. And in this day and age, there are no great efforts being made to make television shows and movies with regular Black American people who act like everyday mainstream Americans; know they are Black American but do not act ghetto in the least; like art and theatre, love good fashion, and can appreciate music other than the type of the strip club dance single "Bands To Make Em' Dance". And so

MICHAEL IRVIN WALKER

long as the numbers remain at 30% educated / common sense and 70% uneducated/no common sense, a Spike Lee Movie, "Miracle at St. Anna", a Denzel Washington directed movie "Antwoine Fisher" will always fall short in sales dollars and ratings compared to Madea Goes To Jail. (*percentage not factual; my guess alone*).

im 1 who knows there is actually some validity to madea. my aunts & uncles n mississippi & north carolina sound just like her.#blackpeople

I've always been one leaning toward the educated, calm and serene, renaissance man type of guy. I was the first of my grandmother and grandfathers' descendants to graduate from college. My aunts and mother, the 6 of them were born and raised in Mississippi and are not as articulate as I am and cannot communicate in the fashion that I can.

My aunts sound just like Madea (I got Iphone voice memos to prove it). On a particular voice memo, my aunt had trouble saying the word "prescription" she stuttered and said, "pa-su-sckription" and in pronouncing the word "hospital' she says, "hospillal". I can appreciate the preservation and dissemination of the dialect and tongue by Madea because that is what I came from, it is what many Black Americans came from; hence, the popularity of Madea. Will I ever speak like that and do I encourage children to speak like that, No. Will I denounce it as a dialect that has no relevance in American history of speech, to be shunned as a pejorative, never to be heard outside of our coterie and esoteric Black American communities?

#blackpeople everybody seems 2 state & know we do not stick 2gether, so y doesn't that make us stick 2gether & promote health & wealth?

On any given day you can have a conversation with Black American people and ask them what is wrong with Black American people, why can't they take initiative to better themselves within their own community and their own families? You'll get the same answer most of the time, "BLACK FOLKS CAN'T/DON'T STICK TOGETHER!" I have heard this phrase at least 100 times throughout my lifetime. Being that this is a proverbial phrase among us, it would seem apropos that at our own volition, we'd reverse the situation which is causing us not to get ahead in America. But for some reason, that is not what is happening.

Black American people for the most part, just as within any group share many of the same cultural shibboleths; most of us can dance, fried chicken was or is a main staple dish within our weekly diet, most of us like the same type of music that has been passed down to us by our parents: Marvin Gaye, Al Green,

MICHAEL IRVIN WALKER

Stevie Wonder, James Brown, Michael Jackson; that music in return grew into a new R&B and Hip Hop music phenomenon that a generation or two, shares and loves. We have great parties together listening to all of the communal music and eating BBQ during the summer, but we do not talk business at these parties and connect on a professional level.

Most Black American people share the same dialectical tongue passed down from our grandparents, parents, to us. And for the most part, the majority of us share the same sentiment and pain in finding steady gainful employment and then go through similar situations on the jobs we do obtain. You'd think with all of this cultural sharing between us, WE'D STICK TOGETHER AS A SUPPORT GROUP FOR OUR STRUGGLES AND BUILD UPON THAT! BUT WE DO NOT! And that leads me to say BLACK AMERICAN PEOPLE ARE STUPID! We keep banging our head upon the same wall, actually see the wall and know it will hurt to bang against it again, but yet, we RUN RIGHT INTO THE WALL AGAIN OF BLACK FOLKS NOT STICKING TOGETHER!

@LennyKravitz realized ur music wasn't as rocked out as i thought it was. It was more like r&b/rock. Back then i was a hip hop head though

#blackpeople do u like lenny kravitz music
or he some sell-out mulatto rock dude?

Every single Lenny Kravitz released - I only
remember two - "It Ain't Over Till Its Over" and
"American Woman", I liked. I always intended to get
his debut album, but with a new Hip Hop album being
released every Tuesday back then, Lenny just got
pushed back further and further; eventually the desire
to obtain his album or albums was effaced. Usually,
I'd copy a CD from a friend, but not too many of my
friends had any Lenny Kravitz music. We were all so
Keith Murray, Eric Serman, Redman, Nas, Jay Z, De
La Soul, Souls Of Mischief, Gangstar, M.O.P., etc,
Lenny Kravitz didn't stand a chance.

In 2012, while over a friend's house going
through his ITunes library, I discovered he had 30
Lenny Kravitz songs, all of which I copied to three
CDs and listened to late into the morning when I
returned home. What I discovered was, just like his
singles, most of his songs are smooth easy listening
rock & roll. I particularly like "Sister", "Flowers for Zoe"
- his daughter by famed television star Lisa Bonet
from The Cosby Show - and many other tracks. His
music was just as I had imagined it would be, smooth,
funky rock that I would have enjoyed back then during
the time of its current release dates as well as now,
years later when I downloaded it.

At the time of writing this, Lenny Kravitz was
appearing in great Hollywood movies: "Precious",
"Hunger Games" and I'm sure some others I'm unable

MICHAEL IRVIN WALKER

to name. I like Lenny Kravitz, always thought he had a cool look and I've never heard any embarrassing news about him. Besides that, I liked his mom Roxie Roker, who played Helen on the television series "The Jeffersons". In real life, in 1962, 12 years prior to "The Jeffersons", she was true to her character on the show of marrying a White American man; thus we got Lenny (half White American). Most people, once they get ultimate fame and money, they fall in love with people who would have detested them like a sickness just a few years prior. Suffice to say, I admired Lenny Kravitz's mom and thought she was a dark and lovely, beautiful Black American woman; I admired Lenny Kravitz's 1st wife and had a crush on her and I admire Lenny Kravitz himself.

stop gettin tatoos like ur rich & don't need a job, stop speaking hood, dresssing hood, unless the hood is going 2 make u some $$$ #stupid

Lil Wayne has tattoos all over his face and neck, but Lil Wayne has been a Hip Hop star since he was 15 years of age and has net worth short of or above $100 Million or more. A few NBA basketball players have tattoos - a craze which was kicked off by the legendary Allen Iverson - all over their arms and a few have them on their neck, but NBA basketball players make minimum, upwards of $500K - $1Mil a year and much more if they are of star status.

Jimmy Jr. who is 17 or 18, has not enrolled in college nor does he plan to, doesn't have a job, etc, yet he likes to wear True Religion jeans, Montero coats, $250 NIKE sneakers & Ugg winter boots; what are the chances he will be able to make a legal living that affords him an apartment or house of his own, a nice car of his own and still maintain his high-end expensive dress style? Of course, there is a slim chance that he will create his own job, be an entrepreneur who can support himself in all of the above categories, but without proper education, it will be mighty hard.

Let's say Jimmy Jr. decides to enroll in college and wants to study a respectable profession and get a job for some company upon graduation, who is really going to hire him with a tattoo sprawling up his neck? Not even I would hire him as much as I love Black American people and think they should be given chances. In order to get that chance, even in my company, I'll need my prospective employees to be upstanding (to a certain degree) Americans. (*tatoos are no longer anathema in society; they have been fully embraced by the mainstream; I do however draw the line with FACE TATOOS!*)

What is an upstanding American, particularly as the term pertains to a Black American male? Someone who speaks the proper English of this land we were born into; dresses in a fine fashion with some acceptable swagg; wears his hair in an acceptable fashion (neat dread locks are allowed) and

- 114 -

MICHAEL IRVIN WALKER

acts as a civilized normal human being under regular sober circumstances.

As I look around at Black American people, my main problem stems from the fact, we seem to want to be this separate society all of its own: talk slick street language or the form of broken English seeming the natural elocution born into many Black American households, particularly those with ancestors from the South; wear certain clothes in a certain way (saggin' pants); wear our hair in funky popular styles, etc. There would be no problem if we as a people stuck together and somehow came to economic prosperity together, or if like Lil Wayne and/or NBA/NFL players and boxers, we had the wherewithal to maintain our seemingly endless philistine livelihood.

Take Hasidic Jews for example, they walk around in black and white garb, black yarmulke on their head and a stringy curly lock extending from each temple of their head, they speak their own language, etc. They stick together economically, pool their money together within their own community, purchase land and property and support each other's businesses in the very neighborhoods they purchase land and property.

If we as Black American people would do this amongst ourselves, sure, speak all the, "yo son, nigga," language, walk around in our drawls, shave our hair on one side with parts in it and let it grow out the other side, go to work for our own business at 10AM and leave at 4:30PM (though, as I'm sure other

races of people wishing to gain respect in America
learned, only prodigious hours and attention to detail
in TCB {taking care of business} wins over even the
hardest racist and changes opinions.)

Since Black American people do not stick
together and most of our economic gain depends on
White American people employing us; White
American people employ us based upon their
perception of us and our work ethic; therefore, the
extreme images and language some project,
inadvertently affects a job applicant whose attitude
and actions as to their own lifestyles are antipodes of
the aforementioned.

So as the tweet says, STOP BEING HOOD,
UNLESS THE HOOD IS GOING TO MAKE US
ECONOMICALLY INDEPENDENT IN THE
GREATER SOCIETY AS A WHOLE! Rap, Basketball,
Football, Acting, Clubs and Parties IS NOT TAKING
CARE OF THE HOOD!

#blackpeople u c how every1 shuns us,
shuts us down, will not hire us, so y when
we get $$$ we hire them.
#wearethestupidest #race of people

@tarajiphenson can't get her image
alongside her co-stars on NBC, treated like
shit but I bet her cpa & lawyer/agent r
white & paid well

MICHAEL IRVIN WALKER

I say this due to my experience in finding employment within the corporate world. I say this due to my experience as a CPA networking with all people to try and get independent CPA work.

From 2003 to 2006 I was unemployed with a bachelor's degree and four consecutive years of work experience on my resume to my credit. I was not unemployed because I was not looking, but rather, of the many calls I'd gotten from recruiters and company HR departments, no one would hire me. I'd go at least once or twice a week to an interview, but nothing. Also, during that period of time, I would go out for drinks and meet different people who claimed they could help me submit my resume somewhere but nothing ever became of it. I know what you'll say "that's because, as you've formally stated, your work ethic wasn't the best and you were terminated from a few positions". Actually, I was only terminated from one position. Even still, a White American CEO can be fired one day for a horrible record at a particular company, leave with a lot of cash and stock, and get another CEO post within a few months or a year; I was unemployed, while searching for work for three years.

I had moved out of NY back home with my mom to contemplate my next move. After two weeks of living back home, the job I did land, came to me after a Black American woman working in the HR department granted me an interview, which I went on and two hours later she called and said they were very interested (I have no doubt she had great

- 117 -

emphasis and input into that decision) and then she went about helping me to get paid a higher salary, which the department heads were trying to tell me they made a mistake in their listing and were really offering $15K less than the ad I answered. Even my first job, when I think about it, came at the hands of a White American woman with two children from a marriage to a Black American man. My third job, there was also a Black American woman who conducted my initial HR interview. I know these individuals did not have executive power to make the final decision, but still isn't it ironic "like rain on your wedding day and a free ride when you've already paid" (Alanis Morrissette) the jobs I've had, these particular individuals were present from stage one, or maybe the companies had great diversity initiatives?

Once I passed my Certified Public Accountant examination, I thought I'd quickly get another position in Corporate America with a $20K-$30K raise. No such luck and it seemed as if recruiters were downplaying and even ignoring the fact I had passed the exam; meanwhile I'd read blogs which stated "passing the CPA exam showed great work ethic, discipline, higher mental aptitude and ambition." I guess for a Black American man passing the exam, it says nothing. And even in networking with business owners at various events around New York City, I never landed any clients or work with them or their network circle.

MICHAEL IRVIN WALKER

Everybody, individuals and corporations alike shun Black American people, even if we are seemingly intelligent, articulate and have the education to boot. I was recently told a story of R.J Reynolds, the tobacco company headquartered in Winston Salem, N.C. An employee there, a Black American woman says they flew in a Black American man from Houston after a few rounds of phone interviews. In the last final decision-making meeting, they sat him down and said, "you are well spoken and highly qualified, in fact, too qualified, you'd be bored on this job because it will not allow you to use all of your skills." She also imparted the wisdom that RJ Reynolds is reluctant to hire a Black American man over a Black American woman; yet in still, within the company, they will promote a Black American man into the executive ranks before a Black American woman; even still, he has to be the type who has no bass tone to his voice and speaks extra proper English, i.e. Brian Gumble; more likely than not, of the ilk married to a White American woman and who does not identify with any ethos of traditional Black American life.

Black American people, particularly Black American men have to jump through all of those hoops to get hired and promoted within a top American Fortune 500 Corporation. But when Black American people get some money or official business about themselves; even after all of the covert and at times overt racism they've faced in their lives and in the process of getting to the position where they can hire other people; they do not seem to take the time to seek out qualified Black American individuals to handle the most important aspects of their business.

For example, Jay Z has a song on the "Blueprint 2/Curse" album entitled "Diamond is Forever" he laments, "Its true / how society don't want me to move / into the pen house building with spectacular views / they're like / he's a menace / he could never be a tenant", but yet, a White American man, John McNeilly is his business manager and advisor.

You have to look at this from two points of view. 1. Black American people do not think other Black American people are capable of doing that great a job as White American people will or have been proven to do. 2. Black American people think other Black American people do not have the connections to get them where they want to be in particular situations. This just seems to be accepted practice; there is no work or initiative being implemented to help change this reality or perception which hurts Black American people as a whole.

Taraji P. Henson once lamented on twitter after her name and pictorial presence was redacted from a TV Guide article for the television show which she'd been added to the cast, "Person of Interest"; she tweeted, "see the bullshit I have to go through as a Black woman in this business?" Even after her picture and name were excluded from that article, I'd rarely see her image in ads on television along-side the two White American men, who also star in the show.

MICHAEL IRVIN WALKER

They'd have the two White American guys standing back-to-back but no Taraji P. Henson, who is a great actress who can display emotion on screen with the best of them.

At every turn, Black American people, celebrities alike are covertly trampled upon by greater American society, but once these very same Black American people get some fame and/or money, they depend on and pay substantial amounts of money, to the very persons who trampled upon them just six months ago, to handle their most important and trusted business dealings, leaving many qualified Black American people whom they claim to identify with, on the outside looking in to their success stories.

goodfellaz "u know who gets caught & goes 2 jail, nigger stick up men, that's who. they don't have things organized" this is what they think

we're not dealing with Christians mamm, these people, black peopoe don't have the same sense of family as what we do "this is what they think"

There have been many racial affronts aimed at Black American people in movies. The God Father, "in my city we would keep the traffic in the dark people, the colored, THEY'RE ANIMALS ANYWAY, SO LET THEM LOSE THEIR SOULS." In the movie "Ragtime" there are lines that go something to the

- 121 -

effect "We're not dealing with Christians mamm. These people, they don't have the same sense of family as what we do."

These racial epithets were not born out of thin air and imagination. There are quite a few people here on this land approaching the 2nd decade of the 21st century who think in this manner. And I think the placement of this type of language and films about slavery, Jim Crow and modern-day mistreatment of Black American people: The Help, Red Tails, Django Unchained, 42 "Jackie Robinson Story", Fruitvale Station, The Butler, 12 Years A Slave; are released to remind Black American people of our inferior status and that we will always be held or looked at in an inferior light by other races and cultures of people. Do you notice these types of films are the most heralded and touted films involving Black American actors and/or Academy Award buzz. At the 2014 Golden Globe and Academy Awards, 12 Year A Slave won best picture at both awards shows respectively.

Spike Lee has a problem with Quenton Tarantino for his seemingly over use of the word Nigger and Nigga in his movies. And I agree; what's the point proven by releasing all of this racially charged art? Spike Lee doesn't put out movies starring a great cast of Black American people calling White American people "Honkey, White Trailer Trash, Redneck, Cracker, Dirty, Smelling Like Wet Dogs, Racist, Prejudice", etc. And when he did do something to that effect in "Do The Right Thing", It was smartly done with the exhortation that we as

MICHAEL IRVIN WALKER

Americans need to stop using such racial affronts both in private and in public. But most importantly, my point as raised before, we know these people covertly detest us and see us as other and always will, yet, we're the ones saddling up to them and giving them all advantages when it comes to working with us socially and most important of all, economically.

#blackpeople u look stupid coming out of the projects with true religion jeans & ugg boots and montero coats; just plain #dumbass like

#blackpeople u r trying 2 live the life of some1 else when u never had the social, economic or intellectual advantage they've had. #think

#blackpeople white & european people buy those clothes bcuzz they get paid more than u & some r rich, living off interest from investments

#blackpeople u r trapped n2 being a consumer while others r saving, investing & studying making far greater economic & intellectual gains....

@BLK_PEEPSTOP

black people ur spending ur money time & energy trying 2 prove urself equal all the while coming up short. he buys what u do+stocks+house.

black people i'm a millionaire or work a job making $100,000 I get married & have 2 kids, does that = u, making $50,000 married with 2 kids?

black people i have a job making $100,000 buy $120 shoes 4 my children & drive bmw. does that = ur $50,000 job, buying $120 shoes, drive bmw

I fell victim to this epidemic growing up in my early 20s buying $77 - $98 Tommy Hilfiger shirts, $110 Girbaud jeans, $110 Polo shirts, $68 Nautica shirts, even a $525 Nautica goose coat and multiple pairs of $120 Timberland boots. That was all in my closet and if I wasn't wearing it, I felt of less value. I eventually started to support the new urban craze of the same type clothing being designed by Sean Jean, Dada Supreme, Maurice Malone, FUBU, Phat Pharm, etc. I'd literally spend all of my money on clothing and boots.

I realized at a certain adult age, I was still in the same vicious cycle, but with more adult, metro sexual swag. I did not own a home; had no money in a bank account and I was not holding a management position at my job. I LOOKED LIKE AN ASS! I was the best dressed person at my job, but for damn sure

- 124 -

MICHAEL IRVIN WALKER

wasn't the most executive nor most wealthy on the job. It was then I realized I needed to buoy my professional credentials; thus, studying and passing the CPA exam. Even after that point, finding my career moving slowly and not making the money that I knew others were being paid and that I deserved, I looked around at all my clothes and they were the only thing I owned.

Other people I knew, who didn't dress so well, owned homes, nice cars and took trips out of the country, etc. I could not afford those luxuries. I felt my status in life was weak and needed to change. I made a pledge not to shop as much and save more because, though clothes do make me feel better and people may view me as stylish, there are many Black American women in relationships with scruffy White American guys because they have a bank account and assets; cash, equity! Assets are much more sexier than clothes.

I began taking a look around at Black American kids in Bedford-Stuyvesant Brooklyn, NY wearing True Religion jeans, Ugg boots, $1,000 (or maybe they were fake) Montero coats and $200 Nudie jeans. They were in a deadly, wealth sucking cycle copying White American people and trying to make themselves feel as worthy American citizens by the brand of their clothing. But what I didn't and what they did not realize is WE LOOK LIKE FOOLS!

Many (not all) White American people who purchase those clothing are either highly paid on their jobs, have domestic partners who are just as highly paid on their jobs and have no kids. Or, they are wealthy, living off of trust fund interest money that will be enumerating into their bank accounts the rest of their lives. Black American people on the other hand, we spend all of our economic resources trying to match White American people's wealth that, unless we stick together socially and economically, we will never be able to achieve. We have been sucked into the American system of philistine materialism and riches when, outside of sports and entertainment, we are the proletariat on the social and economic totem pole to receive upper middle class wages that will help us maintain our lifestyle.

At some point, you have to do some math. A family of four: husband, wife, two children and a dog; family income of $250,000; live in $550,000 home, drive $50,000 - $100,000 cars, and wear $2,000 outfits which include $250.00 shoes, $1,100.00 suits, $250.00 shirts, etc. Compare those numbers to a single person with none or one child making $65,000 a year, paying $1,500 a month rent, driving a $50,000 - $70,000 car, wearing $1,500 shoes, $600 - $1,500 purse etc. The income of the family is $20,833 per month compared to $5,416 a month for the single person with child who is trying to live the same lifestyle on a completely disparate income. The single person struggles to keep up the image stacking up credit card balances. The family is comfortably

MICHAEL IRVIN WALKER

making those purchases or saving their money in equity stocks and real estate.

Trying to keep up with the family and their image or even a celebrity or single person who makes $250,000 or more annually is ludicrous; yet, it seems this is exactly what we as Black American people try and do, to our own detriment.

To put this into further real context, I have attached an actual payroll journal of an actual company I worked for. I, a CPA, was being paid $95,000 a year at time of termination. A 25 year old white design engineer was being paid $125,000; a 42 year old lawyer was being paid $185,000 a year; a 42 year old COO (WITH NO COLLEGE DEGREE) was being paid $300,000 a year.

I was living in my car at the time I secured the job; saved only $15,000 into the stock market which grew to $27,000 in 9 months to a year. I took the original $15,000 and paid off my car, as to not have any debt while unemployed once again at the hands of White American people who never appreciated my talent, damn sure did not pay me for it and tried to palliate my spirit at every attempt to contribute my education to the company.

#blackpeople do u no what interest & capital gains r? taxed at 15%? do u no what a complex trust account is? paris hilton will never b broke

I suppose this question should be posed to all who were or are apart of the Occupy Wall Street movement. It is really a simple concept, that if the average person took an hour to study, they'd more than likely understand.

Certain persons earn their MBA, JD, CPA or who are adroit enough to organize their strategy and start a brilliant company, earn CEO, COO or CFO positions in large corporations or their own company. These people also, at times benefit from nepotism and/or politics of being alumni of certain prestigious schools such as Harvard, Yale, Stanford, PENN State's Wharton Business School. Due in part to politics and nepotism, but also by working prodigious hours in their respective positions, they get paid high salaries and stock options. The stock options are what often times materialize into instant wealth.

An option to cash in on 500,000 shares of stock when the price of those shares reaches $30, nets an executive $15,000,000 which (s)he pays taxes on upon converting the shares to cash. After that point, (s)he has $10Mil or a little less to place in an interest bearing account. The interest that gains on that money is called a Capital Gain, which is only taxed at 15% (the rate at the time of Occupy Wall Street). (S)he may leave the capital gains interest in the account and never pay the 15% tax (or whatever the going rate may be) until they turn the market shares into cash. In that case, until the shares are turned into cash the interest gained in the account accumulates more interest year over year. The

MICHAEL IRVIN WALKER

concept is called compound interest and for those who come into a lump sum of money, it is a very lucrative concept which keeps money flowing forever more.

The same process pertains to a trust fund; Paris Hilton for example. Her father, probably long ago, put multi-millions of dollars in an account to earn capital gains and interest and more compound interest. Once Paris reached a certain age, she received after-tax (because the trust income also covered the tax liability) cash payments from the interest and other income from the trust and will receive those payments for the rest of her life and it can even be set up to benefit her children once she dies, etc.

The problem is, most people do not work hard enough to gain those type of riches and wealth; therefore, never get to practice the concept or even think about it. But that my friends, is how the 1% make their money and I am not mad at them. What I must do is build me an empire, or get with my own people (Black American people), to accumulate some funds, start a legitimate company, run with good management skills, branding and advertising to build goodwill; once, I or we can do that, we too can enjoy being taxed an effective tax rate of 13% on $20,000,000 income for the year. READ, STUDY, PRACTICE and IMPLEMENT!

#blackpeople can u calculate the %change between old price $50 & new price $55? do u know where to search 4 the answer or how 2 look it up

I told a friend of mine and all of my face book friends, that if there is any information you want to know or study you can easily look It up on the internet. The internet has a lesson about every subject: math, science, accounting, finances, taxes, etc. But, it seems true as the old saying goes, "if you want to keep something from Black American people, put it in words for them to read or in a book"

Percentage change is how a company measures their performance in revenue, expenses and even stock price. It is a very simple formula: (new price – old price) / old price. So ($55 - $50) / $50 = .10, ten percent change.

I suppose my passion comes from me being the type of person who wants to know something about anything that I find interesting or which I do not understand. For example, I studied transfer pricing, a tactic used by companies with foreign subsidiaries to avoid or significantly reduce U.S. income taxes by the use of Inter-company loans to repatriate minimally taxed foreign dollars back into the U.S. I also guess that is part of my profession, and it is my duty to study and know everything about my profession that I possibly can. But my point is there is no cause of mass ignorance in todays' society; for, you can get a pretty good self-education on the internet.

MICHAEL IRVIN WALKER

#blackpeople mark z created fb, steve j created apple, bill g created microsoft, all billionaires. what $Bill idea have u created? #stupid

Black American people take a look around; if you want to be in true competition with White American people, if you want to dress in expensive brands of clothing and shoes White American people wear, why isn't anyone interested in competing educationally and intellectually? After all, brand building of million dollar companies is where they (White American people) are crushing us and mainly where they accumulate most of their wealth.

Mark Zuckerberg went from a college student, at Harvard no less, to a billionaire in a matter of 10 years. He started his company idea when he was 18. Steve Jobs created Apple computers. The company damn near dropped off the face of the earth until he created IPods, IPhones and IPads, which boost the company brand and stock price out of the stratosphere. Bill Gates, at a very young age, created Microsoft which at one time was the only software suite in any office worldwide. What have Black American people created over the last 30 years, BET, DEF JAM, BAD BOY, No Limit Records, all of which (maybe with the exception of DEF JAM) are either defunct, in a serious trough or in the hands of major White American corporations (BET/VIACOM)

All of these companies: Facebook, Apple, Microsoft are sold on the public stock market and their owners, creators are all billionaires and their children, grandchildren and maybe great grandchildren will never have to worry about money and financing a materialistic lifestyle at no time in their life. But one thing you must notice about these three gentlemen is that neither of them in their public life are/were very materialistic or wear/wore fancy clothing. If anything, they may drive a fancy car or live in a comfortable spacious and palatial home which they can well afford to purchase and upkeep.

#blackpeople have the nerve 2 balk when said #whitepeople r smarter than us. there is only 1 oprah & for lack of better words, she's just lucky in entertainment. #stupid

Most jobs you've worked on, who was the owner of the company? The majority of companies whose stock is sold publicly on the stock exchange are owned and operated by whom? The companies that many Black American people support religiously: Levis, NIKE, COACH, Ugg, etc, are owned and operated by whom? The many new bright ideas that have popped up over the last 10 years: Groupon, Twitter, Instagram, MySpace, Facebook, Whats App, LinkdIn are owned and operated by whom?

MICHAEL IRVIN WALKER

A list of well-known billionaires in America: Oprah Winfrey, Bill Gates, Mark Zuckerberg, Warren Buffet, Steve Jobs, Mark Cubin, Steve Balmer, Martha Stewart, Sam Walton, Robert Johnson. Two are Black American and they each got their billion from entertainment and from damn near the entire Black American population being behind them and supporting their brand, the others got their billion from products they sold or creative factions of their own brain.

Every form of entertainment Black American people have ever created: Rock & Roll, certain Dances, Hip Hop; who controls the distribution, marketing of it and released a paycheck to the Black American people, if at all? WHITE AMERICAN PEOPLE! Black American people look around and ask the question regarding everything useful in your life and for entertainment - who ultimately controls it?

Sure Benjamin Banniker made many products from the peanut; he nor his family ever received a dime for its invention because, as still holds true to a degree today, Black American people give away their work, are afraid to charge high prices and/or get into litigation.

Take for example Beats by Dre headphones. You think Dr. Dre engineered those headphones, tweaked the specific parameters to make them sound nice and that he is the sole proprietor, paid individual of those head phones. WRONG! He's partners with Jimmy Iovine, an Italian (read White American) guy

- 133 -

who's a legendary artist manager, music producer and record company executive, responsible for managing and marketing Dr. Dre, Eminem, 50 Cent and many others on Interscope Records. Dr. Dre is just a name for all the fools, many who are non-Black American, to latch onto and identify with the product; a concept also developed by White American people: product mental and physical association to give an individual a personal feeling with the advertised product.

Product association is one of the many reasons you did not see too many Black American people in television commercials in the 1960s, 70s, 80s promoting products we ourselves used in our own homes; White American people detested us and would not feel a mental connection to a product if a NIGGER was on television telling them to use it; that concept was discussed in the popular show about the advertising business in the 60s, Mad Men.

But back to the point, BLACK AMERICAN PEOPLE, some whom I thought were owners and operators of their own destiny, DID NOT AND DO NOT CONTROL SHIT! "Puffy" "Puff Daddy" "Diddy" was not the sole creator, owner, distributor and marketer of Bad Boy Entertainment, Sean Jean, nor CIROC! There were and are White American people with a controlling majority stake and brain ingenuity and distribution in all of those brands. Correction, Bad Boy was Mr. Combs creation from his own ingenuity, but to bring it to the world in the fashion he did, a White American man, Clive Davis put up the cash and

MICHAEL IRVIN WALKER

mentored him through the process. Bad Boy eventually went on to lose all its original acts due to a switch in White American owned distributor companies from Clive Davis' Arista to Universal, which was Bad Boy's downfall from its most successful hey-day of CRAIG MACK, BIGGIE, TOTAL, FAITH EVANS, and 112.

I bought all of the beginning releases under Puffy's direction: Mary J. Blige "411" & "My Life", Graig Mack, BIGGIE, 112, FAITH EVANS, TOTAL! WHY? BECAUSE OF PUFFY, THE BLACK AMERICAN MAN, the 50% stake and White American owned distributors of the music were A NON-FACTOR, meaning I WOULD HAVE BOUGHT IT REGARDLESS, SO WHY NOT HAVE IT TOTALLY CONTROLLED AND DISTRIBUTED BY BLACK AMERICAN PEOPLE? BLACK AMERICAN PEOPLE ARE NOT SMART ENOUGH TO PULL SOMETHING LIKE THAT OFF? Black American people are only smart enough to let White American people pay them a small percentage of the profits, sometimes half, FOR THEIR TALENT AND SKILL? (even me, if Penguin Books or Random House wanted to publish this book, I'd probably jump aboard. But then again, I'm not claiming to be a publishing wizard or owner/operator of my own publishing house).

Not too many Black American people have adroitly benefited nor highly profited from the creations of White American people. In fact, behind every successful Black American person, you can find them in a picture smiling, shaking hands and making a deal with a White American person. I HAVE NEVER SEEN MARK ZUCKERBERG SHAKING THE HAND OF ANY BLACK AMERICAN PEOPLE!

#blackpeople oprah gave all her money 2 1 jewish man 2 manage & profit off of. I don't think she suggested he hire 1 #blackperson. #stupid

Eli Broad was who I originally thought Oprah Winfrey hired to be the sole money manager of her $2.4Bil net worth. But upon further research, she hired Peter Adamson, whom is no doubt a White American man because if he was Black American I would know that; everyone would have been beaming with pride and talking about it as a major step in the right direction for the Black American race of our people giving ourselves a chance to help ourselves.

I'd be willing to bet, while this guy is managing Oprah's money, there is no stipulation that he hire or seek out Black American people to work closely under him as an apprentice/successor or intern; nothing of the sort. And that is SAD! You would never catch a Black American man being the sole operator of a White American billionaire's business affairs with a team of all Black American men on the help staff, without that White American billionaire saying, at the least, his son, daughter, niece, grandchild has to hold a learning or full-fledged top position in the operation; IT WOULD NOT HAPPEN, IT DOES NOT HAPPEN, IT WILL NEVER HAPPEN!

- 136 -

MICHAEL IRVIN WALKER

A company like Modell's Sports, a Jewish family owned and executive managed company which will ultimately be passed down to the owner's sons to be chief executive officers; a Black American will never be CEO, COO nor probably even CFO of that company. But here you have THE MOST POWERFUL BLACK AMERICAN, WOMAN IN AMERICA, not giving such an edict regarding the operations and management of her money. An area, I'm sure many Black American Finance majors, CPA majors, Economics majors, would love to have an opportunity to dedicate themselves to in work, study, learning and growth.

Sure, Oprah has hired many Black American individuals to work on the production of her syndicated talk show and many Black American people have positions within her school for girls in Africa. Gale King, Oprah's best friend was given a leg up in society due to their friendship, (which I can't understand why Gale would stab Oprah in the back and go work for ABC, BUT THAT'S ANOTHER TWEET!).

Maybe Opera considered Chris Gardner for the job of managing her wealth, since after all, he was on her show to publicize the highly touted movie starring Will Smith, about Chris's life and pedantic assiduous work ethic to learn the business of the stock market at which he excelled; maybe Chris didn't want the job; maybe Chris demurred due his innate Black American "power distance index", meaning though he is powerful in his own right, he didn't deem himself worthy of Oprah's respect of his profession to ask her to do some work for her. Maybe he did inquire about doing some business with her and he either is working for her in some capacity or she politely turned him down; another stab in the chest of A Black American man by his own people. I honestly don't know. And the fact that I do not know is another faux pas; I know who the COO of Facebook is, Sheryl Sandberg, a Jewish woman given a powerful position at a powerful company by a Jewish man.

A friend of mine recently said something to me in regards to Black American people; WE TRULY DO NOT THINK WE ARE EQUAL AND THAT WE SHOULD BE EQUAL IN THIS SOCIETY TO WHITE AMERICAN PEOPLE! So, for all the love and support Oprah claims to have for Black American people; all the love and support Jay Z claims to have for Black American people; THESE PEOPLE DO NOT TRULY THINK BLACK AMERICAN PEOPLE ARE EQUAL AND CAPABLE OF ACCOMPLISHING WHAT WHITE AMERICAN PEOPLE CAN AND HAVE!

From my point of view, the way I see it, "HOW DID J.P. MORGAN BECOME J.P. MORGAN?"; by abdicating his craft and skill to everyone else around him, deferring to the competition? NO, HIS MISSION WAS TO DISTROY THE COMPETITION! "HOW DID ROCKEFELLER BECOME ROCKERFELLER?" "HOW DID PROCTOR AND GAMBLE BECOME PROCTOR AND GAMBLE?" "HOW DID NIKE BECOME NIKE?" "HOW DID STANDARD OIL

MICHAEL IRVIN WALKER

BECOME STANDARD OIL?" "HOW DID PHILLIP MORRIS BECOME PHILLIP MORRIS?"

These top name super companies did not become who they are today, ingratiated an ingrained in the psyche of me and every other American by; making 50% deals with the competition; the competition managing them nor working with the competition. These companies established their brand and ran with it to RUN OVER ANYONE WHO GOT IN THEIR WAY! They put together teams of intelligent WHITE AMERICAN MEN to put strategy in place, do things, at times unethical and questionable, to get ahead in their market and compete with and CRUSH THE COMPETITION! EAT OR BE EATEN!

I hate when another race tries to be black.....they act so ghetto.....all black people are not ghetto

This was a retweet of someone on twitter. But when I think about it, it is, for the most part a true statement. Take Tina Faye for example, if she imitates a Black American person, It is always in a ghetto inarticulate outlandish manner. Granted, as I stated before, the majority, about 70% of the Black American race is ghetto and does act like that, which is probably the crux of why those are the main depictions White American people try and portray of Black American people, but 30% of 39 Million is 11 Million, which is a pretty broad swath of people. Why can't that group of Black Americans, who speak regular articulate English, have college degrees, do various things for extracurricular activities and are average people, be depicted?

I suppose, for comedic effect, it needs to be ridiculous, which is the point of comedy. And while writing and thinking about it, in comedy or just general thought you tend to think the majority is a representation of all. For example, when Black American comics depict White American people they always straighten up their posture and talk in a quirky high-pitched proper articulate manner. That is how the majority of White American people talk. They rarely depict a Honey Boo Boo.

To answer my own question, if Black American people do not want to be depicted as churlish reeds, I suggest they start better educating themselves and work on their enunciation, elocution and use a variety of words from the English lexicon.

Kids should know successful Black people personally. they shouldn't have to go to the TV for role models. #WakeUp

This, I retweeted from @TheBlackVoice. I think the reason many Black American children, especially young men do not do well in school and do not want to pursue a career which requires college education, determination and work ethic, is because they do not know many men in their families who have done that. I do not think it takes a close personal relationship to

MICHAEL IRVIN WALKER

spur this engine in a young man, but just a vision and sight within the family circle and an inkling of a relationship and connection to a successful person.

I got my impetus to be successful from seeing my aunts' boyfriends' (later to become her life-long husband) family of men and women. They had beautiful skin (dark, light and brown skin), were quiet and civilized in demeanor, had nice homes and drove new cars. They never really talked much to me in the spirit of having a great relationship outside of asking me how I was doing in school and the usual family dinner contact, but just being in their presence, made me want to emulate them and be like them to some degree.

Most of them worked for General Motors, which is totally opposite to my career path, but still their success ignited me towards success. If I had not been exposed to them, my immediate family consisted of all women and one man. Most of the women were on welfare, the one man couldn't find work to support a wife and three kids in the 80s so went into the armed service and the one woman who had the semblance of a successful job at a steel meal was laid off my entire child hood till I reached age 13 or 14.

My eldest cousin was in and out of prison for selling crack from the time I was 16 to my late twenties, and the neighborhood I grew up in was a drug infested ghetto as well. But being able to see success and knowing that being on welfare was a

- 141 -

pejorative life situation, I followed success because I knew and had the chance to be around successful people.

KidsE'lan Brown ᴴ @eian_terrellB KidsE'lan Brown @eian_terrell black people biggest Problem today Is we afraid to work as a team & build we're too selfish & in competition with each other we all can't win

Retweeted by BLK_PEEPSTOP

@eian_terrell we're all trying 2 buidl our own individual brand. notice there r only 3 main sneaker brands, 4 with under armor coming

@eian_terrell we need 2 stop & think 2 support 1 brand; have subsidiaries under it. but every 1 supports the parent brand #solid

@eian_terrell colgate-polmalive owns so many brands & u probably thought they were separate. no, they r all colgate. they play game well

MICHAEL IRVIN WALKER

@eian_terrell same with coca-cola, many brands all under the coke corp brand umbrella. this is y education is so important 2 learn that shit

It's funny how many Black American people think alike, but yet we are still unable to come together and make something happen as a concerted effort for the betterment of our people. We are just not great organizers, maybe not even me; therefore, we talk of great ideas but do not know the next step to bring the ideas into fruition. @eian_terrell has a point that Black American people are afraid to come together. We let the claims of reverse racism stop us from making important moves which could potentially help raise our race to higher heights.

My tweets reference an idea I came up with in 2012. While out on the event circuit in New York City, I'd met many photographers, stylists and PR representatives with their own brand of PR firm; literally 50 to 100 or more. It dawned on me, if you take 50 individuals who have their own separate client base whom they make money serving; each person probably has 5 to 10 clients and makes approximately $10,000 to $20,000 from their respective client base. $20,000 for one individual in New York is not much income to live on and/or support that person's business; If you take 50 times $20,000 that equals $1,000,000. With $1,000,000 revenue reported under one conglomerate brand, that opens it up for outside financing from banks, venture capitalist, etc.

This is how many great company earnings are reported; they report the revenue, expenses and net profit from all their subsidiaries up to the top brand; in fact, in an annual report of a public company, for insignificant subsidiaries which do not comprise 10% - 25% of the total combined revenue, there is no requirement to break it out and/or make detailed notes about its operations; but to say they are insignificant operationally at this time. It is the top brand who has the line of credit from banks, finance houses and hedge funds, etc; pays for the advertising, administrative support and operations of all the subsidiaries.

As I stated in my tweet, Black American people are not educated in this manner to do something like that. Or, as eian_terrell stated, they are frightened, selfish individuals competing with one another and NO ONE IS WINNING!

@4StarZ_Ken what the fuck is considered good hair. its 2012. I thought those statements were dead in the 90s. #brainwashedass#blackpeople

Good hair is supposedly opposite the hair, of dark skinned Black American people, who do not have too much mixed White American blood in their DNA. Good hair is soft, shiny and curly, as opposed to being dry and kinky and or knotted up in balls. Good hair is considered that of Half Black/White

MICHAEL IRVIN WALKER

American people with a natural curly shine due to the addition of a little moisturizing lotion and without having to process it with chemicals.

The good hair statement came along with the brain-washed thinking of Black American people that if a person was White American or if a Black American person was light skinned or Half White American or had Indian in their blood, THEY WERE BETTER THAN THE AVERAGE DARK SKINNED, NON-HALF BLACK/WHITE AMERICAN PERSON! White American/Light is right!

In 2012, while the statement still had life, and there are still brain-washed individuals who only date White American or light skinned people or think that having a child by someone light will give them a better looking baby, many Black American people do not follow that line of thinking anymore and find the "Good Hair" statement offensive, and most in the race try to promulgate the idea that all Black American people, nappy hair and all are beautiful people, and that light skin or half White American does not automatically equal beautiful or better. Many Black American women refuse to process their hair with perms anymore and they style their own natural hair; in addition, many Black American people started back in the 1990s wearing their hair in dread locks, which seemed to help their hair grow to massive lengths that no perm or processed hair could grow to.

@BLK_PEEPSTOP

@BLK_PEEPSTOP

I am so tired of black cool being fetishized
by people who ignore actual black people.

@Karnythia i was tired of it in the 90s. go
to clubs, all white people dancing to hip
hop, ask a white girl to dance and she runs
from u

America is considered a melding pot, where all races of people have come together and live in this land as equal individuals with equal opportunity. And with the advent of Hip Hop music, which was created by Black American people in the ghetto neighborhoods of Bronx New York, many people of all races were sucked in by the music: White American people, Chinese people, Korean people, French people; all of whom may have had some racist views instilled in them by their parents; views such as, "you'll be a pariah in the family if you date or marry a Black American man", "you can be friends with Black American people, but don't ever let them in close or top positions of influence of your business and friendly circle."

Hip Hop brought about a vicissitude whereby people of all races, some racist and prejudice, were listening to, buying and going to concerts of Black American artist, rapping about Black American issues in a Black American vernacular and dialect; this technically means the music is by Black American people, for Black American people, IT'S BLACK AMERICAN PEOPLE MUSIC.

MICHAEL IRVIN WALKER

If you like Black American people music, are coming to party with Black American people or having a party yourself where you are playing only Black American music, you must be open to all possible social relations and understanding of Black American people: invite them to the party, dance with them, grind with them, kiss them, have relations and sex with them.

As a result of Hip Hop, all of the above has taken place, but still a majority of White American people who claim to love Hip Hop music and dance to it in popular clubs in Manhattan's Meat Packing District, when a Black American man in particular goes to dance with a White American woman, she will get cold and closed to the idea of a Black American man dancing with her or in her circle of friends. A proverbial excuse for this could be, "she was not attracted to the guy". I suppose a White American woman is allowed to not be attracted to a Black American man; the thought of attraction in that instance never crosses her mind and/or it makes her uncomfortable.

People/Corporations have been doing it for years, taking from Black American culture and popularizing it, making millions of dollars, while the Black American people who created the original idea do not receive a dime. Of course, that started to change with the emergence of Russell Simmons, Steve Stoute, Jay Z and 50 Cent.

Russell Simmons was one of the first individuals in Hip Hop to take the clothing rappers were wearing: Tommy Hilfiger and Ralph Lauren Polo shirts and put his own urban brand to it, Phat Farm, on the same grade, quality and for the same price. Steve Stoute is the man responsible for setting up many of the corporate sponsorships between brands like Reebok, Jay Z and 50 Cent, with the S.Carter and G-unit sneakers respectively. Jay Z, currently has the power to make or break a brand by bringing millions of people to be loyal customers or making millions of customers leave a brand alone as he did with Mitchell & Ness sports jerseys in 2004 and Cristal Champaign in 2006.

But to the point of the tweet, just because someone sings the lyrics loud and proud of a Black American artist, does not necessarily mean they will have Black American people in their home or circle of friends. Sad, but true and maybe it's just human nature or the nature of White American people.

@FunSize_Steph but #whitepeople started the shit & still practice it n more sleuth ways, because of them #racism will never die, just evolve

Someone was tweeting that Black American people are racist too. Black American people have only become or became racist as a natural response to the way White American people treated us upon

MICHAEL IRVIN WALKER

emancipation from slavery and thereafter to this very day.

Black American people started out wanting to work alongside with and for White American people, but White American people despised us. As time went on White American men declared war on Black American people: beat us, castrated us, hung us and set us on fire. As laws were put in place and enforced to stop such non-sense, the White American people then took to more covert ways of racism: requiring literacy exams to vote and to obtain simple employment, that with little instruction anyone could perform; denying Black American people bank loans for businesses and home purchases and/or denying Black American people the right to purchase homes in certain neighborhoods; denying Black American people entrance into schools and universities; denying Black American people well-paying jobs even in the advent they had the proper education and skills to fulfill the jobs.

In 2013, it was (and probably still is in 2022) documented that it takes a Black American man longer than any other prospective employee to find a job in America (I have personally literally felt this systemic racism myself), longer than: Black American women, White American women, White American men and Asian women and men.

Covert racism is still in play in the United States of America, even as more and more people have married interracially, congregate and socialize with one another, most of the power and money in this country is controlled by White American men and/or large corporations. Though, these White American men are letting many White American women into the executive ranks, the number of Black American males to join the ranks is still few and far between.

When I was a senior in high school, I was in a relationship with a young beautiful White American girl. Her parents were kept oblivious of the relationship because according to her, they would not approve of her dating a young 17 year old Black American boy. So even in our teenage years we become aware of the prejudice and racism of White American people. It was known, and certain White American kids would tell you, they were forbidden by their parents to date someone of the Black American race, or that they would never think to do that in the first place even if their parents hadn't planted the deadly seed of race separation into their brain.

Growing up, sure there were comments made about White American people in my home, but never was I advised that I would be punished if I dated a White American girl or to not socialize with them. When I was in a love relationship with the White American girl in high school, I was given admonishment of fear of what White American people might try and do to me for being in an inter-racial relationship in our small provincial town; this was long past 1961.

- 150 -

MICHAEL IRVIN WALKER

It is White American people who continue to perpetuate clandestine racism in America. For Black American people, we laugh at the differences between White American and Black American people, but the majority of us would love to just be equal, receive equal opportunity in employment and other matters and share this beautiful melting pot.

White American people want to hold on to all of the power, and as their population continues to get smaller, with Latinos becoming the majority population, they are going to hold on tighter and become more and more racist in their ways in America. It is this systemic racism towards others which mainly breeds it in return within other minority groups.

@Me_and2Girls tell that to the young white woman who walked n the street of a well lit road 2 pass me rather than pass me on the side walk.

This tweet was in response to someone saying, "not all Black American men are criminals and not all White American people are racist and view Black American people in a bad light"

One night while walking down Fulton St from Nostrand Ave, headed to Tompkins Ave, I decided to look back to see who may have been walking behind me and just to check out the scenery in the rear. I saw this young White American female approaching me,

- 151 -

but she must have been 30 to 40 yards away. I wasn't walking fast but casually strolling down the street. About 5 minutes later, I see her walking past me in the street. Now mind you, the side walk was approximately 12 yards wide itself and Fulton Street is a very well-lit area. Instead of walking on either side of me; the side closest to the street or the side closest to the wall of stores, SHE WALKED IN THE STREET ABOUT 2 FEET AWAY FROM THE CURVE!

I cannot remember what I was wearing at the time, but since I do not have any thug habiliment in my wardrobe, I'm sure that was not the purpose of her caution. She saw a Black American face and automatically assumed I was a danger or threat to her and that she needed to walk in the street and be prepared to have a wide running area to escape because ALL BLACK AMERICAN MEN ARE A THREAT AND DANGER TO ROB, ASSULT OR KILL A WHITE AMERICAN FEMALE even on a well-lit street.

@KayanaRich if we started acting like we have common sense and stop doing all this culturally ignorant shit, maybe we could love each other

I truthfully think Black American people hate each other and do not love each other. We do not love ourselves, which is why we cannot support each other in business ventures and other areas. Even with the word Nigga, which many of us claim is a show of

- 152 -

MICHAEL IRVIN WALKER

affection, it is really a reflection of us turning the hate the White American man placed upon us during slavery times calling us that derogatory term as a self-esteem killer, and placing it upon ourselves. When most people use the term Nigga, they use it in a negative pretext.

Black American people, especially with much of the derogatory things we do in everyday life to ourselves and others, we truly hate each other. For example, the young Black American males wearing their pants on their thighs and showing their underwear is a sign of self- hatred to say, "no one cares about me and my future, I DO NOT CARE ABOUT MYSELF!" But then again, they could just be emulating current day Hip Hop artist who wear their pants like that in society and on stage because they are rich or making what they perceive as a good amount of money and they could care less.

When Black American women, as well as men do not exercise, eat properly nor consciously look after their health it is a sign of self-hatred. When Black American people do not educate themselves properly, speak broken English and talk ignorantly at one another loud in public it is a sign of self-hatred. When Black American people fight and kill each other at a higher rate than any other race of people it is a sign of self-hatred. When Black American men and women only date light skinned or different races of people with lighter skin tones it is a sign of self-hatred. When a Black American man performs domestic violence acts against Black American women at a higher rate of any other race it is a sign of self-hatred. When Black American people only buy name brand clothing and shoes, especially if they spend the bulk of their income on those items and go into serious debt to purchase them it is a sign of self-hatred. When Black American celebrities do not have Black American lawyers, accountants and assistants it is a form of self-hatred. BLACK AMERICAN PEOPLE, WE HATE OURSELVES!

@Lil_Chanzy @Clapzshizzayne actually, i'm black and never been stopped and frisked in ny. its all about how you present urself

I have lived in New York City for 13 years. I have never been harassed by the police neither in my car, nor while walking the streets. There is this big to-do about the "Stop and Frisk" policy in New York City; that it is racist and Black American men are a target of the policy. I think the reason it is targeted toward Black American men is they are the main population committing crime in New York City. Black American men are the individuals committing the shootings, the assaults on old ladies in elevators and slapping White American women and taking their purses. Black American men are the main population on the streets illegally selling drugs and guns. It could be stated, this is a contradiction to the aforementioned polemic that White American women or people should not perceive Black American men as a threat to them. Where the

- 154 -

MICHAEL IRVIN WALKER

dichotomy of thought process comes in is that police have hard-coded facts of who commits crimes and what they look like; a White American woman goes off ignorant ethnocentric fear and makes snaps judgements, usually incorrectly.

If the Stop and Frisk policy was truly aimed at Black American men and harassing them, of all my days I've walked the streets of New York City, I would have been stopped and frisked by now. What I think the program does target is people dressed a certain way, with a certain uneasy or suspicious look about themselves in the presence of police walking the beat.

There was a young man who documented himself being stopped and frisked in Harlem, New York City. He had been stopped and frisked twice in an hour or so. The second time he was stopped, he was very piqued and adamant in asking them, "why are you stopping me, you just stopped me 30 minutes ago?" The policeman said, "when we ride by you, you look back and forth at us in a jittery suspicious manner as if you are worried about something." The young man said that was because the police always bother him, so he watches them to prepare himself for when the police will get out of their car and stop him. The young man had a legitimate point and natural reaction to the police, but at the same time the police had a legitimate point in that he acts suspicious.

When I see a cop in my rear-view mirror or walking past me on the street, I do not change my demeanor one bit or do anything out of the ordinary

- 155 -

just because I see a policeman in my presence. Most of the times while walking around, I'm coming from work and have a presentable appearance with my hair cut, face shaved, clothes and shoes clean which does not heighten the senses of the police like it would if I was unshaven, clothes big and baggy and/or dirty and had a mean or disturbed grimace on my face, and maybe smelt of alcohol/weed. Other times when I am not going to work, even if dressed in baggy clothing, I am always clean and presentable; therefore, I HAVE NEVER EVER BEEN STOPPED AND FRISKED!

notice when u hang out
with #whitepeople they alway want 2 pay 4
ur drinks. y, cuzz they no companies offer
them more money than #blackpeople

A young lady @ my old job heard her
hiring manger offer a #whitegirl $20,000
more than she 4 the same position. she
was pissed #blackpeople

Maybe you've noticed, maybe you haven't, but when Black American people go out with a lone White American person or in a group for a beer or dinner, the White American people always offer to pay the bill.

I can recall my first job out of college, I asked for $25,000 and that is exactly what they paid me, no more, no less. What that tells me is they were really budgeted to pay more. I have my CPA Lic and 10

- 156 -

MICHAEL IRVIN WALKER

years of experience, often see jobs on the market for my experience level paying $90K to $120K, yet when I have meetings with recruiters from employment agencies, they all tell me that the highest I would possibly be paid is $90K and even that is a stretch; they really try to convince me to take $80K. $80K is a pretty good salary, but White American people my age with my same credentials live in Manhattan in $3,500/Mth Apts; that's more tax-free cash spent on rent than I brought home in my paycheck on my last job making $66K. White American people know this; that most Black American people are paid $.50 cents on the dollar to what White American women make, $.65 to $.75 cents on a dollar paid out to White men.

I came across a salary raise sheet at one of my jobs. A young White American female, younger than I, who started the job the same time as I did in a different department started out making $17,000 more than I did. By the time I reviewed the raise sheet, she was getting paid $21,000 more than I was. She had received a 13% raise in a range of 3 years, I only received a 6% raise in that time period and they acted as if they did not want to give that to me. In essence, you'd pay for the drinks or the dinner bill of persons you knew were getting paid $20,000 less than you also, wouldn't you? I came across another payroll journal of a company I worked for; all of the younger White employees were being paid $15,000 - $30,000 more than I was. (see payroll journal attached at end of book)

I'm realizing that these feelings I tweet may just B my unique experiences feelings not shared by #blackpeoople

- 157 -

These tweets and subsequent analysis of them may just be due to my personal experience and are not shared by the majority of Black American people. Perhaps many Black American people do not share the same stories of being blindsided in corporate America when it comes to starting pay, raises and promotions.

Maybe no one ever thinks about the billions of dollars Black American sports players and entertainment individuals make and how it could be used to boost other careers and economic statuses of other professional Black American people outside of sports and entertainment.

The majority of Black American people may think it just fine to wear ostentatious and excessively expensive brands of clothing and shoes, yet are not in a management position at their jobs nor do they own a home; and lest we forget, that very few Black American people can obtain employment in the stores or corporate offices of these luxury brands.

Maybe no one cares about young Black American men walking around with their underwear showing hurting their own current self-image as well as the future image of themselves and other Black American people.

It may be just human nature and brain chemistry which keeps Black Americans dependent on White American and Jewish people for the organization of their business; maybe Black American people know these other races of people (from Jews

- 158 -

MICHAEL IRVIN WALKER

to Asians) are smarter than Black American people themselves and politely demure and abdicate positions of intelligence, authority, byzantine analysis and inextricable detail to these other races, and truly believe even if a Black American holds the same degrees and professional certificates as these other races of people, the Black American people are still lesser and incompetent in their particular field of expertise.

Maybe Black American people are capitulating cowards and accept defeat in matters of competition which involve creating new brain pathways with excessive thought and study of a new subject or creation of an idea, adroit machination and strategy.

I do not know what I have read, what thoughts in solitude have led me to have the audacity to think Black American people can excel in other areas of life besides: singing R&B and Pop music, Rap music, Basketball, Football and Entertainment; that we can have the nerve to covertly or rather overtly coalesce into a powerful people who can own other possessions besides NIKEs and cars; to think we can own land, property, commercial property, build behemoth brands, send our children to colleges (HBCU or otherwise) and have our own corporations/brands waiting to employ our children upon graduation.

Maybe other Black American people look at these thoughts and ambitions like, "THIS NIGGA (though I do not promulgate the use of that word) HERE IS CRAZY!"

#tamar&vince only money #blackpeople have is from music then they spend it all. this is what we promote as a nice life 4 our people

#dumb#tamar&vince these shows where people r supposed 2B so rich, but we never c meetings with financial advisors & or cpa #stupid#blackpeople

#tamar&vince we never hear what the xtra characters do 4 a living. does anybody have a real job or profession? r they on welfare #blackpeople

I was watching the Tamar & Vince reality television show on VH1 one night. Tamar is the sister of the famed R&B singer Toni Braxton. Vince is the manager of Lady Gaga's music career (Black American peoples' only claim to fame and riches or wealth is MUSIC).

In watching one episode of this show, it dawned on me most of the reality shows involving Black American people were all centered around sports, music and entertainment: Basketball Wives,

MICHAEL IRVIN WALKER

Love & Hip Hop (Atlanta), Tamar & Vince, The Braxtons, Hollywood Exes. The shows were based upon people who were extraneous beneficiaries of someone else's sports contract, music career, etc. No one was self-made without the help of sports, music or acting or having been involved with sports, music or fashion in some form.

The shows usually showed the characters spending money, going on trips, out to lunch and dinner and having a grand ole time interweaved with other drama and fights.

Something else also clicked while watching these shows, which was that no one ever seemed to have a meeting with their financial advisor or CPA, not even to get their taxes done, which is something we all must do. These shows put forth a vision of money from nowhere, spending it and no plan to save it, invest it and/or bequeath it to an estate at death.

The thinking of Black American people seems to be (especially as of the image promulgated by these shows), "I'm going to have money for life and never have to worry about it running out and I'm never going to die", WHICH IS NOT REALITY AT ALL; while great entertainment, these shows provide a bad warped sense of life's reality to an amenable individual who may be influenced enough to believe the show represents how reality should actually be lived.

Also, as a main part of these shows, are friends of the reality stars who are introduced, tied in to some dramatic event happening to the stars of the show and the friend is their confidant. For example, on Love and Hip Hop Atlanta, Stevie J's girlfriend Mimi had a friend who supported her when Mimi needed to talk about she and Stevie J's problems. This friend, it was never stated what she did for a living and how she maintained her life; she's just there when Mimi needs her. Suppose some young pliant, incorrigible girl was watching the show and saw this particular young lady on the show who seems to have no job, but yet she is cute; it could implant in a young girls' mind, "I can be cute, a good friend AND NOT HAVE TO WORK FOR LIVING"

u seem 2 think just because u have on a pair $150-$250 Air Max or Jordan's with an f'd up outfit u look nice & stylish. #blackpeople

u'll c the most broken down men & women with a pair of nike's on their feet and they're walking tall & proud like they're rich #blackpeople

#blackpeople look down when u pass other black people. how many pair of nike's u count n a week? how many #blackpeople work 4 nike #stupid

MICHAEL IRVIN WALKER

#blackpeople how did we become so loyal 2 the nike brand of shoe. people seem 2 think a pair of nike's on their feet makes everything right

You can go into nearly any ghetto in America and look down at the residence feet; a majority of the residence will have on NIKE brand of sneakers: Air Max and Air Jordans mainly. Most of the people, both men and women, will have on the same sneaker and colors as if they all went to the sneaker store down the block on the same day. You'll see these people, some women with scarves on their head because they do not have proper hair styles, their jeans may be dirty and/or ill-fitting or they'll have on out of shape sweat pants; take a look at their skin, which may not appear to be in the healthiest condition and their teeth may be crooked or yellowing or missing or all three.

Even though these people may not have the grandest financial situation on earth; the one common factor which seems to make life fine is if they can show they own a pair of NIKE shoes which cost $150.00 or more. NIKE has branded Black American people, ingratiated the brand so much so, Black American people do not realize how religiously they purchase the brand. BRAND-WASHED! I myself, as a teen up till my late 20s, I would not purchase a sneaker brand outside of NIKE. The majority of sneakers I have owned in my lifetime, were indeed NIKE!

@BLK_PEEPSTOP

It occurred to me one weekend I took a trip to Columbus, OH and visited a late night Black American strip club; I happened to look down and every patron in the club had NIKE sneakers on their feet. I began to ask myself the question, "how did NIKE ingratiate itself with Black American people so well and indefatigably?"

"If Black American people suddenly ceased to purchase NIKE sneakers for a year or two, what effect would it have on the brand and its stock price?" I have not purchased a pair of NIKE sneakers since 2002; not necessarily as a protest, but rather my personal style outgrew the brand.

I mentioned at one time to a friend of mine, "Black American people need to boycott NIKE so they may see the power they hold with how they spend their discretionary dollars." He argued, "NIKE gives Black American sports players such as LeBron James, $90Mil contracts; therefore, Black American people should not boycott NIKE."

What he doesn't realize and what I told him is, while NIKE is giving LeBron $90Mill. NIKE will make $300Mil or more gross profit from the sale of LeBron NIKE shoes. And while they make that $300Mil gross margin profit, how many regular educated Black American individuals or Black American designers of their shoes do they actually employ at their corporate headquarters in Beavertone, Oregon and particularly in the corporate office executive suites?

MICHAEL IRVIN WALKER

Black American people and Black American sports players seem to be the back bone of NIKE sneaker sales, but Black American people aren't receiving any stock options, nor are they getting paid $250,000 or more as executives of NIKE.

#blackpeople can u all please stop shopping at the same stores & all buying the same sneakers (colorful airmax)

the only thing #blackpeople seem 2 do n solidarity is by high priced clothes that their life/job/income level do not match. #stupid

#blackpeople the sales people follow u around is a myth which pigeon holds u n2 shopping at the same stores. shop where ever, don't pilfer

#blackpeople chinese sell us food, nails& hair n our hood, arabs own the corner store n our hood, jewish own the property. we own nike shoes

I noticed in the year 2002, living in New York City, most Black American people, even me, dressed the same. At the time, I was wearing oversized carpenter jeans of various shades and brands: Old Navy, Guess. Levis; rugby shirts: Enyce, Sean Jean, Phat Pharm; Timberland boots or NIKE Air Force 1 classic white sneakers. It was around this time I started to search for other type of brands and a different fit of clothing to wear.

Due to having a girlfriend who worked in the fashion industry, she put me on to different jean brands: Diesel, Adriano Goldschmeid, Gstarr Raw, Joe and Seven. For shirts, it was a little harder to make a change but I eventually transitioned to v-neck and crew neck fitted tees in the summer and different print sweaters in the winter. It took me two to four years to perfect my craft of style away from the quote/unquote Hip Hop baggy style, but eventually I did and my friends started calling me metro-sexy.

Metro-sexy was fine with me, especially since I started noticing I'd get looks and stares from beautiful women on the streets and in clubs. One particular Saturday night at a weekend music industry club party, I had on GStarr Raw jeans, a fitted sweater with an interesting pattern and collar and a pair of Adidas Somoa sneakers which matched the sweater; this beautiful, thick, sexy young lady came up to me and said, "you are dressed so nice and cute and different than most guys. If I wasn't involved with someone else right now, I'm very intrigued and would want to date you."

I started my quest for "different", shopping at ZARA, which is where I purchased the sweater the young lady in the club loved so well. I then branched off to shopping at Penguin, French Connection, Ben Sherman and ATRIUM. I'd buy nice jeans, slacks and

- 166 -

MICHAEL IRVIN WALKER

nicely fitting rugby shirts, not the oversized ones I was wearing before.

I noticed when shopping in these stores, at first, coming in, not wearing brands or styles that the store sold, the sales people were a little reticent, but when I approached them, they were friendly and when I truly had an intention to buy something, was trying it on, etc., the sales people helped me kindly and I never noticed the, "sales people follow Black American people around the store to make sure they will not pilfer any clothing items" myth. As I'd shop more and buy brands that were similar to the store brands I was walking into, the sales people would approach me right away asking if they could help me with anything. Many Black American people truly believe in the myth, "Store sales persons follow Black American people around in the store and treat them badly in high end fashion stores". To a certain extent it is true, and to another extent it is not.

I can recall in 2003 when I purchased my first pair of Farragamo loafer shoes which I paid $325; when I made the decision to purchase, I blatantly heard the guy who fit them for me say, "I didn't think he was going to buy them" not talking to me but to other salesmen in the store. To top that off, as I was walking out of the store, an Asian guy, I do not know if he was a security guard or not, made a comment as I walked by him, "YOU MADE IT" which was a direct insult to me, pointing to the fact, I thought I had made it to the big time of money and wealth just because I could afford to or splurged to purchase the shoes.

The store Barneys on Madison Avenue in New York was blasted with claims, they'd send out security agents to stop Black American people on the street after leaving the store from making a purchase and harass them regarding their debit card and/or where'd they get so much cash to purchase a $300 - $750 item.

Besides my particular isolated Ferragamo store incident, I have shopped in Saks, Bergdorf Goodman and other luxury brands stores without so much as a weird look, comment or sales person following me around the store. They all asked if I needed help with anything, as is a part of their job.

In some instances, it is Black American people projecting the mirror image of the myth upon themselves; if a sale rep asked them do they need help with anything or stick close by them to potentially answer any question they may have and to get the commission, the Black American shopper will presume this as racial profiling when in actuality, it is a part of a sales persons job.

In addition to insecurity with store sales people hampering people from shopping in certain stores, the way the majority of Black American people dress is a vicissitude, a natural extension of where they come from and their environment, also it represents the affordable price range $150 - $250 in which they can shop, but there are many who save and purchase more expensive items outside that general range,

MICHAEL IRVIN WALKER

though it may still be an ostentatious brand or item known to the Black American culture or their peers.

People feel comfortable all dressing the same and are a little intimidated to step even slightly out of the box. When someone comes around wearing something different, they get looks askance as if they are from another planet. I noticed this myself in changing my dress style, which I find it particularly vexing in New York, the fashion capital of the world; with so many stores and brands to choose from, why would any certain group of people all wear the same things? Why aren't people going to different boutiques and buying something to slightly differentiate themselves from the rest of the crowd?

To dress different, takes a little courage and it may be more expensive to do so. But when you think of the cost of the average hot ticket items in the Black American ghetto hoods of New York City throughout 2011-2013: True Religion and Nudie Jeans: $250; Ugg boots for women and the unisex Ugg boots with the rubber front and white fur on the inside which can be seen upon flipping the sides down: $225; Montero Coats, for an original (not knockoff) waist length bubble coat:$1,100; Polo Shirts in multiple monotone pastel colors and/or striped patterns: $100 - $130; as of this writing, Prada sneakers at a cost of $325 a pair were a popular brand amongst popular Black American socialite zeitgeist which has died down (currently back on the market at $660 a pair); people are already paying a high price, but still like locavores, all seem to cling to one or a few expensive brands, and the whole entire neighborhood will all go out and buy the exact same things.

Maybe this goes to show the average person with normal to low self-esteem will take from the environment around them and ratify the validity of their choices based upon the fact that the majority of other people around give it an imprimatur by endorsing the same. The above-average person with high self-esteem does not need validity from those around her; she follows her own creative path and often ends up in a better place and space for doing so.

If a person can notice a pattern of Black American people purchasing particular brands of sneakers or jeans or coats, it means they all consciously or unconsciously are collectively supporting these brands. If Black American people would collectively pool their money with the same ardor to purchase property within their communities such as Bedford-Stuyvesant Brooklyn, NY or purchase the stocks of the brands they wear faithfully, for the purpose of family and future generational wealth building or to support the building of a lasting Black American brand and corporation, maybe Black American people would earn greater respect among ourselves first, and then the respect of other nationalities in this land who come to America and make money in a particular industry: Arabs (corner stores); Chinese (Chinese food, nail salons, Black American hair care products and boot leg luxury goods).

- 170 -

MICHAEL IRVIN WALKER

BLACK AMERICAN PEOPLE CAN NOT SEEM TO UNDERSTAND THAT LANGUAGE! All Black American people do is collectively spend BILLIONS OF DOLLARS WITH OTHER NATIONALITIES MAKING OTHERS RICH WHILE MAKING OUR OWN COMMUNITIES POORER BY THE DAY, YEAR AND GENERATION!

#blackpeople complain about gentrification. since u buy cars/clothes nstead of land/houses u have no power 2 do anything about it #stupid

During the years 2006 – 2013 and beyond, there was a massive gentrification process going on in both Harlem, NY and Brooklyn, NY. I can recall during some type of festival in Harlem, there was a panel with a radio host and some other community activist speaking about what was going on: White American people moving in, buying up vacant and/or dilapidated properties, renovating them and renting them out to other White American people or moving into the properties themselves.

Mind you, in the late 80s to early 90s, there were so many vacant properties in Harlem, the city or banks were trying to give the properties away for $1.00. At the time the neighborhood was crime laden with drugs, murder and robbery and not much of a police presence to hinder the crime; no one, not even rappers with money or common working folks who

- 171 -

could have gotten a renovation loan for $150,000 - $200,000 and fixed up the properties, made a move to do such. It is my suspicion that many of the people who lived in the neighborhood at the time, were living in rent-controlled apartments, with bad credit and could not afford to apply for any type of loan or knew they would be instantly turned down if they did.

My harangue regarding this issue is back in the late 80s to early 90s was when NIKE Air Jordan's started selling at the highest price of any sneaker ever sold on the market; guess who clamored to buy those sneakers, the same Black American people living in rent-controlled apartments probably on welfare.

Those same people who were at the rally crying about White American people taking over the neighborhood, the increased police presence and the neighborhood losing its cultural Black American roots, had lived in the neighborhood for years, you could catch them all out on 125th St on the 1st and 15th shopping, buying named brand clothing, leather jackets, gold bamboo earrings and neck chains with their working, welfare or drug dealing pay.

While they were all on 125th shopping, they should have been organizing, pooling that money together to buy some of the property in the neighborhood, changing the landscape of the neighborhood and/or changing their future wealth prospects as well. Spring forward 23 – 25 years, NO ONE OWNS ANY PROPERTY!

MICHAEL IRVIN WALKER

If you own NO PROPERTY, you cannot legitimately complain about who is moving into the neighborhood, BECAUSE YOU HAVE NO POWER TO CONTROL WHO PURCHASES THE PROPERTY AND/OR MOVES INTO THE PROPERTY. Arguments and complaints about gentrification are futile, falling upon deaf ears of persons who truly seem concerned, who very well know, within the back of their mind, THERE IS NOTHING NO ONE CAN DO ABOUT IT!

Allow me to explain what I think is the mindset of Black American persons in their mid to late 20s in the New York City metro area; personally, and culturally, our priorities are in the wrong place: first, we spend a healthy amount of our paycheck on name brand clothing; second, we spend the next portion on saving for trips and cars; add a baby out of wed-lock to the mix and there is nothing left for investing in the future of a home purchase.

Another important part of the equation, out of the control of Black American people, is we have been and currently still are getting paid $.50 to $.75 to every $1.00 that the majority of White American people - who we are trying to imitate in life - make on the job, and that's if we can get a job, which is often hard due to lack of education, connections, incessant systemic racism and/or nepotism.

If a person has $2,000 a month tax free cash for living expenses: $600 rent, $800 spending / clothing, $600 car and insurance, equals MONEY GONE! Change the formula up or down for rent

- 173 -

and/or spending because many lived/live in rent-controlled apartments with their family - my ex-girlfriend lived in the Astoria Projects with her mother, father and aunt; made $60,000/Yr rent free, SPENT ALL MONEY ON CLOTHING! This leaves no room, much less the desire to save $10,000 to $20,000 for a down payment on a home loan. Then there is the fact, a home loan would drastically increase the rent/property tax payment to $1,000 - $1,200 taking away from the all-important shopping/spending/car budget.

IT'S A NEVER-ENDING CYCLE of owning clothes and cars, not land/houses; thus, no control of the neighborhood. If Black American people would come together and start pooling their money for the political power statement rather than the individual ownership and individual riches/wealth building, minority ownership could be much, much, greater.

In Bedford Stuyvesant, Brooklyn, NY, it was rumored a young man could not walk down the street in the late 80s with a gold chain around his neck without getting it taken by force of hands of a gang or by gunpoint. The neighborhood has always been a dichotomy of nice brownstones, both on the inside and outside and not so nice grimy brownstones or sloppy vinyl front/row duplexes. Many families owned/own their brownstones in Bed-Stuy and many families did/do not.

MICHAEL IRVIN WALKER

The gentrification process began by a strong police presence in the neighborhood that had never been seen before when Black American men were killing each other via gun violence and innocent by-standers, including children were getting injured or killed as well.

Then, Jewish property owners started raising the rents on apartments they were happy renting before to Black American families at a cheap and/or section 8 rate. Once they evicted a family or the family willingly moved due to the high rent, the property owners began renting the apartments to White American people at the higher rate, as well as to Black American professionals who could afford the higher price. Black American property owners followed suit with raising rents and/or moving White American people in.

Black American families who owned their brownstones were hit up by investors to purchase their properties for cash; to a family, living in a run-down brownstone, who could not afford to fix it up and were barely making the property tax payments and/or defaulting on 2nd and 3rd mortgages, cash in hand was very appealing. A family would sale a four-story brownstone for $215,000, an investor would take it over, renovate it and sale it for $750,000 - $850,000 or rent out each separate floor for $1,200 - $1,800 a month to a majority of White American individuals: professional and/or students and a minority amount of the apartments to professional Black American individuals. Bars and restaurants, internet café baristas and wine stores owned both by Black American and White American individuals started springing up on Bedford, Nostrand, Lewis and Stuyvesant Avenues.

As of Jan 2013, you could not walk down any block in Bedford-Stuyvesant without there being a gutting and/or renovation project going or seeing a For Sale sign, and White American families walking down the blocks checking out the properties and also testing out their comfort levels with walking down the block, often hand in hand in the presence of Black American people with less economic status and wealth.

#blackpeople #hiphop numbs ur brain n2 thinking u can bcome an overnight success. u can't. stop dreaming. start reading & studying #stupid

"Let me start by sayin' / You wanna leave / go head / I'm stayin" (Daddy O of Stetsasonic "In Full Gear") I used to be an avid fan of Hip Hop, the music was my life, I literally lived by the KRS ONE mantra, I AM HIP HOP" My top artist as they applied to my generation: 1. KRS ONE 2.JAY Z 3. NAS. I could get into a long-protracted list and explanations about top ten list, who's there and who's not; if someone has one or the other rapper on their top ten list, my understanding or not as to why they put them there, etc.

MICHAEL IRVIN WALKER

When Eric B and Rakim received a $1Mil contract in the late 80s, they didn't brag about it, rap about it by throwing it out as "I got $1Mil you got two hundred thousand so I'm better than you".

Around the year 2003, I noticed Hip Hop began to have an effect on me. It started to put an avarice fire in me to be rich, to be able to obtain cars and clothes, etc. Many of the lyrics were about: $300 Evisu jeans, Rolex and Jacob watches and lines by artist Foxy Brown, "If you ain't pushin' what I'm trying to be pushing next year, you're talkin' for your health." I'd look at the artist, young Black American men and women just like me who had done nothing special but had a skill to write rhymes – a skill which I had once upon a time - be at the right place at the right time, preparation met opportunity and got signed to a recording contract, put together a nice record or album and voila, within a year, they were rich and heading on a path to more riches; all while enjoying themselves and bragging about their riches.

In the real world, to acquire the riches of Hip Hop artist/rappers, people obtain a bachelor's degree, work countless hours navigating a path of political pitfalls, go back to school and get a graduate degree/MBA, become an executive and somewhere in their mid 40s to mid 50s they hit a stride where their work seems to become easy management to them and the riches rain down constantly. It's the process of getting degrees that Kanye West made flippant skits about on his debut album "The College Dropout".

When I used to turn on the radio in NYC to Hot 97 FM (and probably still), all of the rap songs, by artist such as Rick Ross, for example, made it seem as if life was so golden; not only was it golden, they pushed to their audience through lyrics: I lived in the hood, I never had a job (well, Rick Ross was a prison corrections officer), I sold drugs, I made a demo tape or mix CD and BOOM, HERE I AM LIVING THE GOOD LIFE!

They make it sound so easy and attainable; with little effort you can live life like this as well. I think it transfers into everyday working-class peoples' psyche, they do not have to work hard on their jobs or in life to get ahead or obtain half of what the Hip Hop artist have; they think it is easy or that it is owed to them by the universe. When reality hits and things do not come as easily; when set-backs arise instead of advancement, it leads to depression and greater life problems.

Hip Hop lyrics with tales of riches and the easy good life, are noise which clouds Black American peoples' brain as to what struggles and sacrifices must be made to obtain any measure of success in life. If you really want to be successful, watching and listening to fake reality on television, music videos and radio stations is a hindrance to, not a promotion toward your dreams; unless that is, your dream is to become a Hip Hop artist yourself.

MICHAEL IRVIN WALKER

#blackpeople y would u buy art from a rich white kid of the westside of manhattan justin bua. he profits off our cultural sensitivities

u'd think the painting of black people with long arms and big lips djing or tupac or biggie would b from a black artist. they r not #stupid

@justinBUA my point exactly. eminem heralded as 1 of the greatest wealthiest rappers, kool g rap/talib k has probably 001% of em's wealth.

black people funny how every other culture takes our culture, dance, etc & become famous. i.e.korean guy dancing like morris day & the time.

Around the year of 2000, I noticed these prints of art being sold on 125th street in Harlem. They were comprised of a brown skinned Black American man, with large pronounced lips and a funky look on his face, long curvy arms and fingers, playing the piano, trumpet, guitar and DJing.

At first glance, especially since these prints had a Black American man as their subject, a person would think that was Black American art and logistically the work of a Black American man or woman. WRONG! Those prints, which I've seen in more than a few Black American peoples' homes are by a White American guy named Justin Bua. Justin claims to be down with Hip Hop because he was a break dancer and graffiti artist back in the early to late 80s. And who am I to judge, after all, Hip Hop is a music of the people, ALL PEOPLE!

Here is where the problem comes in for me. It always seems to be a White American guy who profits in arbitrage of the talents created and or shaped by Black American people and culture: Elvis Presley, Pat Boone, Beastie Boys, New Kids On The Block, Vanilla Ice, Mark "Marky Mark" Whalberg, Justin Timberlake, Robin Thicke, Eminem, Clive Davis and Jimmy Iovine and add Justin Bua to the mix.

Black American people are always on the cusp of innovation; the White American man comes and organizes it, sells it, gets some White American people out in front of it and profit the most from it. Of all the Black American graffiti artist and Black American artist period, out of New York City, why is it that Justin Bua is noted for paintings of Black American men; which he copied the style of Black American artist Ernie Barnes! Justin also sales paintings of Tupac and Biggie.

These people are masters of infiltrating Black American peoples' circles, speaking our language of the "birth of the cool" and becoming huge successes off of our innovation: from singing, rap, dance, to artistic paintings. And the thing about it is they actually make great livings. Black American people struggle and struggle to make a living; a White

MICHAEL IRVIN WALKER

American shows up and becomes a millionaire off of the same dream some Black American had years earlier and may, at the same time the White American boy is making a huge profit, the Black American is still trying to figure out a way to eat, buy clothing and even better still, a car or house from his artistic endeavors.

Many Black American people have also profited from their own innovation, but yet, it seems just a little too easy for a White American individual to copy-cat Black American culture and become popular, rich and loved by the masses of America. Another note on the subject is Black American people who desperately try to simulate within American culture, while there are many successes, many more have/had a long road and stories of their education and talents ignored, passed over for promotions, etc.

I have no problem with the human beings Justin Bua or Charlotta Janseen. I'm sure they are nice individuals and it may be fun to hang out with them, and it truly is not their fault they were or are able to profit and make a comfortable living off painting very nice images of Black American people and Black American culture.

How could I blame anyone for taking advantage of a profitable situation, but my lament is with the system and how unfair it seems to Black American people with the same talents who do not receive half the reward and/or glory, but are left to suffer as talented afterthoughts of the arts who just happened to catch a bad break or no break at all.

- 181 -

#blackpeople the book 48 laws of power by robert greene will teach u how white & even light skin people play u 2 their advantage

#blackpeople even the statement of "light skin & dark skin is still all black" is a testament 2 the 48 laws of power working on u

#blackpeople who believe that skin color doesn't matter is the reason we r at the bottom of totem pole in cultural success & class

#blackpeople skin color matters n america, trick is 2 promulgate it doesn't matter but behave n major ways like it does #whatwhitepeopledo

#blackpeople best way 2 gain advantage on opponent is 2 guide n2 a me-too position while advancing ur future position far greater than (s)he

The 48 Laws of power is a very popular book within the United States of America because Americans are totally consumed with money, fame and the power it seems to bring oneself. What fascinated me about the book is it goes totally antipode of what my grandmother and mother taught me in my household: "trust in the Lord, Pray and EVERYTHING WILL BE OK."

- 182 -

MICHAEL IRVIN WALKER

According to the 48 Laws of Power, a human being needs a lot more than spiritual faith to survive in any society. Even more shocking was that the adroit strategies talked about in the book go back to BC times and 1700, 1800 and early 1900s. What that tells me is that people have been practicing artifice, deception and power brokering since the beginning of time. However, Black American people seemed to have missed the boat on these teachings or ways of living; including allowing themselves to be sold into slavery by White American men posing as their friends.

Many Black American people know for a fact that skin color matters in these United States of America as well as abroad in other nations. It seems no secret that light skinned Black Americans get advantages over dark skinned Black Americans: i.e. Beyonce v Kelly Rowlands' music career; Halle Berry v. Angela Bassets' acting career and the countless 1st Black American individuals in history - Thurgood Marshall, the first Black American Supreme Court Justice - are very high yellow. The first Black American person from New York to be elected to Congress, Adam Clayton Powell, was also a very light skinned man descending from mixed Black/White American parents.

Take the antithesis example of light skinned persons being first and receiving advantages; abroad in Europe, the first Black Italian Integration Minister Cecile Kyenge having bananas thrown at her during a rally in Cervia, and Italian Senator Robert Calderoli calling her an orangutan. She is a dark skinned individual with a short coif, black in color. I seriously doubt she would have received that type of treatment if she had the features of Valerie Jerret who is/was Senior Advisor to President Obama, or Susan Rice who was the United States Ambassador to the United Nations during President Obama's tenure. Speaking of President Obama, the first Black American President of the United States is half White American.

Every time this particular subject is broached, many Black people say, "that is some real color struck, slave minded, Black American separatism, Willie Lynch shit." Light skinned people will come out to their own defense, "we have it just as hard as any other Black Americans; we're not given any special privilege or treatment." All the while before the new millennium, it was hard to get a dark skinned person in a mainstream television commercial or show; on The Fresh Prince of Bel Air, the dark skinned mom was replaced by the light skinned mom (but we've later learned this was due to other factions, not just skin color); on Damon Wayans television show "My Wife and Kids" his original dark skinned daughter was replaced by a light skinned daughter, etc.

The subject of "Colorism", the proper term placed upon my skin color lament, was broached upon Oprah Winfrey's OWN Network show featuring Ayanla Vanzant which is called Life Class. Before the airing of that show, I had never formally heard the subject discussed in a dogmatic format.

MICHAEL IRVIN WALKER

In the 48 Laws of Power, there is law 21 "Play A Sucker To Catch A Sucker – Seem Dumber Than Your Mark" it goes into warning of how it is better to speak the language of those you hope to keep on your side and be friends with; never seem superior in sophistication or intellect to those you come across and want to persuade in your favor. THAT IS EXACTLY WHAT LIGHT SKINNED PEOPLE DO TO DARK SKINNED PEOPLE, pose as their friend in suffering, all the while gobbling up the riches and advantages for their own light skinned family.

White American people also use the light skinned/dark skinned strategy to create a divide amongst Black American people to keep them fighting so as they can never fully come together, discuss the true nature of the plot and overcome it for the sake and good of ALL BLACK AMERICAN PEOPLE! Actually Law 21 speaks to how White American people always infiltrate every aspect of Black American culture that has a profitable end: side up to your mark, play into her culture, dumb down your superiority, get what you want, become rich and RIDE THE WAVE.

#blackpeople let's look at this light skin thing: thurgood marshall, ceo of: bet american express, adam clayton powell, potus. all light

#blackpeople let's look at this light/dark skin thing: ceo of: xerox, mcdonalds, merck & co, tgif cref, condi rice. all dark

#blackpeople let's look at this light/dark skin thing: destiny child highest paid artist & most successfully married.

light #blackpeople let's look at this light/dark skin thing: collin powell, valerie jarret, eric holder, charlie rangel. all light

By my count that is a 9 to 3 count of light skinned/half White American people promoted to powerful or historical first positions over regular dark skinned Black American people. The issue when discussed on Oprah's Life Class show did not go deep into discussion and questions of why is it, that Kelly Rowland is a very beautiful woman, but she has yet to snag a very rich and famous husband or find the musical success in the United States as Beyonce has? Why is Soladad O'Brian, who literally looks like a White American woman, whom you would not guess is a half Cuban/Black American woman; why was she the face of "Black In America" on CNN, a very popular news channel, and has since ran with the brand after resigning from CNN? Why doesn't Brenda Blackman, a quote/unquote real easily identifiable Black American woman, have that job of representing and/or questioning what is the status of and problems with being "Black In America"?

MICHAEL IRVIN WALKER

Has anyone asked the question? Why is it that a majority of White European Americans, especially those in powerful economic and political positions will continue to promulgate within their family that persons of African descent are "other" and are not to be brought closely into the family network and business, nor are they to be treated as total unabridged equals; especially not to be married and to start a family with?

At the same time White European Americans perpetuate racist ethos, they often make concessions for lighter/half White persons of African descent. They seem to have a proclivity toward and/or are more comfortable with the lighter hue of African/Black American people, accept them and/or push them forward in all aspects of life.

Take a look at these persons, some aforementioned: Adam Clayton Powell, Collin Powell, Thurgood Marshall, William Haste (the guy who John F. Kennedy would have chosen to replace Thurgood Marshall if Mr. Marshall didn't make the senate conformation cut), Ken Chenault, Valarie Jarret, Susan Rice, Charles Rangel, Debra Lee, Kathy Hughes and lastly President Barack Hussain Obama. What do they all have in common?

Per Malcolm Gladwell's "Outliers", the last chapter, entitled "A Jamaican Story", in the Caribbean, Slave masters would buy slave women and publicly have relationships with them; the mixed Black Jamaican/White children were born free and were entitled to part of their fathers' estate upon his death. Since all cultures sway toward money and power which these Black Jamaican/White children had or would have, people often gravitated toward them for marriage and/or child birth; it was the same in American slavery for the most part (but without the public relationships and entitlement to estate).

With colorism today, many Black American people of lighter hue, with less effort than those of darker hue, get advantages - not necessarily WHITE AMERICAN PRIVILEGE - and my argument is not that they (lighter skinned Black Americans) do not work hard, but they seem to get in better places and in a better (no pun intended) light.

HOWEVER, there is a paradigm shift approaching. Ursula Burns, Donald Thompson, Roger Furguson, Shonda Rhimes, Wonya Lucas; what do these persons all have in common? We are starting to see more - darker than paper bag brown- persons put into positions of power. Take the fawning over Lupita Nyong'o during the 2014 Hollywood awards season, to the grand finale of her actually winning the most highly coveted prize in Hollywood, an Academy of Motion Picture Art and Sciences Oscar for her role in 12 Years A Slave (though, I'll never watch that movie).

It's the pushing forward into the spot light of persons who look like Lupita as opposed to Halle Berry; Idris Elba today as opposed to the past Harry Belefonte, until the scale is a little less tilted and there is more parity such that our young children or our

MICHAEL IRVIN WALKER

grandchildren will not notice that the darker skinned mother in "The Fresh Prince Of Bel Air" was replaced with the lighter skinned mother; that Halle Berry won an Oscar for "Monster's Ball", and Angela Bassett did not win for "What's Love Got To Do With It"; that our 1st Black American President of The United States is ironically half-White American. When these color lines start to be blurred, colorism has a far greater chance at being eradicated.

#whitepeople: apple twitter microsoft walmart facebook google netflix groupon myspace nike mcdonalds underarmor ford chrysler

#blackpeople fubu phatfarm cross color ebony/jet tyler perry studios bet motown laface badboy tracey reese dudley hair products

Take a look at the list and think a moment. All of the companies started by White American people are public, multi-billion dollar companies, have been or are the most popular in their respective industry. Take a look at the companies supposedly started and run by Black American people; none of the companies have been taken public, most of them are defunct or have lost market share and popularity in their respective industry. Many of the Black American companies, which revolved around the Hip Hop crowd in the late 90s had a loyal following among Black American people, but somehow lost vision, forward thinking and management.

FUBU for example, started out making T-shirts and hats, gained the celebrity endorsement of LLCOOLJ, quickly moved to jeans, rugby shirts and high-quality fleece tops and warm-up suits; even formal dress suits and sneakers (though the sneakers were a direct knock-off of other popular brand sneakers of the day). FUBU revived the Fat Albert gang, by placing the characters on T-Shirts, jeans and warm-up suits. Seemingly after the Fat Albert sweat suits, that was the last innovative idea they had, and interest – both the company's itself and the consumers - seemed to surcease in the brand. I always thought they should have decreased the size of their logo a little and reduced the bold designs, a supine step back in an effort to move forward from the Fat Albert trend, but they did nothing.

Take a company like Apple which started in the early 80s as competition to Microsoft. The company gained market share, went public selling stock for financial leverage, and founder/CEO Steve Jobs was on top of the world. Apple, with its boxy monitors and software, which could not compete with Microsoft - whose software quickly became ubiquitous in offices across America - quickly began to lose market share and its stock price plummeted. CEO Steve Jobs was ousted from the company by the board of directors and it seemed Apple would never revive itself ever again into a top player in the hardware desktop computer and tech market place.

Apple, instead of going debunk like Black American companies - FUBU, PhatFarm, Cross Color, Karl Kani – bounced back in early 2000s with new innovative products: Ipod, Iphone and Ipad. The stock price reached an all-time high of $705 a share in 2013, up from $28 a share in early 2000. Upon Steve Job's death in 2012, the company began once

MICHAEL IRVIN WALKER

again to lose market share due to lack of change in design and also lack of innovative technology in its products.

Take a look at the comparison of products just named off the top of my head in the tweet; the Black American companies are all centered around fashion and entertainment. The White American companies on the other hand span the gamut of automobiles, athletic products, technology products, fast food, new and innovative techniques to release old products like DVDs into digital streaming; ALL PRODUCTS WHICH BLACK AMERICAN PEOPLE INDULGE IN, WANT AND NEED, but yet Black American people do not create or cannot seem to get a footing in the creation of companies which provide these types of products universally used by millions of people, and take the companies public to everlasting sustainability.

A kid on the corner has a better chance of becoming a cpa, lawyer or doctor than becoming a rapper nba or nfl player. how is that not sexy

If u go 2 a jewish family and ask who is there hero, the kids might say loyd blankfein, ceo of goldman sachs

There seems to be this attitude within the Black American community, among our youth, that they do not have to work hard, that they are going to instantly make something of themselves one day; many have

- 191 -

hoop and football dreams, many have rapper dreams and some have drug dealer dreams. This is mostly among the young men.

The young women, a good majority of them seem to have motivation to get an education and try and obtain gainful employment to feed their shopping habit and desire to drive a luxury car.

Among the young men, they do not seem to have the same motivation and/or do not see any role models of what they would like to be in life and that's because there are not many role models in one concentrated area of law, accounting, ceos and doctors.

Perfect example, just look at my situation of passing the CPA Exam, yet could not get a fulltime job making six figures in New York City. I am not living in a nice house, at least not one that I own, nor am I driving a nice car; As yet, my 15 years of accounting experience with a Certified Public Accountant license has not redounded to the things it supposedly should. As I run my own accounting and tax firm (SYSTSEMIC RACISM WON AGAIN and the idea has become defunct) and work harder, surely my ultimate success will come, but technically it should already have been here. That's what it boils down to, WHAT CAN THEY SEE?

In a Jewish household, Lloyd Blankfein is reported in media to make upwards of $16Mil a year. Lloyd Blankfein is visible and tangibly teachable to a Jewish kid. Sheryl Sandberg is COO of Facebook,

MICHAEL IRVIN WALKER

one of the most popular companies of the 21st century. The only persons making that kind of money in the Black American community are professional sports players and entertainers; so, you can see the desire and proclivity toward these professions.

I suppose the odds are not being laid out for Black American men in school and their educational programs. The teacher is not grabbing their ear and telling them, **"YOU HAVE A GREATER CHANCE OF MAKING A NICE STABLE LIVING AS A LAWYER, CPA, DOCTOR OR JUNIOR ACCOUNT EXECUTIVE OR SUPERVISOR AT ANY JOB YOU CHOOSE TO CONCENTRATE ON, THAN YOU DO TO SUCCEED AS AN NBA/NFL PLAYER OR RAPPER! YOUR CHANCES OF MAKING IT AT A GLAMOUROUS PROFESSION ARE JUST AS GOOD AS THOSE OF WINNING THE MULTI-MILLION DOLLAR LOTTERY PRIZE! VERY INFINTESIMALLY SMALL CHANCE"** This message is not being fed.

Frankly, I do not think anyone cares or is paying attention to what our young Black American males are being taught in their high-school curriculum as it pertains to their life in the future as a man, husband and father. And somehow, these young men are not tapping into their inner strength to overcome obstacles and odds to BECOME SOMEBODY!

#blackpeople media makes it seems as if entertainment & sports provide a great life. hard work n other fields provides a great life also

Take a look at the media: American Idol, X-Factor, NCAA March Madness, NFL, NBA, TMZ, Entertainment Tonight, OMG Insider, The Voice. All of these media shows focus on success as a celebrity or star who already has millions of dollars, to the celebrity or star in the making who will soon possibly make millions of dollars. Is there a wonder youth, particularly Black American youth want to be in the ilk of sports stars, rappers and singers; not only that, the media makes it seem INSTANT!

There is no showing of the grind to make it, nor a showing of the people that went through the grind to make it, but never got there. In that spirit, there should be a show that chronicles a person with a dream, their day-to-day life, their home life, their preparation process, their performances, auditions, many failures or rather the attempts to strike gold without ever seeing any light at the end of the tunnel; the process of the success. The media does not promote a process.

There is a process to all success whether the process is mental or physical preparation. Take Fantasia, one of the many winners of the American Idol music show. Before she reached that show, she had to hone her singing skills some place for many years, she didn't just decide to get on stage and

- 194 -

MICHAEL IRVIN WALKER

figured out she could sing, ran with it and WON THE ENTIRE SHOW!

Take Rick Ross the rapper as another example, he didn't just show up at a record label, they signed him to a contract and he was an instant star. In fact, his real stardom didn't blossom until around his 3rd nationally released album; before a record label released his first album with the renowned single "Everyday I'm Hustling", he perhaps had been performing, rapping and recording music for 5 to 10 years prior to that.

Success can be had in other fields of work such as accounting, law, medicine, science, technology, etc; at times success in those particular fields happens more instantly than in music. Mark Zuckerberg for example wasn't exactly dreaming and working toward FaceBook while attending college courses at Harvard; he had an idea, the education and skills to put it into action and within 3 years he had millions of people using his invention and was on his way to becoming a billionaire 10 years later.

Sean "Puff Daddy, P. Diddy, Diddy" Combs and Jay Z have each been in music and product/brand endorsement for 20 plus years and STILL ARE NOT STAND-ALONE BILLIONAIRES! The creators of Twitter also used their education and execution skills to bring a product to life and found themselves multi-millionaires within a short period of time.

A life cycle of a CPA: go to college at 18 years of age, graduate at age 23 or 24, work 2 years while obtaining your graduate degree, pass the CPA Examination, work either for a CPA Firm or a corporation for 3 to 5 years and put in a hard work ethic, long hours and you'll find yourself making a six-figure salary in your early 30s, which believe it or not, is still very young in a professional corporate work career.

The path laid out above can be followed in just about any field of study and it is almost statistically proven to provide you with a stable living and income for the rest of your life. This is not pushed forward enough in the media. Even the people who do the reporting on the celebrity and sports player lifestyles, they have decent livings and incomes and fulfillment within their life.

Celebrity status is not the only way to live in America, but if you turn on the television to your local free station from 6PM to 8PM, the world of television and news STOPS AND ALL ATTENTION IS ON CELEBRITY LIFE! This fuels a vicissitude of lethargy and a longing for a sinecure, life of glamour, money and instant success.

There seems a great imbalance within the media between real life, which often times is not grandiloquent, and celebrity/sports star life which seems often times than not an instant amelioration of real-life circumstances. The real truth is not being put forth that all success takes time, humiliation,

MICHAEL IRVIN WALKER

emotional fortitude and preparation, but the easiest road to a reasonably successful life is education and hard work on a job or on a road of entrepreneurship.

#blackpeopople please do not listen 2 this hype that a college degree is not worth it. with it u barely get n the door, without it, ur dead

#blackpeople the thug is not a threat, 4 he'll either do nothing 2 help his people or go to #jail. the intelligent college grad is a threat

There have been reports that surfaced in 2011/2012 that a Law Degree is not worth the debt students get themselves into because they graduate and cannot find a good paying job. There have also been reports that a college degree in any field of study is not worth the debt. The studies are detailed and quite convincing.

What the studies are leaving out is, we are coming to a day in which White American people are becoming the minority, republican presidents are becoming a thing of the past. As their population becomes smaller and smaller, White American people will try and hold on to maximum power at all levels of life and the pursuit of happiness. Their main discriminatory tactic is and always will be, DID YOU GRADUATE FROM COLLEGE? Without a bachelor's degree – it's coming to the point where one needs a master's degree - they will eliminate any and all non-White American people, particularly Black American males from consideration of gainful employment.

The reports of "a college degree is becoming useless" are only an adroit tactic of White American people to eliminate competition from theirs and their children's dwindling numbers in the population. As this pertains to the Black American male, White American people know they have done the Black American male wrong and kept him from the resources needed to succeed at a top-quality level in this country. White American people know once the Black American male gets power in succession with other minorities, in recrimination, he may go about denying opportunities to the White American male as reverse discrimination for the many years of original discrimination against the Black American male.

The New Jim Crow, a book which speaks of trapping Black American men within the legal system with felony convictions and extending them long prison sentences for non-violent crimes, is a prime example of a control and guarding of power tactic among White America. This is the reason there is not an advocacy to educate Black American men and there is this newfound promulgation of college education as a waste of time, which rings loudest in the Black American mans' ear; an elimination of competition. In essence, America is not threatened by the thug, for they know, they will easily lock him up for years and years, destroy his public record, his credit and thus, HIS LIFE!

- 198 -

MICHAEL IRVIN WALKER

Take an educated Black American man; even if White America continues to deny him opportunities, he'll, sooner or later start his own small to mid-sized company and may promote a racism/nepotism system which White American men and women will be pariahs and precluded from. As these types of systems are built nationwide and the White American population continues to atrophy, THAT SPELLS TROUBLE FOR WHITE AMERICAN MEN AND WOMEN!

It is only a matter of time before the reputation of the Black American man, especially among other Black American people is turned around to that of a hard-working, ethical, detailed oriented, non-lethargic upstanding individual who can get things done and is good at project management, finance, law and operations. And an education, reading and studying is the only way that is going to happen.

What I think of education: it has prepared me to write this book, conditioned my mind to read and soak up information, made me analytical and able to understand the stock market on a certain level, made me observant of power moves, politics and tactics involving work environments, Washington, DC Capitol Hill politics; last but not least, has allowed me to think of ways to employ myself, handle clients with congeniality and professionalism and think of ways to expand my business once I have the proper resources or to think of creative ways to gain the resources needed for my ultimate success. Without education, I think what you'll find yourself doing is

- 199 -

BEING STUCK IN A CIRCLE OF THE SAME DAY
TO DAY PROCESSES, BRINGING YOU NOWHERE
AND NOTHING! Education allows YOU TO BREAK
THAT CYCLE!

#blackpeople how u build ur vocab, read a
newyorker magazine, every word u do not
know, underline it & look it up, write def

#blackpeople I used 2 read & come across
words I didn't know (1 word don't make no
article) till 1day I realized all the words I
didnt know

#blackpeople words I didn't know: lament
livid abdicate pariah debauchery coitus
consanguineous dichotomy tumultuous
paramour facetious

#blackpeople on 60 Mins, they just used a
vocabulary word - adulation. Do u know
what that mean

#blackpeople @kiganhoda show just used
a vocabulary word. delectable. do u know
what that means

#blackpeople president obama said
something about a "despot" gvnr romney
just said something about having this
"tumult" do u know the vocab

- 200 -

MICHAEL IRVIN WALKER

#blackpeople everybody has smart phones with downloadable apps such as "http://dictionary.com" which will make you smarter, use them

      In 2003, I was having a very hard time finding employment in White American Corporations in New York City. It was then that I realized, thanks to my girlfriend at the time, I had a southern drawl to my speech, I was not enunciating all of my words wholly and fully. I also realized my vocabulary was limited. I immediately started trying to speak more clearly, pronouncing my "ERs", "INGs", not using the words "BE" and "AIN'T" in my sentences and concentrated on pronouncing words with more than three syllables without stuttering, like Sanai Lathan's husband, Rockmond Dunbar, in the movie, "A Family That Preys" was doing and she made a note to him; her White American lover and father of her child, Cole Hauser, aka "William Cartwright" did not do that; he was intelligent and articulate.

      Being that I was trying to get a job within Corporate White America, I thought better of speaking in my natural Black American, southern drawl dialect. And just as you hear many Black American people who try to speak proper English, even President Obama, I was stuttering and stumbling badly when communicating with my girlfriend at the dinner table. She would say to me, "just speak naturally, plainly and clearly", which you can see the conundrum in that.

Often if you listen to Black American people talk, the majority of us, unless we've trained ourselves not to, cut off the "G" in "ING" words; for that is the way our ancestors talked and learned English coming over from Africa, without being able to read, as it was against the law. They were prevented to practice proper English at any great length; they were forbidden to emulate the proper language of their slave masters and others whom they heard speaking; for if they did, they'd be vituperatively scorned for being an "Uppity Nigger!"

The broken language has been passed down from generation to generation. Many view it as ignorant, without a place in the proper English language, especially corporate business dialect. Take "Sweet Brown" for example, the lady who in April 2011 almost burned in an apartment fire and became famous on YouTube for her speech to the news reporter about her escape; her final words, "AIN'T NOBODY GOT NO TIME FOR DAT"! The way she spoke, many, even me, view as ignorant and uneducated language. But in all actuality, it is a natural dialect tongue for Black American people to speak.

Up until this point in my life, the only time I'd focused on vocabulary was in 11th grade English class at the age of 16. So, one day I sat down with a large "W" fashion magazine and was determined to read through the entire magazine and underline or write down all of the words that I didn't know as I read. What most people do when reading an article is

MICHAEL IRVIN WALKER

skip over a word or think they'll get the meaning of it through the context of the remaining sentence. Once I truly paid attention, I realized that was a shortcoming of me and most Americans in building a memorable vocabulary. The proverbial saying is, "I know vocabulary words because I READ!" Well, in my case and I fear most people, especially Black Americans, reading alone is not enough.

What I discovered in reading is that words, at a glance, I thought I knew the meaning of, or took a guess at it from the context of the remaining sentence, once I actually looked up the word in the dictionary, I did not know the definition; add to that, all of the various words which I came across repeatedly which I never ever recalled coming across in my entire educational life, especially not in everyday disquisition with my friends and family: tumultuous, esoteric, banal, auteur, despot etc. (these words are common in fashion magazines), I realized my vocab was very weak.

Once I started getting my hands on free New Yorker Magazines at my media company job during the years of 2006-2010, I felt like a 2nd grader reading it; the New Yorker Magazine crawls with vocabulary words from front to back, every article. As a weekly publication, those who can keep up and read it in that time are some very vocab savvy and intelligent people, or at least the magazine presents such a picture of its readers.

What did I do? I did what any educated individual would do who wants to learn something. I began to write the words down on a piece of paper and write out a brief definition. I'd recognize if I had come across a word that I'd written down prior, and if I didn't know it, I'd look at my paper sheet and recite the definition to myself. When I acquired a smart phone, I began to keep track of the definitions in my note pad and put them in alphabetical order and I would go over them every so often when I had nothing else to do or while riding the train. While it is quite impossible to know all the definitions to all the words in my phone at one particular point in time, it does provide a quick reference point for words and often times, it actually helps with word association in sentences to recall the meaning of a word you've written down or come across recently in another book or publication. A word like "abdicate" is etched in my brain because it is the first word in my vocabulary list.

Now, of course in this day and age, Black American media personalities such as Steve Harvey and Sheryl Underwood have campaigned to say, "why must we change the way we speak and operate in everyday American life for White America to accept us." They have won that fight in respect to themselves as she is co-host on a very popular daily television show, "The Talk." Steve Harvey is host of an eponymous radio morning talk show, "The Steve Harvey Morning Show", Steve Harvey television talk show and also a very popular American television game show, "Family Feud." I however do not think

MICHAEL IRVIN WALKER

this fight has been won as it pertains to Corporate American Board Rooms, Accountants, Lawyers, etc.

I'm under the opinion that though, Black American people have a natural germane, passed down, elocution; it was born out of keeping us ignorant to American education, reading, history and culture of The United States of America. As I was born in America, educated through college, a bachelor's degree and professional CPA certificate in America, I prefer to speak the proper language and know the vocabulary in the lexicon of the mainland. But even still, I have not perfected speaking the English language Brian Gumble style; that takes a class which I believe is offered in undergraduate or masters in journalism programs at universities; serious practice or having grown up in an environment and/or home where enunciation and articulation was common. I grew up with my mom and aunts and they sound, believe it or not, like Tyler Perry's Madea.

#blackpeople must train our children 2 have longer attention spans 2 concentrate & study longer, think & figure out the byzantine subjects

#blackpeople we must train our children 2 figure out the convoluted subjects: medicine law electrical engineering accounting science #think

#blackpeople we must teach our children if they do not figure out the problems some1 else will. that some1 else will b respected & paid more

These thoughts came about when I started studying for my CPA examination. Going over the information as I was reading it seemed simple enough and that with little concentration, I should have easily been able to retain the information and pass the exam. This was hardly the case. I found myself, after I had passed Financial Accounting and Reporting, what many perceive to be the most difficult part of the exam, I was failing the other parts which were supposed to be less arduous. I actually failed each part once and two of the parts twice before passing on the third try.

My thoughts began to wonder if Black American people, myself included, have the intelligence capacity and emotional fortitude to become, in greater numbers, CPAs and Lawyers. Many people, after failing twice will not go in for a third try. John F. Kennedy Jr. took the Bar Exam 3 times, passing it on the 3rd try.

I began to think of other subjects: Engineering, Science, Medical, etc which are great professions and pay very well, but it does not seem that young Black American people tackle these subjects to completion of a successful career. My cousin for example, started her college degree at a popular university in Mississippi as an engineer, which I was very proud

MICHAEL IRVIN WALKER

she was following that particular punctilious course of study, but she later switched her major. My fraternity brother also was in school at the time we pledged, as an engineer major; he never finished school.

I recognized early on in my career as an accountant, that I would defer the most challenging subjects to a White American counterpart on the job or let them take on the bulk of the work while I kept it simple.

Passing the CPA exam was the most arduous feat I'd ever accomplished in life, and after I passed the exam I felt I could tackle any subject on earth; even thought about applying to law school. As I fought so hard and spent countless hours studying to pass the exam, I began to wonder were many Black Americans doing this type of studying or willing to put in that kind of prodigious time to better themselves educationally within their respective fields of study.

I was friends with one gentleman I met in Brooklyn, he said at one time he thought about studying to pass his Certified Financial Advisors examination, but once he got the book from which he had to study, he quickly realized it would take great effort and time away from his social life that he was not willing to give up, so he dropped the idea. He'd laugh at me, when after two years of seeing me on the train, I was still studying to pass the CPA exam, which was because I did self-study for a year before I took a prep course, which took me another year and three months to complete, study and pass the exam.

But he's the prime example of what I'm speaking; he'd rather party and relax than take a year and a half or so to pass an exam which could bring him more status within his career, more income and possibly more social status.

It seems many Black American people's attention spans do not last long to put forth a florid effort, very hard work ethic and get something done; they'd rather let someone else take care of that, which is exactly the reason Black American people are in the position in America we're in today: least desirable to employ, getting passed over for promotions, being underpaid or NOT BEING ABLE TO OBTAIN EMPLOYMENT AT ALL! I think the total numbers are skewed to the latter scenario than that of Black Americans who have been or are happy with their Corporate America experience, or have made it to CEO/CFO/COO. Yes, racism exist and persist, but "it's only so long fake thugs can pretend" (Jay Z "Takeover" Blueprint album, 2001). It's time I/we look at the man/woman in the mirror.

#blackpeople it's cool to be smart. it's cool to like rock & roll. it's cool not to dress like everybody else in your hood. be you

#blackpeople what I discovered a long time ago about rock music. It's not so abstract & different as some may think.

MICHAEL IRVIN WALKER

#blackpeople it's cool to like jazz. it's cool to go to the metropolitan opera at lincoln center. it's cool to go to a broadway show. be you

A rock and roll band, I recently had an impetus to explore, especially after they were honored in the 2013 Kennedy Center Honors, is Led Zeppelin. During the night they were honored on the show, I text a White American female friend of mine about a Led Zeppelin box-set I knew that she or her former spouse had in their possession. She told me she had a few Led Zeppelin albums and that I should experience Led Zeppelin by album, not a greatest hits compilation. She began to e-mail me the first two Led Zeppelin albums.

Upon listening, what I realized is that they produced some very funky music with groovy bass lines and guitar riffs. Two songs in particular, "What Is And What Never Should Be" which starts off as basically an R&B song, when listening to the timbre of the singers voice, "If I say to you tomorrow / take my hand child come with me" combined with the bass line and acoustic guitar strum; then when it gets to the hook, he starts this funky scream, "WAY UP HIGH IN THE SKY / BUT THE WIND WON'T BLOW / THE RIVER SHOULDN'T GO / IT ONLY GOES TO SHOW / THAT YOU WILL BE MINE"; after all of that, it settles into a calm "WOOOOOooooooooooo" I WAS BLOWN AWAY, and quite disappointed that I had not been exposed to this music prior. "The Lemon Song" is more Rock & Roll with a screaming/scratchy voice

- 209 -

@BLK_PEEPSTOP

type of singing and a funky electric guitar riff and bass line, but the beat behind it in the beginning of the song is very Hip Hop; after about 30 seconds, it gets into this sped up rock mode, which is not at all displeasing to the ear if you love music; but it eventually calms back down to the funky Hip Hop groove, or shall I say, Hip Hop comes from this type of music, sampling the beats and bass line riffs of Rock & Roll.

I discovered long ago, watching Mtv that I loved the videos by Aero Smith, "Janie's Got A Gun" "Rag Doll" & "Love In The Elevator" (the latter, a funky favorite of mine). I recall talking on the phone with a friend of mine one day as I was playing back an Aero Smith video I had recorded and she could hear it through the phone, she commented, "what are you listening to, is that what you've learned to like from going with that White girl?" I said, "No, I like the song, it's pretty funky so I recorded the video"

There seems to be this unspoken word that normal Black American people cannot like Rock & Roll music; that type of music is something "other"; when in all actuality the rockers admired old Black American Rock & Roll and Blues musicians so rock music has more in common with Black American music roots than one would think.

I can recall many songs which struck me as having a groove I could vibe too: "Guns & Roses: Welcome To The Jungle, Sweet Child Of Mine & November Rain", "Pearl Jam: Jeremy Spoken &

MICHAEL IRVIN WALKER

Black", "Bon Jovi: Living On A Prayer, You Give Love A Bad Name, Wanted Dead or Alive" "Green Day: Basket Case, When I Come Around" "Stone Temple Pilots: PLUSH (AN ULTIMATE FAVORITE OF MINE!)

It seems Black American people want to pigeon hold themselves to particular activities and a certain level of intelligence. At times many Black American people admire from afar someone who is smart, intelligent and articulate, but up close and personal in their own circle, if they are not of the same intelligence caliber, they may not be so accepting of the smart kid or educated and articulate adult. I feel smart, educated and articulate people should be embraced by our culture, even if it is opposite of what we are used to in our particular upbringing or circle.

The main problem may be people are uncomfortable with that which is not the normal for them. They do not know how to step outside of their comfort zone (the same as described above with dress code). So, if everyone in the crew listens to Lil Wayne when riding in the car or at a casual get together, a person would not feel comfortable playing Charlie Parker in the car or house gathering and making their friends listen to that, even as a suggestion to try something new from a different zone of Black American culture.

Art of all kinds has no race or face. Any artist will tell you their works of art are to be enjoyed, viewed, listened to and analyzed by the masses; while the art may come from a particular space of culture, it is not culture specific as to who can and will enjoy it, and it's up for interpretations of anyone. That statement is contradictory to my Justin Bua harangue, yes, but to my defense, I think certain art forms, the originators or persons who created it, or are the subject of the art should benefit most from its arbitrage, but as to who can enjoy, purchase, love or hate it, there should be no discrimination there. I would never say a White American man can't "Throw ya hands in the ay-er / if you's a true playa". To that point, of the millions of Black American people in the New York Metropolitan area, you do not see many of them at art museums such as the MET, Guggenheim or Whitney Museum of Art. While I understand that may not be part of many Black American people's comfort zone; at times, it is cool to step outside the comfort zone and learn from doing so, analyze yourself and your reactions to the art, analyze the other people in the museum and analyze the art - the details or lack thereof - itself.

A concept talked about in the book, "Who Moved My Cheese" references a similar, me-too, non-differentiation ideal. Most Black American people cannot seem to take an alternative route to find new cheese; thus, keep banging their head against a steal wall and remain in the same status circle (educationally, socially, economically) leading to nowhere. The majority of Black American people, though they bristle when it is said, "are not above average, detailed oriented, critical thinking, analytical people." And there may be some validity to the

MICHAEL IRVIN WALKER

statement, "White American people are cognitively smarter than Black American people"!

#blackpeople it's cool not to wear weave. it's cool to jog a few miles three days a week. it's cool to not have a fat round stomach

One of my main issues with Black American women and has been since the mid-1990s, is WEAVE! At one point I used to think it was cute, the braided hairstyles worn by female rapper Yo-Yo and female Hip Hop dancer Josie Harris in music videos. After some point in time, it began to get redundant, but Black American women never gave it up. As the new millennium approached, long straight/perm weave became a staple among Black American women. By that time, I had long decided I would not be in a long-term relationship or marry someone who considered putting weave into their hair.

While braids to a certain extent represent a cultural hairstyle of Black Americans, long straight/perm weave represents a self-hatred of ones' own self. I say self-hatred because typically long straight hair naturally grown down to the middle of ones' back is something that is natural among White American women, East Indian and various other cultures; while there are Black American women who can grow their hair to such lengths, the number of them when taken from the Black American community as a whole, is very minimal.

I am not on the side of this hair thing that if a Black American woman perms her hair and it grows long, she is doing something that is anathema to her own culture and Black American roots; not at all, is that what I am saying. But to purposely buy hair, sew it into your hair, trying to fit a quote/unquote image of American Beauty; I find something psychologically wrong with that process. I do not see countenance, serenity and beauty in the process, but rather a longing to be something that one naturally cannot achieve. I'm a firm believer in the song lyrics, "If it don't fit / don't force it / just relax and LET IT GO!" /Just cause that's how you want it / DOESN'T MEAN IT WILL BE SO! (Kellee Patterson)

#blackwomen it's cool 2: wear something 2 work other than the express dress pants; wear thongs with tights or the jersey summer dress

One thing, as I said previously, education has taught me, is to be observant and analytical of my surroundings, trends, etc. In ten years of working in Corporate America in New York City, one thing I noticed is the lack of dress style of Black American women in the subway on their way to work. A major staple outfit among many females on their way to and coming from work in New York is the simple flat front,

- 214 -

MICHAEL IRVIN WALKER

wide leg loose/tight fitting pant slacks, cheap and ugly flat shoes and a button-down waist length shirt either tucked or un-tucked. I particularly noticed this outfit being worn by Black American women the most, while I'd see White American and Asian women wearing different cut skirts and dresses, designer jeans and various designed sweaters along with some nice knee high/ankle high boots or flats ranging in brand and style, as well as high stepping in four inch heeled shoes as if they were comfortable sneakers.

The great disparity in dress code I quickly attributed to the bottom pay scale from which Black American women are being paid, the type of jobs they hold; many of whom I spoke with said they were receptionist or executive assistants; maybe also, it was due simply to a general lack of style. The average American male or female is not stylish, whether that is trendy style or classic style; in middle-America, the standard outfit for a regular Saturday out at the mall is jeans, t-shirt and a pair of sneakers or brown/black comfortable leather or synthetic material shoes of some sort.

While pay range and price tags may be a challenge, with many stores such as H&M offering very stylish alternatives for the office at reasonable prices, price couldn't be the main problem. What I think the problem is within New York, the fashion capital of the world? I came up with a dress style and trend hand-me-down chart: Europe starts the trends, New York White American fashion cognoscenti, White American and Asian women get them next and two

@BLK_PEEPSTOP

years from when New York White American and
Asian women get it, the majority average New York
Black American women get it and then the trends
spread across to the rest of the United States of
America; once again, in White American to Black
American distribution channels.

In the spring/summer of 2009 is when I first
started seeing White American women in New York
wearing full-fledged knee length leather boots with
shorts, skirts and dresses. It was not until spring 2011
that a majority of Black American women started
wearing the trend in mass in New York. I noticed
women in Ohio and North Carolina on Facebook in
2014 complaining about seeing women embracing the
style.

As it pertains to professional work attire, Black
American women have yet to catch up to the
chic/professional/sexy current looks that are detailed
in Essence magazine for easy proselytizing. Many
Black American men (out of the so few there are, or
maybe I should just say, ME), on the other hand set
the trends in the office and have everyone from the
CEO down to the mail boy trying to keep up.

Black American women, I do not know the
cause of their lag in wearing different colored
pattern/material dresses, especially in summer time.
The one-dimensional, one-color jersey dress which
lays so fine over a woman's body and shows every
spare tire and panty line (if you do not wear a thong),
is a tired look. There are other dress

MICHAEL IRVIN WALKER

patterns/materials, of other lengths, with the right shoes/sandals/boots (2022, sneakers with dresses is the trend), which will make you look even sexier than you may want to be.

Last but not least, if you are going to wear a jersey dress, a tight dress, tight jeans or tights/jeggings, or a jump suit which tightly grips your ass or smoothly/loosely lays over your ass, WEAR A THONG! Believe me IT LOOKS MUCH BETTER, SMOOTHER, SEXIER! Jay Z said it best in a song that was a hit. "No panties and jeans IS SO NECESSARY" (Jay Z "Change Clothes', Black Album). I guess many Black American women missed that line or thought it was a joke.

#blackman u seem stuck on being cool. 1 of the coolest things u could do is if u have a child u do not live with, visit & spend time with it

It's known within the Black American community, that there is a certain innate swagg (as we are calling it today) within Black American men. In fact, it is a natural occurrence within our culture, i.e. the way President Obama and/or Denzel Washington walks with a certain cool. I think there has been a study on this very subject, "Black American Man Cool" and how trying to be so cool is deleterious and destroying our culture, keeping us unemployed, lacking education (because studying and getting an education, to many Black Americans, is not cool), destroying our family structure, etc.

When I was about 9 years old, I could recall my aunts sitting around playing spades with friends, and I can vividly remember a particular conversation where they were saying they loved a man with a distinctive cool walk about him. Ever since that night, I began practicing walking with a diaphanous dip and drag of my foot, to where it became natural and I no longer had to think about it or practice it anymore.

In summer 1993 working as an employee at Bank One, a Black American woman who worked there in the credit collections department mentioned that I walked a certain way and that walk would not take me far in Corporate America (as of 2021, sad to say, she was right, I HAVE GOTTEN NO WHERE IN CORPORATE AMERICA).

My girlfriend in 2001 remarked to me that her mother liked my walk and thought it was sexy. In 2007 when I was walking down the hall to enter the back door to work at a particular job in New York City, this young White American guy was coming down the hall toward me. He started to mock my walk; dipping and moving from side to side very demonstratively, to the point I had to question if I really walked like that? The walk I practiced to perfection, which is probably why I have never ever had a problem walking around in any ghetto, has been a rapier to me; great in the ghetto and sexy to some Black American women, bad in the Corporate American system which I have tried to make my life and advance to no avail.

MICHAEL IRVIN WALKER

In addition to the walk, there are other facets of life of Black American man cool; for example, the "saggin" craze among young Black American males and Hip Hop stars is just a part of Black American man cool. But the worse cool of all within our community, seems to be that of having multiple women and producing children with them and not remaining loyal and standing with any of them and/or disavowing from the entire situation all together.

When I had my child, after taking a hard look at the possibility of marrying the mother and deciding against it, I haven't produced another child since; I never considered not providing financial resources to and/or speaking/visiting with my child. In fact, when I was visiting with my child, I felt the ULTIMATE COOLEST I'd ever felt in my life. My child was with me during visitation, not dropped off to my mother or some baby sitter during the day. I spent the entire day with my child, playing with her, feeding her, taking her to visit family members and if she was left with a baby sitter it was only when I would go to a bar which she was not allowed; trust, if she could have gone to the bar, she would have been right there in the children's section or sitting on my lap while I was having a drink. In fact, I have a picture of my daughter and I when she was two years old, we were at a football tailgate party; me Budweiser in one hand, my baby in the other.

While it is not cool to have multiple babies out of wed-lock, or to have babies out of wed-lock PERIOD (something that needs to be said and practiced within the Black American community), if that should happen to be a Black American man's situation, it is imperative that you spend time with your children whenever you are granted the freedom to do so. There is no better, greater or cooler image in America than that of a father with his child or children. A father, believe it or not carries great influence in a child's life, is listened to and modeled after. Fathers within the Black American community could stop teenage pregnancy by knowing the game and schooling their daughter to it and telling her how to protect herself from such precipice; as well as preparing their son to not make such a long-term life changing mistake.

Men will be men. Dan Marino, Arnold Swarzenegger, Sean "P-Diddy" Combs, Elliot Spitzer, JFK; men love women and to have more than one is more natural than to not do so; that is not the problem. The problem is blatant repudiation from the responsibility of being a part of your child's life: P-Diddy hasn't married as of age 45 and has 4 biological children by three different mothers, but he is present in all of his children's lives.

You should, once you produce a child (you should not produce children outside of a marriage), at any price: lawyer, court, visitation, custody battle; FIGHT IF YOU HAVE TO, BE APART OF YOUR CHILD'S LIFE, AND THAT, IS THE ULTIMATE COOL!

MICHAEL IRVIN WALKER

#blackwomen most unattractive thing u could do is if u have a kid out of wedlock, put obstacles n the way of the father's time w/the kid(s)

We all know the story of the bitter Black American woman, who has been left alone by different men with whom she has had children. The men do not do much to support the children or they may do everything to support the children monetarily through child support or with clothing, food, pampers, etc., but does not provide enough financial support for the woman to live comfortably in an apartment or house or to drive a nice car, etc. Or, she's bitter and scorned from the rejection of the break-up. Whatever the reason, the mother of the children, in many situations puts up obstacles between the father visiting and spending time with his children; denying him visitation once he shows up for pick-up, especially if he shows up with another woman present; not allowing him to speak with the children over the phone or not allowing him to stop by for 30 mins or so just to talk and be by his childs side for a brief moment if he feels the need, provided this is not interfering with other relationships the mother may have at the time and/or it is not disturbing her with drama or arguments, etc.

When my child was born, the first day she was home from the hospital a big argument ensued because I was being told I would not be allowed to take my child solo to visit my family (*something tells me the Lawrence and Condola SAME ARGUMENT in*

- 221 -

the 5th season of Insecure was stolen from preliminary releases of this book I've shared, lol). After three months and calming of that heated argument, a family meeting followed where I was granted visitation, but no overnight visits. I accepted that arrangement for 9 months until I decided to go to court and get more rights and visitation time, which was the standard one day a week and every other weekend; I spent that time faithfully without fail.

When I moved out of state, I would drive back every other weekend to pick up my daughter early Saturday morning and spend Saturday and Sunday with her. After a year of doing that, I requested of the mother to be allowed to come pick my daughter up and take her out of state with me for two weeks every three months with my mom as babysitter, which was once again denied; once again, I went to court and was granted such visitation.

The mother put up road blocks and denials along the way, has been to court for contempt and denial of my out of state visitation and has created an argument about the situation in almost every instance: wanting to shorten the time due to dance lessons, cheerleading, etc.

Here I was a willing participant in fatherhood, willing to pick my child up, be a part of its life, establish a relationship with my child and pay child support without bitterness, but yet, the mother gave me problems all throughout the process. To my knowledge, she has not had another child, nor have

MICHAEL IRVIN WALKER

been chosen for marriage (*married in 2019*), which probably is attributable to her attitude towards the father of her child, a man who has not harmed her except in a shoving match, and having pushed her to the ground to take my child away from her upon her teasing and threatening to deny my visitation at that very moment.

I have never caused her drama concerning who she dated, never denied her anything the times she/my child asked me for money outside of child support and always, without fail, upheld my visitation and relationship with my child; yet, her attitude has always been as if it was not for the courts, I would not see my child but for four hours when I decided to come to town on a weekend and that would be only if she felt like granting me the privilege of seeing my own child which I was financially helping her support.

In many of the situations I've just described, men are driven away, see it as a load off of their shoulders, one less bother. The women successfully drive the father out of the relationship with the child. Some women move out of state with the child and never make arrangements for the father of the child to visit. Some women out of hurt and jealousy over break-up of the relationship, deny visitation right in the neighborhood in plain view of the child, all the while proclaiming, "your daddy AIN'T SHIT"

If a woman thought a man was responsible enough or good enough for her to carry his child to term, he should be good enough and responsible enough to have his child in his care for uninterrupted smooth visitation of however long, where ever he sees fit at appropriate intervals of times. A woman should not, regardless of financial support or not - ill-will feelings regarding the relationship, in another relationship with other women - never deny a father time with his child.

Sure, argue about financial support or go to child support court, make your feelings known about reasonable discomfort (if you have any) with the character (not the basic principle that it is another person) of another woman; tell him you hate him every time you see him, BUT DO NOT DENY HIM VISITATION WITH HIS CHILD even if that has to be an alternative arrangement, let it be, but flat-out unreasonable denial, NO!

Men who cause drama with the mother of their child regarding having them around other men, especially if they are not a family unit; this is also a NO NO! Once it is over, IT IS OVER and the two adults only concern should be the parents maintaining a healthy relationship with the child and the safety/health of the child. The other woman's business with another man or the other man's business with another woman should be and technically is, a non-factor.

MICHAEL IRVIN WALKER

#blackpeople I (my opinion) the word nigga is a childish slang word, that once u come to certain age & maturity, u sound #stupid using it

While watching the movie "Think Like A Man", I recall the word "Nigga" was placed in the dialogue twice; once or maybe twice when the guy met her at the bar and took her drink, or when he picked her up for a date and drove off because she demanded that he open the car door for her, Megan Goods' character remarked quietly "did this nigga just take my drink / leave me", and the other instance, which I saw as totally unnecessary, when all of the guys were in the van on their way to the one guys mother's house and they had a copy of Steve Harvey's book, Romany Malco's character remarks to the effect of, "I can't believe Steve Harvey went out like that, I thought he was my Nigga". The reason I am bringing up this movie is because it was a nice movie filled with beautiful Black American actors, modern day, educated, svelte savants. Among a star-studded cast, there was no reason to place the word "Nigga" in the movie.

The word "Nigga" is childish and churlish, used amongst kids and the proletariat. Will the word ever die, probably not, but among the educated, upwardly mobile Proustian middle to upper class individuals, it has no place and is totally uncouth when spoken from their lexicon.

I consider myself to be a classy individual, educated, non-provincial, renaissance, etc. I do not use the word nigga, in no instance, when dealing or speaking with anyone: the educated or the uneducated. The word, in my opinion places an individual in a certain light, image and mind set of inferiority.

The word "Nigga" among Black American people has naturally become a part of our lexicon just as certain dialect inflections and elocution have naturally become a part of many of us. Just as it takes a Black American man or woman practice to speak articulately, it will take conscious practice to replace the word "Nigga" in the Black American use of the English language.

I cannot recall the point when I deemed the word inappropriate for use by me, but at some point, without much thought as I am trying to convey here, I just said to myself, "Nigga just does not sound right for the image of a beautiful, college educated, articulate Black American man trying to make something of his life." And I just took it out of my vocabulary and believe it or not, it was not an arduous feat to accomplish.

Jay Z endorses the word in his music lyrics and I suppose in common social interaction among Black American people, but at the same time endorsed President Obama to win the election as the First Black American President of the United States in 2008; it seems like a dichotomy of endorsements.

- 226 -

MICHAEL IRVIN WALKER

I do agree and/or do not mind the use of the word in rap lyrics, but I wonder if in the President's company, did Jay Z ever call Barack, "Nigga" or refer to other Black American people as, "Nigga"? I wonder when Jay Z was speaking with Warren Buffet, Bill Gates and Steve Forbes, was his speech edited when he was talking about his friend Emory who got busted with drugs and sentenced to long prison time, had Jay not been out of town with Jaz, Jay, himself would have suffered the same fate. Was it edited out, where he said, "one of my Niggaz, was a drug dealer, as was I, and this Nigga got knocked on the block. Had I not been in London at the time on tour with Jaz, I would be in jail with him on this very day. What a lucky Nigga I am?" And they all laughed, nodded and agreed, "lucky indeed!"

We as Black American people need to change our image to classy, civilized individuals, even in the face of American racial injustice, prejudice and being pushed down to 3rd or even 4th class citizenship in this country; if you would not feel comfortable using the word, "Nigga" around President Obama or when sitting and chatting amongst billionaires, do not use it PERIOD! What that says is, the niggas you do use the word around, you think of them as lessor or being in a different space than you are in the face of the President of the United States of America, whether a Black American or not; you think of the niggas as lessor and deserving of less deference (such as lesser, to not be your lawyer, cpa, doctor or dentist) than you do White American billionaires. And believe it or not, it shows in how niggas treat and respect and carry themselves in everyday society; uncivilized, 2nd/3rd/4th class "Nigga" citizens.

#blackpeople there is nothing wrong with the term african american. african americans, there is nothing wrong with the term black people

As you see within the book I use the terms Black people and African Americans interchangeably. (actually, I tried to go through and change that to "Black American" in every instance). White America has gone through a series of what they think we should allow them to call us and what we, in return should call ourselves; from: Nigger, Negro, Black to Nigga (yes, there is a difference between the words Nigger and Nigga) to African American.

A friend of mine refuses to use the term African American (as I am also trying to cull the word from my vocabulary). He calls us Black people. I, for one do not see anything wrong with the terms Black American people, White American people; though technically both are not that color, but more like brown and pink. For simplicity's sake, Black American and White American will suffice.

When I think of the term African American, I think of it as a more formal/articulate use in the description of Black people. You can come across some people who do not like the term Black and will always correct it with African American. I am not one

MICHAEL IRVIN WALKER

of those people. In fact, I'd prefer the term Black American people, cause though we are of African descent, many of us have never been to Africa, have no known relatives in Africa, do not know from which part or tribe we came from within Africa. In that respect, take Italians or Greeks, many of them have relatives in Italy or Greece, a few of them speak Italian/Greek and travel to Italy/Greece. I have never been to Africa, neither has anyone in my family. Black people are so far removed from Africa, it is almost condescendingly insulting when you think about it, to call Black American people African American.

#blackpeople it's cool 2 read and talk about other books than the street literature, which some feel is so real & appeals 2 u

#blackpeople the purpose of reading is 2 read, learn & grow from that which u have no knowledge, which may lead u (if wanted) 2 a new life

I can recall in 2003, a book reading in the Hu-Man book store in Harlem, NY. The author was one of urban street literature, which was making a very big splash during that time period; this is/was nothing new, for Donald Goines wrote an exhaustive catalog of ghetto street literature books in the early 1970s. At this particular reading there was a woman in the crowd in her late 30s or early 40s presenting the argument that the new ghetto street literature was not real literature as opposed to books written by great Black American authors James Baldwin, Alex Hailey and Richard Wright.

As you could imagine, everyone, including me, jumped down her throat and our main defense was that teens and young 20-somethings were reading these books and READING IS GOOD, no matter what form. As I think back on it, I believe her argument stemmed from the fact that most urban street literature, even Donald Goines books, do not contain many vocabulary words infused within the pages. The only vocabulary word I picked up from reading 9 Donald Goines books was "dilapidated." Her argument, though she never got to present it, but I believe it was, those books do not expand the imagination much, expand ones' vocabulary or go into much structure of prose, story and character development; the basic principles of literature and writing.

Present day, I have read a few new millennium urban literature books myself and I agree with the woman at the Hu-man book store reading, those books do nothing to spur the imagination or creativity. The story line usually involves a drug dealer, a drug addict, dead parent/parents, beautiful young lady who became depraved or who was sullied from the beginning due to some unsavory incident which took place in her earlier life; murder and/or robbery and the ultimate TRYING TO ESCAPE THE GHETTO for a more relaxed and potentially better life. The books do

MICHAEL IRVIN WALKER

not help expand the vocabulary because they use very limited, simple, easy to understand, words from the English lexicon.

Picking up and reading something different exposed me to a different world which I, in turn applied to an area of my life which gives me a slight sense of fulfillment. As noted before, I started reading fashion magazines sometime around 2003 or 2004. In reading these magazines, I learned about fashion; the bespoke and the sartorial.

Another thing I picked up is how many people were born to parents who at some point in their life started a business - large or small - that was somewhat successful; many people worked for their parents which gave them their entrepreneurial spirit to start successful businesses themselves or continue to carry on the legacy of their parents' success and brand.

I was also exposed to the fact that art, music and fashion are three aesthetic cohorts all around the world, which opened me up to artist such as Jean-Michael Basquiat and Andy Warhol. I was opened up to the despot auteur personalities of famous fashion designers, which if you take the success of many of them, seems like a good trait to have. Last but not least, I was taught how to dress well.

The purpose of literature is to open your mind and imagination to different thought, different experiences and influences which could ultimately change your life if even in the slightest manner: how you dress, appreciate art or enjoy life.

When I'm on the train in New York City, I often peak at the books I see various, mainly White American people, reading and they read all kinds of books from the most popular New York best sellers such as "The New Jim Crow" to oblivious titles I've never heard of.

I asked this one White American young lady working a coat check at a party why was she reading a particular book and she responded, "just for the enjoyment of reading." And though this may sound odd coming from a man who is criticizing all things Black American, I found that response to be quite odd. I read, what I read when I read, because I pick a particular book and the synopsis on the back seems interesting or I start it and it immediately interest me; once I start a book, I usually make it a point to finish.

Reading does open up a world and turn on a light inside a person and teaches you things or life experiences. For example, in reading the book "SLASH" of the legendary electric guitar player of the band "Guns & Roses", I learned, his and the bands rise to fame was purely a lottery win, their debut album had been out nearly a year before it caught on and became popular; I learned rock guys do/did a lot of hard drugs but still somehow, many of them turned out functional and still in the end, rich.

MICHAEL IRVIN WALKER

I may have learned some other things from many other books, such as John McWhorter's "Losing The Race" that he, like I, think most Black American people go about conducting their college careers and their business and organizations with a slight to severe case of lethargy, which should not be excused among ourselves nor anyone else. I may have learned some other things buried within my subconscious, from various books I've read, but regardless if I remember or not, I LEARNED! Pick up a book AND LET IT LEARN YOU!

#blackpeople almost every race of people teaches their children apprehension n dealing with and loving us, y do we seem 2 love everybody

black people, regarding my comments. was I born this way? or is this what white america has shown & developed me into

I can recall when I reached the 7th grade in Jr. High School. The environment was a totally different world. Being that I was a teenager, hormones were starting to flare and girls were starting to like me and write me notes or pass word along through a mutual friend that they had a crush on me; phone numbers began to get passed around in abundance.

When 8th grade hit, being that I was part of the upper classman, and all of the cute Black American upper classman girls who liked me the year before

- 233 -

were gone and I was already familiar with all of the girls in my class, my attention began to shift to White American girls. Along with this shift came the smack in the face that since I was a Black American boy, they wouldn't talk to me in a boyfriend/girlfriend manner, or they did not accept friendly flirting, and they never gave me their phone numbers.

I can recall me and another friend of mine, being dropped off at the school after an away basketball game to wait for our parents to pick us up and we were with two cute White American cheer leaders in our class grade. We all hit it off there talking and joking and it seemed as if we were all equals, no racism, no barriers, etc.

Me with my open and racism-ignorant mind, I went home that particular night with one of the cutest White American girls in the entire school on my conscious, Rachel Strait, and wanting to at least talk in a friendly manner with her and maybe become, if not girlfriend and boyfriend, at the minimal, good friends. I called a mutual friend of ours, Granger Kingsbury and he gave me her phone number. I called her, and just like earlier at the school, she talked with me politely. I cannot recall who answered her home phone, whether it was her mother or father (if it was one of her parents, they politely handed her the phone with no questions asked). After a few minutes she said that she had to finish some homework and we hung up.

- 234 -

MICHAEL IRVIN WALKER

The next day, Granger tells me in class, Rachel called him right after she hung up with me and cursed him out politely saying something to the effect of, "oh my god why'd you give him my number, my father would kill me if he knew I was on the phone with a Black boy."

In my home growing up, I was never taught racism, to dislike White American people, that White American people were better than nor worse than me and that we were totally separate beings that though we lived in society together, we were not to interact with one another too closely. But Rachel Strait, and many other White American boys and girls were and still are being taught just the opposite in reference to Black American boys and girls, men and women.

I can recall a White American family (Bobby and his sisters) who lived in the Highland Terrace Projects right down from us on 4th Street in Warren, OH and we played together often with the rest of the neighborhood kids. When I got to Jr. High School, Granger who had given me Rachel's phone number, I used to talk with him all of the time, every day in reading class as if we were best of friends and he obviously took to me as well which is why he saw no harm in giving me her phone number. When we reached 12th grade I used to go to his house for weekend parties on nights there weren't football or basketball games.

From 8th grade to 12th grade, my voracious appetite to date a White American girl only grew. I had sexual relations with a few, but it always involved sneaking around on the White American girl's part or her parents finding out about our relationship and them scolding her for it.

Even as an adult, though I no longer desire and try to date White American women, I do from time-to-time talk to them and try to be friends and that effort ends up going nowhere. The reason could be attributed to two things, 1. At a certain age people just aren't really that open to making many new friends. 2. It could be plain old racism, no matter that I have a Bachelor's Degree, a CPA License and do not consider myself ghetto or wretched, A BLACK AMERICAN MAN IS NOT TO BE ACCEPTED or held too closely within their White American circle.

In job hunts Black American people are ostracized, in business deals (unless you're an athlete or entertainer) Black American people are ostracized, in Hollywood Black American people are ostracized. In any facet of life besides sports, Black American people seem to get the short end of the stick. But yet, Black American people; movie stars: Jamie Foxx, Zoe Zaldana, Sidney Portier (may he R.I.P.) only date/marry White American. You see many Black American persons, the only one in a crew of White American people, just as happy as they can be. As I've described earlier, many rich Black American people entrust only White American professionals with their business dealings. My question is HOW IS

- 236 -

MICHAEL IRVIN WALKER

THIS SO, when we know these people promulgate racism, nepotism and separatism in favor of their own select racial groups and/or just within those having White American skin?

You'd think the one who is hated and ostracized would have limited contact and dealings with the ones who practice this virulence against them. But it seems with Black American people, the more we are pushed down, the more we want to get back up to be pushed down again, AND THEY CONTINUE TO KEEP US ON A SHORT LEASH of marginalized opportunities and crumbs on the table wages.

I would truly love to live in a non-racial world where in Hollywood they stop casting Black American people as Black American people in films, but as ordinary people who happen to be Black American; where on these popular television shows, just as White American men are sleeping with all of the beautiful Black American women, Black American men can sleep with some of the beautiful White American women as well (this recently happened on the Netflick show "House of Cards"); when I talk to a White American woman in a bar, I don't have to wonder, "does she, has she, will she date a Black American man or think/thought Black American men are attractive?" A world where there is truly equal opportunity in NBA/NFL Basketball/Football coaching jobs for Black American men as well as CEO post of Fortune 500 Companies; a world where maybe the second Black American President of The United

States of America WILL NOT BE HALF WHITE AMERICAN. A world where I wouldn't even have to write that last sentence because the world or the United States would be so RACELESS, I nor no one else would notice such indiscretions.

For now, it seems Black American people are far more open to racial harmony; are, and ALWAYS HAVE BEEN taking the steps across racial lines, to the point of almost abandoning and treating their own Black American race as anathema to their being. It is natural for the minority to clamor to be equal to the majority and for the majority to keep them at bay at a distance in an effort to keep majority status and power.

Granted there are a good/great number of White American people who are race blind in carrying out their life, as well, there are Black American people who are anti-White American (mainly because of the hatred and putrid racism that White American people have spurn out toward Black American people throughout American history), but on a whole and majority, White American people started and continue to promulgate racism, separatism and prejudice and the bad seed just continues to carry itself. MAYBE IT ALWAYS WILL!

MICHAEL IRVIN WALKER

#blackpeople actually we need 2 focus on happiness not upper echelon careers & money. but being churlish on gov't assistance is no option

Black American people, because we have been held down for so long and denied opportunities, we are an innate avaricious people. We crave for riches like no other race of people. But, I've recently read that the Asian/Chinese/Korean culture (I may be mistaken as to which one) is name brand crazy; they buy Gucci, Prada and Louis Vutton like it's a necessity such as water or food; even to the point of saving and selling the paper shopping bags, a practice I find to be purely ridiculous.

Black American people are totally committed to brands: NIKE, Louis Vutton, ADIDAS, AIR JORDAN (which is not so bad, least a Black American family will forever share in the profits of the Jordan brand). Black American people have sporadically boosted many brand sales without the appreciation or acknowledgement of the brand itself: Polo Ralph Lauren, Tommy Hilfiger, Girbaud, True Religion Jeans, Nudie Jeans; currently Gucci and Balenciaga.

Many Black American youth seem to have a microwave mentality; they think you put success in the microwave, in a minute take it out, and they'll have Benz and Bentley cars, Rolex, palatial home, endless NIKE sneakers, Louis Vutton and bank rolls of cash to go to the club and ball out buying bottles of Patron, Ciroc, D'usse etc; as noted earlier in the book, many do not seem to believe in working overtime hours on a job to build their credentials on that particular job, gain the trust of management to be moved into a higher paying prestigious position or even value education and concentrated learning to teach themselves to build a major brand and company to become that million/billionaire.

While we do have our stars who shine in their respective fields: Shonda Rhimes, Ursula Burns, Tyler Perry, etc. Many Black American people and the children of the future generation are not being taught the grunt work that Tyler Perry went through before Madea was a house hold name; grunt work Jay Z went through before he was the proud ghetto millionaire and even prouder grown man American $100Millionaire to Billionaire and beyond!

In Malcolm Gladwell's book "Outliers, he speaks to the facts about hard work ethic. He says of prominent Jewish New York Lawyers, they were mostly born in 1930, their parents were immigrants who came to the United States with merchant skills and garment industry skills and worked prodigiously as entrepreneurs within their communities to make a comfortable living for themselves; the children saw this work ethic growing up and took that vision of ingenuity along with them to law and medical school; that and other opportunities which became aligned caused a paradigm shift in Jewish fortune in the professional industries which they endeavored to become great within.

MICHAEL IRVIN WALKER

Russell Simmons said it best in his book entitled, "Super Rich" PUT YOUR HEAD DOWN AND WORK, DO NOT WORRY ABOUT THE MONEY! TAKE THE JOURNEY OF GETTING THE WORK DONE, BUILD THE RELATIONSHIPS AND THE MONEY WILL COME! BUT IT WILL NOT COME OVER NIGHT! His book helped me to stop dreaming about driving a 2006-2012 Benz S550; to just enjoy my life, WORK, do not worry about the money and the cars and the clothes, let the work take its natural course and soon (5 to 10 to 15 even 20 years later) I'd wake up and THE MONEY, CARS AND CLOTHES WOULD BE THERE! IT IS NOT INSTANT!

Often times those who have completed their college education want a top prestigious job, growth and great responsibility right away; sort of an instant CEO tract, with a six-figure salary. For Harvard master's degree students, unfairly or fairly so, this is possible; for a Kent State University bachelor's degree student, this probably will not happen as fast. But it may happen faster if the end result (six figure salary/money/material things) does not preoccupy your existence; the more you want or hunger for something, the more it eludes you.

I grew up despising welfare and public housing. Welfare is not an option to live on, it just is not. I have not seen a welfare check since I turned 18 years of age, or maybe 19, as I think my mom and grandma encouraged me to file for welfare while in college and receive a check for $100 a month. But even during that time, the questions they were asking on the application (which are to get into your life to be sure you are not defrauding the system), were crazy and I found it degrading to answer them and live like that. When it was time to re-up, I REFUSED and made due with my scholarship and Pell grant money.

As Jay-Z said in Change Clothes, "I don't care what you do for stack / I know the world clued your back to the wall / you gotta brawl / DO THAT!" WELFARE SHOULD NEVER BE A LONG-TERM OPTION; work, go to school, read and study and practice a craft to live by; push yourself beyond whatever situation put you in the position to file for welfare in the first place. Life is not easy, but the fight and struggle, even RACISM and denial of opportunity makes you a better person. WHAT WILL NOT KILL YOU WILL MAKE YOU STRONGER!

#blackpeople or rather people in general, when u visit NY, u r not supposed 2 eat at chain restaurants u'll fin n ur hometown

#blackpeople n new york it's cool to eat at other restaurants besides red lobster, olive garden, bbqs, applebees & t.g.i.f Friday #explore

#blackpeople red lobster is processed lobster and other sea food products. its not exactly the best seafood restaurant in the u.s.

MICHAEL IRVIN WALKER

New York of all places in the world is known for its shopping boutiques, Broadway Theatre shows and restaurants. When you as a person or group visit New York, the last places you are supposed to visit are stores that you would shop at in your local mall or shopping plaza: Gap, Old Navy, Footlocker, Payless, etc; restaurants: Olive Garden, Red Lobster, TGIF Fridays, Apple Bees, etc.

The reason people commit this act of New York treason and dining degradation is a fear of the expense that may be encountered sitting down and dining at an unfamiliar restaurant, especially if it has nice décor. For this reason, many restaurants started long ago, placing their menus right outside their door in the window of the entrance way. Though the saying, "if you have to ask, you cannot afford it" is a bit of an exaggeration, there is an uneasy feeling that comes along with asking the cost of something. But what I've discovered long ago is that the average restaurant you'll walk into in New York, if it happens to be high-end such as Mr. Chows on Hudson Street, will run you at most $250 (2012 prices) for a dinner of two, provided you do not order a bottle of wine. Down lower on the totem pole, on average a dinner bill for two at a decent restaurant with avante guard décor will be $69 - $130 (2012 prices) and that includes the tip; for a trip out of town to one of the greatest cities in the world experiencing new things, $90 is not a bad price to pay for a nice meal on a get-a-way from home or a vacation.

Born and raised in a small town in the mid-west, when I visit a restaurant to dine, the most I've been to the same place to eat on a date with a girlfriend in New York City is twice. I always try to eat at a different place: Mr. Chows, Ruth Chris, Morimotos, Sammys (City Island), Peaches Bedstuy-Brooklyn, Sylvia's Harlem, Rothchild's Steakhouse, Houston's, B' Smiths & Bobby Van's in Bridgehampton, Madisons in Hoboken, NJ and a few other mid to high end locations I forget the name of.

For a local outing, there are many places other than chain restaurants to eat: Black Swan BedStuy-Brooklyn, Corner Social Harlem, Peaches Bedstuy-Brooklyn, Do-or-Dine Bedstuy-Brooklyn. Eating and hanging out at chain restaurants is to do in every city and state BUT NEW YORK CITY! If you're going to hang out at Apples Bees, you may as well vacation in or move to Akron, OH. It's a lot cheaper cost of living to go with the cheap unadorned dining experience.

Red Lobster in 1988 – 1993 was chic, a nova, considered a special seafood dining experience. You'd walk in the door and literally see the chef taking real live lobster out of the lobster tank to cook and serve to the patrons (do they still do this?). THE GARLIC BISQUITS appetizers were simply out of this world; you could virtually fill up on them and not have any room left for dinner. The fish they served was delicious; shrimp scampi, surf & turf and sample seafood dinner platters were all a hit.

MICHAEL IRVIN WALKER

As the late 1990s began to usher in the new millennium, Red Lobster began to taper its price tag down to appeal to the general public without breaking the bank. If you're one to think in a macro-economic fashion, you'd have to question yourself: how can Red Lobster afford to feed me Shrimp and Lobster along with fries and a drink for $20?

If you're ever a business owner, you buy products or materials wholesale and sell them retail at a markup to make as much gross profit as possible. You'll soon find out that your wholesale materials are going to spike up much more in price than your loyal customers will be willing to pay to keep those same profit margins; therefore, you must raise your retail prices and risk losing customers or find an alternative at a lesser expense wholesale and keep your prices the same and KEEP ALL OF YOUR LOYAL CUSTOMERS AND GAIN MORE!

Timberland for example: in the years before the mid-1990s, their boots and shoes all included Gortex material laced under the leather and/or nu-buck to make a sound water-proof seal; the reason their boots cost $119 - $135 which was a high price back then for a casual pair of shoes which many middle class White American families and suddenly Black American Hip Hop kids willingly paid for the quality name and product.

Timberland boots started selling in record numbers to urban youth; the numbers of increased need for speed in production no longer supported the time and quality measures nor cost of lining the boots with Gortex. At some point during the 90s they eliminated their partnership with Gortex (Gortex soon began producing their own higher-priced high quality waterproof boots); Timberland managed somehow to still keep the boots sealed and waterproof. Timberland lowered their cost, making the boots and shoes with cheaper materials but all the while keeping the same price tag; thus increasing their profit margins. Today Timberlands are not made of the old quality leather and/or nu-buck of old but rather synthetic materials; as I stopped purchasing the boots around the year 2001, I do not know their retail cost anymore, but I'm sure it is still $120 and above.

Red Lobster, when you think about it; fresh seafood was a premium that commanded the price tags charged back in the late 1980s and there is no substitute for a lower price. So, the next time you're out on a date there or eating there with your family, know that you are not doing anything exclusive or special but rather eating a reasonably priced meal to fill you, your dates and/or your family's stomach in a mediocrely pleasant atmosphere. YOU ARE NOT BALLIN'!

#blackpeople watching 60 Mins about a company: huawei, that has built its $Bill company by copying & stealing others trade secrets

MICHAEL IRVIN WALKER

#blackpeople building a still company is not always a straight foward ethical benevolent endeavor. even legal scared money don't make none

#deception C #Stupid #BLACKPEOPLE, business is not always straight up white washed business. At times, corners R cuts & deals R made #LEARN

#blackpeople white people: what has narcissistic devilish nepotism ways gained them? what has ur altruism & benevolence gained u? #think

black people we have tried 2 stand with dignity & christian love 2 win our enemies over 2 honor & respect us. Yet, still, they do not. Y

There was a 60 Mins special on about a billion dollar company called Huawei in China, that was in a court battle for stealing computer programming source code of another billion dollar company CISCO; sort of like in the movie "The Social Network" about Facebook, how Mark Zuckerberg stole the Winkleboss twins' idea and when they were in the court deposition, Mark says, "did I use one single line of your code" or something to that effect. Code is computer programming that makes computers and phone apps do what they do.

While watching the 60 Mins show, I started thinking about the teaching of Black American people by our grandmothers' and church, that the meek shall inherit the earth; do not do evil for the evil doers will be damned to hell on earth as well as in the hereafter. And for the most part Black American people - with the exception of 60s and 70s hustlers, pimps and 1980s heroin and crack dealers - lived by this creed.

That credo keeps us from making the many ideas we have in our head into viable marketable products and taking them to fruition at any cost; that credo makes us defer to White American people waiting for them to innovate and create or take credit for almost every brilliant idea that has been created in America and made the inventors and their families billionaires; many of these ideas have come about through the same evil that our grandmothers' and the Baptist church I grew up in, inculcates in us to avoid at any cost; this too shall pass and the Lord will make a better way.

Take for example: Las Vegas, Atlantic City, Bootleg Liquor during prohibition, construction and/or real estate companies; these billion dollar industries were all creations or under the control of mafia gangsters, murderers and muscle men.

Less gangster, but still in some sense, is the Facebook story itself; the idea being taken from a seed idea of the Winkleboss twins at Harvard University; Samsung and Apple at each other's throats over copyright/patent infringement and the

MICHAEL IRVIN WALKER

Huawei, CISCO situation. It seems ethical business dealings are taught in the classroom, but the real world shows us countless times again and again that many White American businessmen throw ethics out the window when it comes to a chance at scoring hundreds-of-millions to billions of dollars: Enron, Worldcom, Bernie Maddoff, etc.

The Deception television show starring Megan Good (cancelled after its first season); it was fiction, but the entire show revolved around the patriarch of the family who owned a pharmaceutical company trying to hide the fact he falsified reports of deadly side effects of a drug so that his company could obtain FDA approval of the drug and be the first to market before the competition; thereby, having the patent for many years and making hefty profits before the patent expires and duplicates could enter the market. Trying to hide the fact involved the murdering of his own daughter, attempted murder of his son and political favors and blackmail.

In business and politics, evil deals which result in billions of dollars are struck between seemingly straight up family oriented ethical White American men; muscle, force, rabid violence as well as small and large favors being repaid to make things happen on a grand scale. And often times Black American people were/are not the beneficiaries of any windfall of industrialist, technological or political profiteering.

Am I preaching unethical behavior? As Malcolm X once said, "when you tell your people to stop being violent against my people, I'll tell my people to put down their guns. YOU'RE SAYING I'M ANTI-WHITE!" I'm simply saying, know or learn the fact of how the wheel is greased in order to go round and use your better judgment as to how you'll put a plan in place to make your wheel go round to build a billion dollar corporation and prosper like the others.

If you lay back reticent, a recluse acting alone and praying for a great outcome; nice guys (even Jesus) finished last, ALWAYS! And unlike the Bible religious teaching passed down from our ancestors; in life, there is no ascending from the grave, or from the adroit hands of nepotism and racism, to a great pie in the sky.

#blackman it's cool to perform cunnilingus, just know, it's not necessarily all about the hole, but it's about the clitoris

Just as Black American men may have the complaint that some Black American women do not perform fellatio, Black American women have the same complaint. I learned long ago, from a Caucasian woman I dated in college, the joys of oral sex, both receiving and giving; it is such a turn on to make a woman climax by performing cunnilingus, especially if her uterine muscles pulsate during the process. After my relationship with that particular woman, giving oral sex became an ordinary part of sex which got me

MICHAEL IRVIN WALKER

further in the mood, which would be further heightened if the oral sex was reciprocated.

I can recall my attitude toward oral sex and the attitude of teenage girls during my high school years was that it was a nasty thing to do and you would never want it to get out on the school yard that you had performed such an act. In fact, I can only recall doing that once in the years since the loss of my virginity until I started dating and living with my Caucasian girlfriend; we pleasured each other in that manner to full climax on a constant basis. Even after that point, an older (as in born in the 1930s or so) cousin of mine told me and his grandson, "do not eat no woman's nasty ass pussy; there is nothing but bacteria down there and it will cause you to get throat cancer." I never took his advice, I've eaten plenty, have not gotten throat cancer and my sex life has been a lot better due to oral sex.

Upon moving to New York City and dating a woman who was my equivalent age, when I pleasured her in that fashion to full climax, she confessed to me that she called her family confidant and said, "I was floating, I thought I was dead and said to myself, THIS N*GG* (and no, I do not promote the use of that word) DONE KILT ME!"

The secret to opening up a woman with this key of the tongue is the clitoris. When I performed the act in high school a few times, I'd stick my tongue in the hole and wiggle it around and/or stick what little of it would go in and out of the hole. While that feels good to the woman, your tongue being down there, she does not get the full pleasure of oral sex until you swirl your tongue around her clitoris for a little while and then expose it fully and cover it with your entire mouth and lick it up down and all around, gently as well as vigorously until SHE EXPLODES!

There is absolutely nothing anomie, nasty, or vile in performing cunnilingus, with the exceptional warning: not fresh out of the shower, a slight odor (on those who practice good hygiene) is to be expected; if the odor is too strong, something may be wrong and it is not advisable to continue with the act. With someone whom you feel comfortable, you're dating or in a long-term relationship/marriage, EAT THAT THANG WHENEVER YOU GET THE URGE, morning, noon or night (or all three); it'll play an important small to large part in keeping your woman happy and keeping you on her mind.

#blackpeople watching t.v. is a mind numbing experience. it hypnotizes u not 2 think & feel relaxed about ur peasant/worker life status

#blackman while ur watching football, the networks, the players (some of them), the team owners r getting richer. what r u doing

MICHAEL IRVIN WALKER

#blackpeople media & entertainment's sole purpose is 2 numb ur brain so u will not create brilliant ideas, companies, wealth & competition

Think about this for a second. "No matter what the name / we're all the same / pieces / in one big chest game" (Chuck D of Public Enemy "Rebel Without A Pause"). Not only are we all pieces, the majority of us are all ponds to be knocked off by the rook, queen or king.

When you are watching television, what are you actually doing? ABSOLUTELY NOTHING: you are not thinking, you are not solving problems, you are not honing your skills at a craft or trade. Watching television, is you sitting there, watching other people who are living and/or making their dreams come true; even the commercials are filled with upcoming actors who have taken one step and are one step closer to making their ultimate dream come true.

Everybody dreams: I want to be rich, famous, an inventor of something, a writer, an actor, a musician, etc. Many people wish they could get out of their current life situation or make it slightly better; obtain a promotion on their job for example. While you are watching television, you are taking zero steps to make your life better, ZERO/NONE! And look at the many mindless shows that are fed to us on regular network television: dancing with the stars, america's got talent, housewives, survivor, the voice, american idol, x-factor, fear factor, big brother, the apprentice. These shows are an exact replica and regurgitation of the same concept: watch this person do this to try and win this, or watch these people argue and fight about petty situations in a pursuit of power and semi-celebrity status.

Is television necessary? Absolutely, at times you need a release, especially if you are trying to accomplish something that takes great concentration and learning. But, to be addicted to a show and habitually tune in or DVR record it every week as if you're getting paid to watch it is a bit ridiculous.

Television is to keep the majority of persons at bay while a select few: hint, the one percent, manage and invent things and get richer and richer from your mindless consumption of what they create. Television advertising (ads period), on its grandest scale is intentional mind manipulation to brand you like a cow: NIKE, Levis, Dawn, TIDE, Cheerios, Frosted Flakes, Wheaties, Palmolive, DOVE, Chevrolet, McDonalds, Burger King, FaceBook, Twitter, Apple; recognize how these names do not need any explanation and are ingrained in our conscious. The executive employees, mostly who are White American are paid hundreds of thousands to millions of dollars a year (the 1%) because we have been oblivious enough to allow them to invade our brain and psyche with their brands and we became/are loyal followers. The brands even change the color and/or construction of packaging or invent slightly new products every 3 to 5 years so we'll think we are receiving something

MICHAEL IRVIN WALKER

dramatically different when in reality it is basically the same product.

The goal of television is to keep you entertained and thoughtless; keep you from writing that book inside that is dying to get out of you; keep you from producing that hit Hip Hop track or writing the next amazing pop chart topper song; keep you from writing and thinking about the business plan for your company idea. All the while, the football and basketball stars are getting paid an average low/high of approximately $2,500/$312,500 per game respectively. Even though you'll probably never earn that amount of money in a 3-hour time span, hard work and dedication to some course other than sitting around watching what others are doing will yield greater fruit and life fulfillment than you may imagine.

#blackpeople realize, we'd b so much better off as a race if we educate ourselves 2 american systems, create jobs & work4/support 1another

When I take a look around, it seems Black American people want to be something other than American; the most hideous part of wanting to be Un-American is living in America under American law, social and capitalistic economic systems with the notion it is uncool to be properly educated and adroit with the inter-workings and machinations of the systems which affect us every single day of our lives.

Black American men, imagine, if along with the Un-American/Un-civil actions of walking around with your pants down to your mid-thigh, you actually were equipped with a law degree, specific knowledge and/or federal and state law precedent to address officers who stop and frisk you and could tell them their limits and manipulate the control of how the stop and frisk will be conducted.

"Well my glove compartment is locked / so is the trunk in the back / And I know my rights / So you gon' need a warrant for that / Knaw, I ain't pass the bar / But I know a little bit / Enough that you won't illegally search my shit" (Jay Z "99 Problems").

In addition to having an education for the purpose of traversing the terrain of American soil without the handicap of being taken advantage of, education can be used to create real jobs and opportunity for Black American people by Black American people. It is a well-known fact that within the White American capitalistic system of fortune 500 companies, Black American men are the least employed despite the company's public service announcement "WE ARE AN EQUAL OPPORTUNITY EMPLOYER." Companies blatantly discriminate against women and Black American men in terms of pay, raises, promotions and promulgation of corporate board membership.

You would think with the overt racism and sexism that goes on, young Black American men would have figured out: "let me Harvard educate

MICHAEL IRVIN WALKER

myself within the systems of accounting, finance, economics, journalism, science and many other fields so that I may one day create a major corporation of my own to benefit the majority of persons who look like and carry on with cultural traits very similar, if not identical to my own."

When you do create that company, you can have offices in Time Square full of educated Black American men with their pants hanging down to their thighs, screaming, "YO SON, meeting in the 3rd floor large conference room tomorrow, we got Sylvia's collard greens, yams, mac and cheese, and bar-b-que ribs. I'ma need dat power point to be on point with the VGA connect to the large flat screen, aaiiight." If you take a look, it is exactly how Jewish people operate: speak their own language, wear their own habiliment, hire entirely (or a majority) their own people to run and operate entire industries which have come to include: Advertising, Hollywood film making and many fortune 500 companies. Without education of politics, logistics, money, power, respect, NONE OF THAT IS POSSIBLE! Black American men will just continue to fill the PRISON POPULATION!

#blackpeople everything, every idea that was or ever is put n2 place has 2 have support of the execution & actual action 2 make it happen

As I've stated earlier in the book, many people have many ideas for brands and products or technology, but many of them remain just an idea. I think it is pretty safe to say, we are past the stage of having to be told, "write your ideas down to get them out of your head." The writing of the idea on paper is an elementary step, which still doesn't serve the purpose of getting the idea into fruition. There are many other steps which must be executed in a professional manner in order for anyone to take your idea serious, and for you personally to set the idea in motion.

When I passed my CPA Exam, I called a website developer and paid $450 to produce a professional website. I wrote all of the copy for the site and proof read it three to four times before releasing it for final publishing. While having the website developed, I created an e-mail (NOT G-MAIL) and www.---.com account through a provider of web .com/.net services; in tandem with the site and email account, I had professional, nice quality grade paper cards made. For the website, cards and email, I thought of two slogans and chose a font/logo for my brand. Once all of those things were complete, I was in full professional business, and it cost approximately $850. A year later, I also wrote a business plan, laying out initial steps and forecast of revenue growth and expenses for the next three years.

If you are not as motivated as I was or creative enough to create your own slogans and descriptive font and/or logo for your brand, those are services

MICHAEL IRVIN WALKER

you'll have to pay a professional to help you develop. In addition to an official website, if there is a product to be developed or sold, steps need to be taken to efficiently and professionally complete production, distribution and delivery. A team of persons to handle various tasks must be assembled.

The steps I described above are rudimentary. I cannot count and probably neither can you, the amount of times I have read a web-site of a sole proprietor or small business and found a typo; run into some guy with a flimsy card with the so-called name of the business, his name and telephone number, a g-mail e-mail address and if he has a www. Web address, it goes to FaceBook. That is not officially doing business. That is being non-resourceful (actually resourceful, but to a non-effective degree) and/or cheap. I see people with a Louis Vutton belt around their waist, Air Jordans, designer sun glasses; hand me a card such as that described above, which means they value their clothes more than officially starting their business.

The next step in building my business and brand is to rent office space, put together an advertising, public relations campaign and client relations team. Without those four things, my brand will never get off the ground, and sorry to say, FaceBook is not sufficient advertising. After I get PR and advertising up and running; the business starts to become profitable, at which point I can solicit investors. Actually, investors are needed before the point of profitability to get started with office space, marketing and sales.

Teams of support persons and EXECUTION, is the key to getting an idea really started. But do not confuse execution with doing anything: g-mail account, web address which points to FaceBook, handing out letters with misspelled words and ill grammar asking for funds to help publish a book; those are steps of a craven charlatan, which are an albatross to your end goal and are very futile to your brand and future success. In all actuality, if your efforts to start and run your business all point to free services you're using: FaceBook, Vista Print, G-mail, it says your idea is, more likely than not, ephemeral and/or will never get off of the ground floor, and that's if you've even bothered to develop an elevator pitch.

#blackpeople do u ever give thought 2 how major tall buildings & sports arenas r built? It's called leveraged & collateralized debt #think

#blackpeople do u know what corporate debt financing is? a corporation borrows ur money & promises 2 pay back with interest @ later date

MICHAEL IRVIN WALKER

#blackpeople many enterprises & operations r run on debt financing. its simple. but we do not trust each other or understand 2 make it work

Have you ever walked downtown in your particular city and looked up at all the tall buildings with great architecture and design, and at new buildings and hotels that you enter and think, "wow, this must have cost millions to build." Your thought process may stop short at that point, "it cost millions." But did you ever think a step further to ask, "is the building paid for, who sold it, who paid for it?"

The answers to those questions, more likely than not are: no, it is not fully paid for, many people in a group sold it (could have been a family such as the Trump family or a Jewish family no one ever heard of). Many people paid for it, maybe even you, via city/state government bonds, which are guaranteed via your tax dollars, being sold to finance the property. The building may have been paid for with a partial cash payment and the rest paid for on credit: bank credit, government credit, non-public bonds credit sold to many various groups of people, which rarely include any Black American people.

The concept is one which you may have heard before, the pooling of money to invest in a project, whereby a group of persons, depending on their financial status put $10,000 - $10,000,000 in a pile (account), the amount you put in is your percentage of ownership (a simple algebraic formula – yes, algebra has real life application after high school). The person or group who holds over 50% ownership is the majority stake holder and gets the greatest return once the building starts making a profit. And that should be your next question, "how does the building make profit?"

Barclays in Brooklyn, home of the Brooklyn Nets. As an estimate, say the place holds 20,000 people, 5,000 on four levels: floor level seats to a basketball game can sell for $1,000 - $2,500 per game. 2nd level seats can sell for $200 - $1000 per game. 3rd level seats can sell for $100 - $200. 4th level seats can sell for $25 - $100. (these price levels have doubled or tripled since Barclays was built). Do the math, and multiply the total by: boxing match events, circuses for kids, concerts of Beyonce and Jay Z.

As this ticket sales revenue rolls in from each event, the bank loans and bond principle and coupon interest are paid back to the investors and creditors. Many of the original investors even sell their investment on a secondary market for a lower than promised percentage return, receive their cash early and move on to another investment. These people have faith in the system of investment and return, operations and revenue, profit and loss.

What happens with Black American people? If a Black American person gives you $10,000 today, he wants $1,000,000 back tomorrow or he wants to run the operations to know what is being done with the money. If you tell this person, you'll give them

MICHAEL IRVIN WALKER

$15,000 in three years for the $10,000 you received, which is a 50% return, much higher than would be received on an average investment, they'll cry three years is a long time to wait to make $5,000. They aren't thinking that IT IS A FREE $5,000 for doing nothing but allowing money to work for them instead of working for it, which in my book (no pun intended in reference to this book) is the greatest idea since King Midas turned anything he touched into gold.

Also, a question comes up of not having faith in the process or other Black American people's management capabilities to make such a return on their investment. That question could simply be due to ignorance, which makes the idea sound like a hoax or a quick - take your money and run - scheme or brain-washed thoughts that if "White American people are not handling the business dealings, there will be no business dealings." (Education, reading and comprehension of ideas and processes would come in handy in alleviating these thoughts and fears of Black Americans as apocryphal when it comes to business.)

With pooling of money, everyone is not going to receive a great return, especially if they did not put a great investment into the pool in the first place. But rather, the purpose of pooling and borrowing from one another within a community is for the greater and larger power brought about by community ownership.

If you live in Bedford-Stuyvesant, Brooklyn, NY and you see a Jewish person monitoring a residential brownstone rehabilitation project, you may have three emotions and/questions: 1. These motherfuckers own the world. 2. How is it that around the majority of building reconstruction projects I see these people with these black circles on the tops of their heads? (lol, for everyone knows those are Jewish people) 3. You have to respect those motherfuckers, they own a lot of shit and obviously have a lot of power. That power came/comes from pooling of economic and political resources/money for the greater good of the community.

I had this idea a few years back to gather 100 young Black American professionals in New York and have them all contribute $1,000 into a pool to purchase a brownstone in Bedford-Stuyvesant Brooklyn, NY; rent it out to pay the mortgage; the group is to contribute a minimal sum $10 per person per month for maintenance. Once the mortgage is paid in 20 to 30 years, keep renting it out, splitting the profits back amongst the group or raffling the property off for a family within the group to own and live in it for a nominal mortgage, which would be split amongst the original investors. The few people I mentioned the idea to had every nay say in the book to throw at me: who's gonna manage it, who's gonna keep the records of the investors, how are we gonna get our money back, how much money will we make, who's gonna live in it or decide who lives in it? I had answers to all of these questions, but no one ever

MICHAEL IRVIN WALKER

gave me a "that's a great idea, let's do it, call your friends and I'll call my friends".

I self-deprecatingly admit, I'm not the greatest rabble rouser. I proposed the idea to a friend of mine who was the president of a great Black American civics organization for presentation to its civics and economics committee. He said that was not within the ambit of the organization to put a project such as that into motion. I presented it to a real estate guy who said it was a great idea and plan but he never mentioned it again. Ideas like this are how we as a community gain power, self-respect and respect of others. There are a long list of other measures as well, we could all take for the greater good of the Black American race.

#blackpeople I here people say they want 2 raise money but do not want 2 give % ownership 2 any1. its ok 2 give ownership, but limited power

Many people may be familiar with the show "Shark Tank" and the concept of giving away a percentage of ownership for a major investment in your business may not be so foreign, as it may have been years ago in 2004.

10 years ago, my girlfriend at the time had a great idea to start a children's clothing line with plush leathers (sometimes harlequin), wools and other materials; "lifestyle and heritage" pieces she called

- 265 -

them, to be passed down to generations of children. She came up with a great name and logo written by her own daughter and she incorporated the company. She started the process of buying materials and making patterns and soon started to realize that it would be a very expensive endeavor. In discussing getting financing from individuals we'd meet at parties or men she'd meet who were hitting on her, she often remarked, "I do not want to give up any ownership in the company." She was not a business major, but rather went to FIT for two years for pattern making.

I'd often tell her, you can give up 10% - 25% or more of the company, just not 51% and also you could insert in the contract that it would be silent ownership, meaning no say in operations and management of the business. She insisted she wanted loans and to provide a return percentage and cut ties with the investors after that. I reiterated to her that even an equity ownership percentage deal could be structured in the same fashion, to be bought out at a specific point in time at a certain return of investment.

Loans or bonds are a way to go to receive investment funds for start-up and operations of a company, but if your idea has any weight, creativity and appearance of longevity, an investor, such as those on "SharkTank" are going to want in for a nice percentage - protracted at times into perpetuity - or want a hefty buy-out premium to cut them away from the business. Whether a loan, bond or otherwise, an investor asking for 10% - 50% silent ownership in a

- 266 -

MICHAEL IRVIN WALKER

great business idea is the nature of the beast. I'd do it myself, except there is the egregious albatross rule in ethics of Certified Public Accountant firms (which actually call themselves CPA firms in their title) that owners must be CPAs or work within the business, which at the outset severely cuts into profits and cash flow because CPAs demand hefty salaries for their time and work; advice to myself, as well as others is, "50% of something is better than 100% of nothing."

y do actresses #evalongoria try & find a sports player boy friend #marksanchez? they bet his contract money will b greater than any actor

y do actresses #gabrielleunion try & find a sports player boy friend #d.wade? they bet his contract money will b greater than any actor

Eva Longoria and Tony Parker and Mark Sanchez (12 years her junior), Gabrielle Union and Dwayne Wade, Halle Berry and David Justice, Kelly Rowland and Roy Williams, Venessa Williams and Rick Fox, Debbie Allen and Norm Nixon (actually a successful relationship). The list is probably longer than I know.

I get it, if you're a beautiful actress, presumably rich, you want a boyfriend/husband who is equally yoked, as was Vivaca Fox's incantation after she married a one hit wonder rapper of the group 69 Boyz and later in life dated (nascent wealthy mogul) rapper 50 Cent. No woman, worth her weight in self-esteem wants to take care of a man, no matter how wealthy she may be; she'd like to see a man earning his own keep. Take for example Mariah Carey and Nick Cannon. I may be wrong but I seriously doubt Nick's net worth closely matched that of Mariah Carey, but to Nick's credit, he was/is host and producer to a few television shows and had/has other endeavors going on and brings in a significant amount of income; he earned his own keep, not merely lived the good life as a Mariah Carey minion; though his exposure did increase in his hosting jobs and stand-up comedian work after the marriage.

      The question comes in when you think about longevity of career. Let us take the Kelly Rowland, Roy Williams situation. He played for 8 seasons in the NFL, signed a huge $54Mil contract in the process, $26Mil guaranteed; take into account the assumption of his spending habits up until his present age 35 – 40 years old, his estimated net worth is $10Mil - $15Mil. For the remaining prime years of his and her life, say to age 65, which is 30 more years, that is a maximum $500,000 income per year to spend; not taking into effect failed investments and/or compound interest and dividends to be earned over the same period. Doing the hypothetical numbers, $500,000 a year for the next 30 years is not a bad living being earned on one side of the equation of an entertainer/sports couple, but you must also add into the equation that this guy may not be able to do anything else with his life outside of football, which will wreak havoc on his

- 268 -

MICHAEL IRVIN WALKER

mental stability and self-esteem. Kelly Rowland has been part of a platinum selling world touring group and solo career for 23 years to date of this writing and has many more years left in her career to provide her with wealth and self-esteem for a life time. Career and self-esteem problems of men are seemingly quelled by partying, using drugs and alcohol; proselytizing and philandering with other young women. Women are a main problem for most rich men who feel powerful and they can have anything they want; thus, Tony Parker texting with some other woman when he had one of the most beautiful women in the world of entertainment.

The actress and sport player relationship typically boils down to the clashing of egos. In clashing of ego situations between men and women, the man must be king and there are numerous ways for a man to make himself feel so, which are the antithesis to a long-lasting relationship. Just as a male sports player seemingly has a better relationship with an ascetic (until she gets the money in her veins) ingénue, it would be better for a beautiful actress to carry out a successful relationship with an attractive guy who makes six figures or better, or a self-deprecating wealthy man who'd be happy to have her. Dating the self-centered sports player, actor or singer/entertainer, as history shows never works out for a beautiful celebrity actress.

#steveharvey #blackpeople little black girls have been dancing and gyrating 4 yrs. little white girls start doing it, they're superstars

#steveharvey these little girls if they do not become princesses, they'll b strippers &/or whores. the only way 2 continue attention getting

There were these two little White American girls, one by the name of Sophia Grace, on Ellen Degeneres and Steve Harvey Show rapping the lyrics to Nicki Manaj song "Super Bass". I was asking myself, what is the big deal? Why are they put on television for this and given a spotlight, if only for fifteen minutes? My next questions, posed on a little lighter note than the George Zimmerman and Travon Martin case; if these little girls were Black American and rapped the song just as well or better, or made their own rap song, would they receive such attention?

I've been hearing of a rapper, Lil Miss Na Na who has been rapping since she was about the age of Sophia Grace and making great original lyrical rap songs, yet the vast population of North America has never heard of her. Famous radio personality and now celebrity gossip television talk show host, Wendy Williams used to play one of Lil Miss Na Na's songs to open her radio show on 98.7 Kiss FM, but that is the most attention I've heard or seen Lil Miss Na Na get.

MICHAEL IRVIN WALKER

When thinking about the Sophia Grace situation and her age, when was the last time there was a successful child rapper or group in the music industry, let alone female? The last, most successful, I can recall was Kris Kross, whom to date, one of the members overdosed on drugs twenty something years after music career apogee and trough.

Lil Miss Na Na, of course came along in the early 2000s before YouTube could make an artist an overnight super star such as it did for Soulja Boy. But even without the internet, she was a formidable lyrical artist who was working very hard, but never saw an inch of spotlight. And the fact it's not a novelty that a Black American can rap, sing or dance is not lost upon me.

What about when Black Americans do things that are not apropos to their culture such as get juris doctorate degrees and MBAs from Harvard or science, medicine and engineering degrees; they are not heralded in Forbes magazine as the next business brain prodigy recruited by GE to succeed the CEO or to be the next mastermind behind the next miracle drug for Merck or GlaxoSmithKline? Johnny Cochran is the only famous Black American lawyer many Black American people know. Lenzy Lowhand's lawyer may be running a close second to Johnny, but it never seems Black American people get publication for anything other than behaving like uneducated, churlish, rube American misfits.

My other question with Sophia Grace and her hype girl, outside of race, is what will become of these little girls' futures? They are getting attention for basically doing nothing, putting in no work ethic in the least bit, but viola, they're on television. What message does the microwave success send to them and other children, "you can recite the lyrics of someone else's song and become rich and famous." In reality, life does not happen like that.

The process to get a professional job after completion of a college education in this day and age requires strategic planning and work ethic. Their (Sophia Grace and her hype girl) success is based on looks (cute little girls they are) and racial anomalous behavior. The message of this type instant success is bad for any little children, White American or Black American.

#blackpeople i'm having trouble with the fact stevie wonder is heralded as a greater celebrity than berry gordy who signed him & ran motown

black people what we prize is backwards. john h. johnson should b our most colossal celebrity, not jay z/beyonce/kobe/lebron/steveharvey

Larry Bird, Kevin McKale, Danny Ainge, Kurt Rambos. These are all very recognizable names if you know your NBA basketball history. When you

MICHAEL IRVIN WALKER

think of these names, they bring to mind a generation of legendary championship winning individuals within the NBA. Something else to note about these names is all four of them are or have been either general managers working behind the scenes of NBA basketball or coaches.

Steve Jobs, Mark Zuckerberg, Bill Gates, Warren Buffet, Jack Welch. These are all very recognizable names if you pay attention in America to who has run the most successful companies in the last 20 years. John h. Johnson, if you asked your average Black American teenager who he is, I'd be willing to bet half of them would not know. The name Berry Gordy carries a lot of weight, but it doesn't seem to carry the weight of Beyonce and Jay Z, when in fact he is and always will be a greater music legend than the both of them. Stevie Wonder is known as one of the greatest musical talents of all time, but is Berry Gordy considered one of the greatest music executives of all time; it doesn't feel as if that is the case.

Black American culture superstars and status symbols seem slightly skewed. And in the case where our status symbols are legendary in one regard, it seems their status does not transfer over to the next obvious step. Kareem Abdul Jabar, Patrick Ewing. Robert Horry, Scotty Pippen, Reggie Miller; do any of these guys have back-office jobs or have become legendary championship winning coaches; Doc Rivers is the only name that comes to mind. Alan Iverson, a great legendary NBA basketball talent, who led his team to a championship run, will he ever benefit the NBA as a coach or general manager to choose and nurture talent that will be even greater than he?

It seems our heroes are entertainers, but unlike Sylvia Robinson did with Sugar Hill Records, our entertainers rarely go on to be owners and celebrated for what their ownership brought to the table and legacy of the game they were once so great at. With the exception of Magic Johnson and a few other notable characters whom I cannot recall (that's how few and underpublicized they are), we are celebrated, heralded and rewarded backwardly. Berry Gordy made Smokey Robinson, Michael Jackson, Marvin Gaye, Diana Ross and Stevie Wonder; Berry Gordy should be aforementioned when speaking on any of them, not après.

#blackpeople many races of people r bi-lingual except us: jews, latinos, germans, russians, italians, chinese, koreans #think about it

Americans in general are probably the least bi-lingual people. America is the dominant imperial nation, the land of opportunity and freedom that everyone wants to live in and learn English, so why bother learning other languages, right?

While this may be the sentiment of the majority of Americans; not even President Obama, Bush, nor Clinton were bi-lingual, it seems a fledging failure on

- 274 -

MICHAEL IRVIN WALKER

our part as Americans, especially when our country is so open to let millions of immigrants across the border to work and live here; people come here with a special code all of their own. In thinking about special codes, morse code has been used to implement strategy in war to gain optimal position and take down the enemy; to alert friendlies that other friendlies were near-by for assistance or if they were captured by the enemy.

As of 2013, it is duly noted that Latin Americans will be the dominant force, population wise within the United States of America; millions of people speaking a separate code all their own and demanding (as early as the year 1999) that services in America be provided and available in their Spanish language.

There are many people who come to the United States, integrate into the society and learn the English language to get along. Black Americans however, we were stripped of our African language upon being brought to the United States as slaves thousands of years ago and beaten if we tried to speak it; therefore, instead of becoming bi-lingual as we learned the English language - which we weren't allowed to learn very well in and of itself because we weren't allowed to read - we lost all traces of our original African language. Whereas you have a vast population of Chinese people who are bi-lingual; Jewish people as well are bi-lingual; Italians are bi-lingual. The majority of Black Americas speak a southern dialect infused, lethargic English, and a small percentage (excluding Haitians) when compared as a whole, speak a second language.

As the population in America continues to become more and more brown, it is imperative for Black Americans to be bi-lingual in the form of Spanish and English. Our children must learn Spanish just as equally as English, which will provide them leverage in the job market especially in management positions, and they will be better equipped to bond with their Spanish speaking fellow minority/majority cohorts.

When I hear persons speaking a second language, it is a bit of cause for envy; for those persons can one-up me at any given time just by being in the presence of native tongue speaking individuals; immediately, I'm an outsider. More and more Latin American neighborhoods and communities will start to appear and often, those who are not Spanish English bi-lingual will find themselves in places and situation where no one is speaking the English language. Living in America, an English-speaking country, having been born and raised here, non-bi-lingual Americans will feel as if they've traveled to another country.

nothing on free t.v. (rachet or sensible) relates 2 #blackpeople. the networks r like fuck ya'll, u want 2 C black people pay 4 cable

MICHAEL IRVIN WALKER

What ever happened to the days when there were television shows featuring Black Americans acting as normal everyday reasonable citizens: Good Times (though there is the argument the show never featured any good times), The Jeffersons (though there is the argument George Jefferson often made a fool of himself), What's Happening and most notably The Cosby Show.

Present day, all shows featuring a majority Black American cast are on cable; a small percentage if any, feature classy, educated reasonable civilized citizens. With the advent of reality television, the images have been getting worse every six months; featuring fighting, loud mouth, gossip spreading individuals who do not seem capable of analytical thought or critical, thought provoking, problem solving which does not involve cursing or violence.

Undoubtedly, the numbers within the Black American population have increased since the year 1973, as all of my grandparent's children are alive and well, they've produced my generation and my generation's children are age 16 to 23. It seems there would be on ABC, CBS and NBC, a show or two featuring a majority Black American cast; to the contrary there is not (preamble to "Black-ish in 2014 and EMPIRE, 2015). There are only the shows which feature one Black American (often times mixed half white), one or two other Black Americans with insignificant parts and the majority of the cast, White American: Scandal, House, Deception etc. All other shows featuring majority Black American cast are

- 277 -

relegated to cable television: VH1, BRAVO, BET, CENTRIC, Bounce TV and TV ONE.

Free television is for all Americans within the United States of America. As of this current period of time in history, Black Americans and Latino Americans are becoming a large swath of the American population; yet, free television does not feature many shows to appeal to these racial groups. What does that say? It says, "expletive" you, you may be a large population, but we hold all of the real power, and as long as White American people hold the real decision making power, White American people will be featured on free major network television.

As of Feb 2015, at the very moment Cicely Tyson hit the screen in the scenes of HOW TO GET AWAY WITH MURDER with Viola Davis, I said to myself, "Things don' changed!" I think Shonda Rhimes is making the ABC network realize and maybe CBS, NBC and Fox with the hit show EMPIRE, that Black American people and our current state of living in American and our dreams, are not something to be shunned and underdeveloped in primetime television. And after I watched the last seasonal episode of HOW TO GET AWAY WITH MURDER on Thursday February 27, 2015, my response was this:

#HOWTOGETAWAYWITHMURDER #WOW, #OMG #UNBELIEVABLE #INCREDIBLE

MICHAEL IRVIN WALKER

I'm going to try and break this down as intellectually as possible:

So what do we have here? WE HAVE IT ALL covered on ALL SIDES!!! REAL BLACK AMERICAN WOMAN, Viola Davis, as opposed to what you say? As opposed to a half Black American or light skinned Black American woman that the media always pushes on the masses as the prime representation of Black American beautiful woman. And us poor brown to dark skinned Black American folks are supposed to fall in line with the, one drop of Black blood makes a Black American, so at least somebody Black is making it; that's all well and good until you start to realize they're excluding a large swath of the Black American population who just so happen, not to be light skinned or half white. The show with Cicely Tyson as the mom, was unprecedentedly, the greatest culturally real Black American, piece of television and acting EVER!

So, Annalise is married to a White American man; Black people can easily swallow that, but when every show with a beautiful Black American woman, and she's sleeping with or married to a White American man, you kind of start to say, WTF! But in this case, the Black American woman is having an affair (not that I condone extra-marital affairs) with a handsome, once again, real Black American brown skinned, non-half White American man. We have a very likable handsome half White American guy, Wes on the show. We have another real brown skinned Black

- 279 -

American woman student lawyer. We have the gay guy/couple. And of course, we have the Omni-present White Americans. I particularly like Annalise's assistant with the short haircut, she's sexy. And I'll also point out Annalise's White American hit man who is very handsome with the beard. I also wish - though I don't really have to, because the beard is in full effect now - White American men, particularly in corporate American board rooms would start rocking beards and job candidates didn't feel as if showing up to an interview with a beard was a guaranteed, NO-HIRE move.

The show IS ALL (not all, but close) INCLUSIVE, from every angle: Black, Half Black/White, White, Gay, Straight! The story line is just enthralling, engaging, captivating, mortifying, nerve biting suspenseful. FALL for new season!!!! DO YOU KNOW HOW LONG FALL IS FROM NOW???

I often say, "I do not watch much TV" I DON'T!!! That's because most TV has absolutely NOTHING to do with or relate to my life, culture, experiences or fantasy. With the advent of #HOWTOGETAWAYWITHMURDER TV is getting better.

My point, when you start being all inclusive and touching on cultural reality, not just what is thought, White American people want to see, YOU FIRE ON ALL CYLINDERS!!!

THANK GOD FOR #SHONDARHIMES

- 280 -

MICHAEL IRVIN WALKER

media & white people have #blackpeople so brainwashed we'll never dig out of the albatross which we so readily allow them 2 place us

#blackpeople. black president challenges strongly, he's about 2 get n2 violent altercation. when white man challenges, he's brilliant/smart

#blackpeople always b aware the media & white people will always perceive u as something negative. they're call debate a prize fight! #wtf

      Ever notice on the news every other night or every night, particularly in NYC an image, of either a blurry video, still photo from a blurry video, a clear or blurry photo of a Black American man accused of doing some crime? In some instances, the video or photo is so blurry the only thing which can be deciphered from looking at it is that the person is a Black American man whom you or anyone else would not be able to identify if the person was sitting at your table having dinner with you. What these images do is demonize and criminalize the Black American male, such that even if he is walking down the street in a three piece suit, a lone White American may clutch their purse, phone or casually cross the street to avoid what they perceive may be a threat, even in broad day light.

- 281 -

The media and the powers that be are the ones who have down played images of darker skin Black Americans to the point of no return where the majority of darker skinned Black Americans do not believe they are worthy; thus, they gravitate toward lighter skinned Black Americans or White Americans in love relationships, leadership business relationships and positions, and sometimes basic friendships as well; it's been termed colorism.

A majority of Black Americans have accepted their position of low-grade status and act as such, hence the behavior of persons in real life as well as on reality television; accepting of the wretched behavior toward one another as normal, the way Black Americans are supposed to act, a badge of pride and honor to promulgate our uniqueness within society.

The only problem with this badge of uniqueness that many Black American people carry is that it is rooted in ignorance and disrespect. A seed is planted deep within the brain, that at the blink of an image of a Black American, you think disrespectfully of that individual which controls all other interaction you have or will allow yourself to have in the future with that person. Whether a J.D., MBA, CPA, PHD, M.I.T. Howard or Harvard graduate, without other information as to their rank, social and/or economic status, you see that person as a negative Black American to be dealt with from a distance; not as your brother or sister to love or support in business and life.

- 282 -

MICHAEL IRVIN WALKER

#blackpeople actually feel guilty 4 supporting a culturally uplifting cause. they let white people make them feel guilty 4 reverse racism

@WSJ: The Supreme Court is hearing a key affirmative action case regarding diversity in universities. Our live blog: http://on.wsj.com/ReHCjC

#blackpeople supreme court is hearing key affirmative action case. they r going 2 strip it away. but yet with it my cpa friend cant get work

#blackpeople do we need affirmative action? yes if we continue 2 support white owned corps who do not hire us when we apply @ corp hdqtrs

#blackpeople we wouldnt need affirmative action if we started our own corps, supported & got support 4 them from our own.

Black Americans have been discriminated against from the very moment we were brought to this land of the United States of America. Discrimination was the law of the land: Black Americans legally could not read, legally could not enter into contracts with White American men nor amongst themselves, legally could not socialize or go to school with White American people, legally could not use the same bathrooms as White American people, legally could not marry White American people, legally could not vote, legally could not fight in the face of blatant aggrievement, legally could not run for public office.

With time and as civil rights laws were passed to give Black American people legal rights to all of the aforementioned, White American people began clandestine movements to deny Black American people every legality which the law allowed: denied jobs, denied equal wages for work, denied home loans, denied equal access to housing in certain communities, obstacles were put up when Black American people tried to run their own businesses or run for public political office.

Black American people have been denied and/or covertly blocked from every area of opportunity that ever existed in America; yet, we've persisted and carried on until many major road blocks have been torn down; today, while we are allowed access, there are still individual stealth machinations which deny us certain opportunities.

When Barack Obama was running for U.S. President in 2008, there were many cries from White American people, "I don't think it is fair that Black American people are voting for him just because he is Black American." And though many Black Americans felt in their heart of hearts, "yes, I'm voting for Barack Obama because he's Black American" very few would ever state that fact. Oprah Winfrey was afraid or maybe contractually un-allowed, on her daily

MICHAEL IRVIN WALKER

syndicated television show, to speak her support for Barack Obama and his run for Presidential office until after election-day.

At a time when Black Americans are still suffering greatly in this country from lack of, and/or access to a great education, lack of job opportunities, lack of access to networks to venture capital and economic support for entrepreneurial ventures; White American people are claiming reverse racism and many Black American people are listening and acquiescing to their laments. All the while it took Black American people 100 years or more to get some form of equal justice on social, economic and political fronts.

White American people try at every possible turn, to cry that Black American people are racist. For example, in the Treyvon Martin and George Zimmerman shooting trial, White American people said, "would this case be getting all the media hype if George Zimmerman was Black American and shot an innocent Black American kid or if he shot a White American kid?" They asked the question, "why are Black American people voting for Barack Obama in 2008?" The question was not asked in reference to John F. Kennedy, Jimmy Carter, Walter Mondale, Bill Clinton or Al Gore. But when it comes to Black Americans supporting our own people and our own causes, we often demure in the presence of White American people and their claims of reverse discrimination, Non-White American privilege and the White American Non-racist; this in turn will forever keep us a weak race of people which White American people will forever hold the power over us.

When 150 of the Fortune 500 CEOs are Black American men and women, 150 are White American men and women, 150 are Latino men and women and 50 other, or some other variation other than 450 White American men; when five to ten darker skin, non-half White Black American men and women become President Of The United States Of America; when Black Americans are Harvard grads in greater numbers and get the best jobs and opportunities in America and abroad; when Black American men, both educated white collar and non-educated blue collar start receiving employment offers in greater numbers and the unemployment rate for Black American men is less than double that of White American men; when Black American men and women who are unarmed, stop getting shot down like wild animals by police officers as well as civilians (George Zimmerman, Michael Dunn, Theodore Wafer), THEN WE'LL TALK ABOUT REVERSE DISCRIMINATION BEING UNFAIR TO WHITE AMERICAN MEN AND WOMEN!

I think at this stage in our great American history, the qualifications needed to meet a certain standard should not be lowered for anyone. SHIT or GET OFF THE POT! But then we have the current situation where so many qualified minorities, with equal or better qualifications are still being passed over for opportunities, based upon mere phone calls and recognition of minority dialect inflections; therefore, affirmative action is still needed.

MICHAEL IRVIN WALKER

The majority of White American people in power cannot, and seemingly will not be fair. And as, which it is already quoted as being so, the number of Black American and Latin American populations continue to grow to majority status, those in power are going to create more ruses and machinations to hold on to their power. Do I want Affirmative Action for my children, NO! Will they need it, more likely than not, YES! Do I think I need it despite 17 years of work experience in my field as well as a professional license in that field, YES!

A guy, Jonathan Trieber, emailed me recognizably very excited about my resume and stated (his exact written words) "*I am reaching out to see if you might be available for an in-person interview on Friday this week or Tuesday next week? We would very much like to find the right candidate and make an offer in the next week Oct 7-11, 2013 due to time sensitivity around this position*". After I met him in person, his story changed to having to meet 10 other people and making an offer somewhere near Oct 31, 2013. If he'd simply kept his story to "we're seeing a few more candidates and you should hear back from us next week" I wouldn't be so critical of him as biased. Ten is more than a few people and Oct 31st to get back to me is more than a week.

The big question with Affirmative Action is in reference to college admissions. Should Black American students be given special consideration in college admissions? This is a heated debate in which many White American students are bringing law suits against college admissions offices for reverse racial discrimination.

I know plenty of college graduates as well as non-college grads who have very sufficiently educated children. We all know or should know what the college admissions game is about: grades, act/sat scores, school activity participation and/or volunteerism, etc. Knowing this, there is no excuse why our children should need an Affirmative Action lower standard to get into the college of their choice. Or, that they/we cannot research the admissions requirements of the college of their choice, and GO GET IT!

The antithesis is we have children whose parents have been given an unfair advantage in being akin to those in power, which provided natural advantage or ease of networking with those in power to obtain great job opportunities. So once again, I say, do I think my children are well educated? YES! Do I think my children should receive an Affirmative Action leg up in college admissions? NO! Are my children educated better than those whose parents are in middle to upper management, (which about 1% or less of those positions at Fortune 500 companies are held by minorities; I DO NOT HOLD ONE, not even at a Fortune 1000 company), and sends their children to expensive private school and/or pays for extra act/sat prep courses? NO! So, all other qualifications equal give or take, up or down a few points, should my daughter receive an Affirmative Action nod to

MICHAEL IRVIN WALKER

enter a top tier university? Would Sonya Satamyor
have been a United States Supreme Court Justice
without affirmative action? NO! AFFIRMATIVE
ACTION SHOULD NOT BE TERMINATED!

For even with affirmative action, minorities still
need to coalesce their interest into supporting and
promulgation of one another on all social, political
and economic fronts; without such support, especially
in the light of an abatement of affirmative action, in
the future we will be in a worse apoplectic blight than
the current day with affirmative action in place.

#thetalk #juliechen it looks like u have an
extra head, behind & on top of your head,
hiden by your hair. lose the weave or
something

#thetalk #juliechen with your beautiful slim
face, less big hair would be best, even a
short cut. guess ur hair-brainwashed like
#blackwomen

#thetalk #theview y r the majority of the
#blackwomen on these shows fat? & the
not so fat ones date/marry white men

#wendywilliams black women on #theview #tweetthetalk (except ayisha, but who cares, she's only attracted 2 white men), & hope. all chunky

#tweetthetalk #ayisha have u ever heard a whiteman say, "viola davis//regina king oh, I love &/or have big crush on them, they r sooo hot"

#tweetthetalk great u have a black man on the show, but still every1 is distant, not like when a white guy is on, every1 cums on themselves

@TerrenceJ @wendywilliams hope u got more love than u did on #tweetthetalk where they treated u like an ugly sweaty slave

#tweetthetalk the show is rep of america: immigrants, gays, white women all get a fair shake. black men get shafted with no vaseline

#tweetthetalk I commend u 4 having a quote unquote real black (not light/mulatto, not mixed married) woman on the show in #sherylunderwood

MICHAEL IRVIN WALKER

#tweetthetalk last yr u were cutting on intro of guest every time a white male guest hugged the black women host glad u fixed that problem

OK. Let's talk about the talk show "The Talk". I started out tuning in because hey, at first glance, five well-known beautiful ladies; second glance, a beautiful Asian American, two beautiful Black American women, both not light-skinned or half White American and one of which is actually dark skinned, two White American women (one gay); a pretty fair representation of America without the obvious bias in racial make-up.

As I began tuning into the show daily, what I first noticed was that every time a White American guest came upon the show, when it was their turn to hug the Black American women on the show, the camera would parry to the audience. As I watched more and more, I noticed that when White American men came on the show (gay or straight) all of the ladies were at the highest heights of apogee; fawning and throwing themselves at the men like pliant little teenagers, which was very cute at first. As I watched a little more I noticed that very few if any Black American guest appeared upon the show and even less, Black American men.

The first two Black American men I did notice on the show were Mehcad Brooks and Terrance J. With Mehcad, he got a fair amount of attention from the ladies, but not even close to that given to a White

American male hunk whose name escapes me. When Terrance J came on the show, it was within the same week or a day after the White American male hunk came on the show, and compared to the attention they showed the young White American male, Terrence J was treated very disrespectfully in my view; not even the Black American women host showed the Black American male guest as much attention as they showed the White American male guest.

The ladies often asked the question among themselves "who do you have a crush on or who's the most handsome man to date?" They all, even the Black American women named a White American male; no Denzel Washington, no Idris Elba, no Omari Hardwick, not even a nod to the ultimate, smoothest Black American man of them all, Billy Dee Williams; Billy is/was a little old at the time, but you get the point.

Watching the show a little more, I found out that Aisha Tyler, with one of the blackest of Black American names, was married to a White American guy, who's also her lawyer, which goes in tandem with my harangue about the majority of Black American people only allowing White American people to handle the most important life and career business (but hey, he's her husband; duly excused).

As I watched a little more, though I appreciated the appearance of Sheryl Underwood as a host, she looked unhealthy weight wise and to place

MICHAEL IRVIN WALKER

her on the very end of the table where she was most visible to both the studio and television viewing audience did not sit well with me; almost as if confirming the myth of "Why Are Black Women Fat?" But you can't say that all together because Aisha Tyler is not fat by far; but anathema to Aisha Tyler being in the clear as an all-Black American woman is her choice of spouse. So, it's like with the two Black American women on the show, it's a case of "you can't have your cake and eat it too".

Thinking a little more on the subject: you have Julie Chen "beautiful", Aisha Tyler "beautiful (but married to a White American man), Sharon Osborne beautiful (but old), Sara Gilbert "beautiful" (but gay), Sheryl Underwood "beautiful" (but a little overweight); the spread about evens itself out which would be great to watch if they'd just stop with the blatant show of preferential treatment of White American men.

While into the spell of watching The Talk, I happened to turn to the talk shows, The View and The Wendy Williams Show. I saw Sherri Shepherd on The View. I saw Wendy's assistant or something to that affect, whose name is Hope. My thoughts then turned to Star Jones, then back to The Talk's Sheryl Underwood. Notice anything similar about these women? ALL OVER WEIGHT or just their curves are not proportionately in the right places. It dawned on me that these shows are sending a direct message to the rest of the world, "BLACK AMERICAN WOMEN ARE FAT!"

To say the least, though I've said a whole lot, I do not tune in to The Talk anymore. Though I applaud its successful attempt at a diverse host/co-host format, the women on the show seem too culturally biased and it oozes from every single one of the host.

do u know you look ridiculous stupid & like an idiot when u stand in front of the mirror & take a picture of urself with ur cell phone cam

This phenomenon started with the advent of the cell phone cameras and being allowed to instantly view the picture once taken. All people do this. Look upon Facebook, Blackpeoplemeet.com or Instagram and you'll see no shortage of persons holding a camera in the mirror while capturing a shot of themselves.

From my experience growing up, it has always been said, 'to be vain and conceited is evil." What could be more vainglorious than taking an obvious self-portrait and smiling while doing it? Not only does it look vain, it also appears as if you do not have a friend in the world, no kids in your home or even a dog who could snap a quick cell phone photo of you. But I suppose the vicissitude in reference to cell phones is they are personal, not to be touched, used or photos-taken nor viewed by any other party than thyself.

MICHAEL IRVIN WALKER

Maybe I hold myself up to a different kind of standard, but I think less of persons who take photos of themselves in the mirror with the phone camera in their hand showing in the picture. I think less of their common sense, less of their education, less of their class and couth.

On the flip side of taking a photo in the mirror with camera showing in hand, is taking a self-photo of your head or upper body, the "Selfie", it has been named; these type photos are not viewed in as bad a light. They virtually look, most of them do, as if someone snapped a picture of you, besides when you see the obvious extended arm showing in the photo, which with a little editing can be cropped out.

To be safe from all judgment, the self-photo, whether in the mirror or the arm extended "Selfie" with your head tilted to the side, is a turn-off. When you hang out with your friends, have them snap a few cell phone photos of you as self-portraits because taking them yourself looks desperate and cast a ghetto pall upon your image. That's just a limited opinion, cause the "Selfie" has grown in popularity with the zeitgeist and there seems to be no turning back. And sure, I take photos of myself, but they are nowhere near egregiously decadent as the "Selfie".

After grad from Yale, Bush Sr. moved his fam 2 West Texas. His father's business connects proved useful when he ventured n2 the oil business

#nepotism G.W. Bush getting a start & n the oil business cause his father made a few phone calls. #whitepeople support of #whitepeople

To Black American, first-generation college graduates, do you recall how you got your first job out of college or received any work experience or internships during summers off from college? Did your parents, aunts or uncles have connections lined up to grant you opportunities in volunteerism and/or paid work?

From my experience, my jobs came through applying, no business connections what-so-ever from anyone. My aunt did speak with a White American lady she knew and got me an interview at some sausage brand company in Akron or Cleveland OH; Sugardale I think was the name, but that was it as far as connections went. I believe to this day, I only received my first staff accountant job at Dairy Mart Corporation because the hiring manager for the position had half Black American children; that, and as a publicly traded company they probably received some incentive for hiring minorities.

- 296 -

MICHAEL IRVIN WALKER

Is it my own fault that at my age with a daughter, I am without a connection in the world; and not for lack of trying? I sent out a text a few years ago to everyone in my phone and e-mail contact list inquiring about a job in my field and nothing came back. I do not have a single connection to set my daughter up once she graduates from college. I suppose I could try to change that.

The question is, "Do Black American people think in nepotistic ways in reference to their friends and family?" Or, is it that Black American people are kept so marginalized in jobs and future employment opportunities, we keep such things under close radar? Or, is it we do not trust in one another's skills to give a good referral? Or, is it that our referrals go in one ear and right out of the other of those we try to make a referral to?

I can recall the company Under Armour whose corporate headquarters is in Baltimore, Maryland, having a Senior Manager of External Reporting roll opening in Sept 2014. A Black American female friend I'd known for some time (as in 20 years) whose husband was a retired professional basketball player, lived in Maryland so I inquired to her about the city. She said Maryland was a great place to live with a beautiful Black American population. I then asked her if she or her husband knew anyone who worked for Under Armour? She said, indeed, an executive of the company lived right across the street from her and that he knew she and her husband and that her husband actually had casual neighborly conversation

with the executive. I asked if she or her husband
could talk to the executive about giving me a referral
to Under Armour HR and/or give him my resume. She
said she didn't speak with the executive often enough,
but she'd ask her husband if he would inquire to the
executive, but she said her husband probably
wouldn't because he doesn't like asking people for
favors; he knows how weird it feels when people ask
him for favors as the millionaire retired NBA player.

I waited a week and asked had she talked with
her husband. She said she hadn't, he'd been busy
and traveling and that she wanted to ask him when
she had his full attention and he would not blow her
off. I said fine, then, I laid out for her a scenario in
how to introduce the subject to him just in case she
felt a little nervous about it. She never responded to
me after that point; needless to say, I received the
proverbial rejection email to my online application to
Under Armour and no less, after I had read through
their entire 2013 Annual Report, and felt confident I
could handle the job of Manager External Reporting.

It is situations like that which keeps a Black
American man, with 15 years of work experience and
CPA License, under and/or unemployed. A great
referral from a neighbor and ex-NBA player would
have probably given me a great leg up or even a
shoe-in for the Under Armour job, but Black
Americans are leery to make such connections and
referrals for one another.

MICHAEL IRVIN WALKER

I can recall thinking I had a pretty good passer-by/working relationship with an owner of an outdoor advertising company in NYC. A friend of mine applied for a job to his company so I went into his office and spoke with him about my friend. He mentioned to me that someone else had also previously spoken to him on her behalf. This guy had two great unofficial references in addition to any she may have included on her application; he still did not hire the young Black American woman.

There are many industries built up through connections and nepotism and favors: film, gambling, sports and advertising to name a few. Black American people need to understand the power we hold within ourselves to change our overall bad situation. In these times going into the future, we must present ourselves, our friends and family as viable candidates to fulfill opportunities of all kind without any doubt and with an expectation that our referrals be taken seriously and request granted.

Everyone else does it: Irish, Jews, WASP, Italians; many in these groups make a phone call and their children are employed, even if that's only for a summer. Black American people need to build up their personal networks through all of the partying we do in major cities; it seems we party and network without building an actual useful network.

Could it be we are useless people? No one thinks that of themselves, but think about this; can you call upon a friend or family member, can they call

- 299 -

on you for instant access to an interview for a job or a resource to help economically? If the answer is "NO" YOU AND THEM ARE USELESS! I AM USELESS!

black people u can read & study how white people became billionaires. but without support of black people u'll never make it 2 that level. expand

Many people pick up books for the enjoyment of reading, to kill time, to educate themselves with general useless erudition or for true motivation to put a plan in place and execute. I can recall reading the book by Ram Charon "Execution: The discipline of getting things done" before starting a new job. I was gong-ho on the literature and determined not to let anyone just provide me with lip service in reference to solving a problem which was my responsibility to solve. I had also read in a few business magazines about being candid in communications.

What I found is that being candid and gong-ho on execution on top of being a Black American man was not working in my favor; anytime I pressed someone for details, especially in a candid manner, I was reported to my manager as being aggressive and/or threatening. In acting in that fashion conducting my own personal business, White American people: my landlord in trying to negotiate a stay of current rent given bad economic times in 2008; fiduciaries at TGIF-CREF (though TGIF has a Black American CEO) in trying to roll-over my IRA to

- 300 -

MICHAEL IRVIN WALKER

Fidelity; a lawyer running her own PR firm in trying to get me to work for her for free; these people were taken aback by my business acumen and aplomb manner of speaking with them and were quite perturbed in trying to get a one up on me on details regarding proper procedure and/or deals/compromises.

As I mentioned prior, I've tried speaking with many Black American sports figures, artist and managers regarding a simple meeting to hear me out regarding my firm and services; no dice. It seems the selling and influence techniques I've read in books and/or great CEO's (Steve Jobs {a known hard-nosed, difficult person to negotiate with and/or work for}, Jack Welch, Donald Trump, Clive Davis) memoirs; in trying to project their CEO-esque into my own life and company brand building, nothing seemed to work.

Why nothing worked it seemed is because I do/did not have a rooted network, which speaks to the fact of Black American people not sticking together in networks; I can name a bevy of persons with some particular status in industries which I was trying to be a part of; I either know personally from a soft connection or know indirectly through other people; yet, no help!

Due to Black American people trying to hold on to their sliver of power they may have, or their jealousy of someone who has ambitions greater than their own; reading all of the CEO, Power, Sales and

Influence books in the world will not work without support of your own race of people. At times there are anomies, and persons such as: Ursula Burns, Stanley O'Neal, Ken Chennault, Roger Ferguson, Donald Thompson, James Skinner - who become the all-powerful, rich with stock options/grants, CEO, but those are only one in thousands and the numbers are greater when accounting for the ambitions of many other Black Americans who wanted to be power CEOs of some sort but whose efforts were thwarted and prostrated.

Looking on the flip side of the coin, almost every company of any significance in America has a White American CEO. Why? Because those people work hard and support each other's efforts; give and receive opportunities to work with and for one another; have solid networks where a phone call gets them a presentation of their ideas on building new companies, introducing new products, merging and acquiring existing companies.

For, without support of those who share the same ethos and commonalities as yourself, reading Steve Jobs and Jack Welch books will not benefit you.

1st, 2 bcome a millionaire u must provide something people need, not what u think they want or u want them 2 have, but they need regardless

MICHAEL IRVIN WALKER

2nd, once u provide what they need, n addition 2 paid advertising & promotion, people need 2 support & push that need 2 other people

In the economy today, it seems we as a people, all people, have everything we need. Then, WAMMO, a billion dollar idea hits the market. - i.e. Facebook - and it is the impetus for many failed ideas to come behind it. The reason for the failed ideas is due to the fact most persons try to create something which they think people will want as opposed to what people need - i.e. clothing line, new magazine, web-site or mobile phone idea - based upon an already existing popular idea.

With the creation of a product or service which people are already using, it takes prodigious marketing, advertising and branding to solidify a place in the hearts, homes and everyday usage psyche of the average consumer. If you think of a business operation as: "if I open my door with a product inside, people will come in and buy it" your business is destined to fail.

The exception to the rule is if you open your door with a product inside that people need at that particular moment in time. For example take Facebook. Before Facebook and MySpace, college students socialized with one another in the student recreation center or at parties on the weekends starting Thursday night. At those particular socialization points there was no way to really stand out as an individual unless you were exceptionally beautiful/handsome, had a great extrovert personality, were a part of a popular group or fraternity, or were a known celebrity's kid and/or known rich kid. Once you left the rec center or the party was over, it was back to being a single individual on a campus of thousands of other individuals.

With the advent of Facebook and MySpace, it provided a platform for an individual in their downtime to connect to a large group of persons at will, by entering a username and password; an instant audience for their pictures, to make comments and to philosophize on self-induced topics or topics of the world and vice versa for them to view others as well.

The social media platforms played into everyone's clamoring desire to be a celebrity or news broadcaster or an opinionated pundit on one or various topics: music, politics, celebrity gossip, local provender etc. Hence, though it seemed like a product or service someone would want, it was actually something college students and in turn, the world, needed.

Tapping into the conscious mind of making the average person think they need your product or service is key to great success. Outside of convincing persons they need your products, there is the actual instance of selling a product or service people actually do need: tax preparation services, housing and home products, transportation, food, mobile phones (as of

MICHAEL IRVIN WALKER

the new millennium), cleaning products (both skin and home/material surfaces).

As for the services everyone needs, the market is well saturated; in that case, ingenuity and artifice come into play to get the market to recognize your product or service in a sea of others. The ingenuity takes major marketing dollars and strategy along with support from those who share a cultural commonality with you and/or your product (i.e. the movie "Keeping Up With The Joneses); for, without those, you will never see a million dollars.

#blackpeople. know what a variable prepaid forward contract is? do u care? it's these created transactions which keep them ahead n the game

#blackpeople build websites, ask do u no flash, no. black people r financial advisors, ask do u no variable prepaid forward contracts, no

Many people bestow the wisdom upon persons, especially in the Black American community, "get an education; it is the most important thing to have; they (racist White American power structure) can never take that away from you."

As years have gone by in my life I've discovered a way education can, in fact, be taken away from people; simply create new transactions and factions which are not highly publicized as standard knowledge for one to have in order to maintain his/her basic level of education.

The Internet; though a bad example of a faction not being highly publicized, is an example of how to take education away from someone like my mom who has a 12th grade education, which as years have passed, has been downgraded to even less than a 12th grade current education level. A person like her with virtually no computer skills except to know what a computer physically looks like, is out of the loop when it comes to applying for modern day jobs, which many require filling out an online application.

I forget what year it was, but I was at a public library in Youngstown, OH and a woman approaching middle age was trying to open a Facebook account; she had no clue where to start, how to upload a picture to her profile or how to navigate the site to post comments, etc. To her and her current education level, Facebook was a foreign language too difficult to understand, even though all the instructions were printed in plain English upon the site; she had no clue where to start on reading and executing the instructions.

From 2003 to 2006 I was unemployed. In 2004 A recruiter called me and asked, "are you familiar with SOX or Sarbanes Oxley"; befuddled, I replied I'd never heard of it. I thought it was something she simply made up to throw me off the employment trail of the position. As it turns out Sarbanes Oxley was

MICHAEL IRVIN WALKER

real, an act/law created as a tool to hold management of companies accountable for their financial reporting results and internal controls. Why was I oblivious to the act/law which so greatly affected my field of work and study? As stated in reference to Facebook, it was a highly publicized enactment of law attached to a highly publicized company, "Enron", and fraudulent on-goings which brought the company and all its employees down with significant loss of value on their stock equity retirement funds.

I was blindsided by Sarbanes Oxley due to my own ignorance and lack of networking and non-membership to any organizations within my field of study and/or lack of keeping up with reading daily news publications nor having a subscription to The CPA Journal, which may have kept me abreast of such an epoch within the accounting industry. Though SOX at the time was nascent and not mandated to be input into company's modis operandi, the recruiter used it against me as being unqualified for the position.

In essence, it is not so much that knowledge is hidden or clandestinely published, as it is due to Black American people's own ignorance and non-application of continuing education (self or institutionalized continuing education), which perpetually buries us in comparison to the competition (i.e. that person who takes Excel advanced classes and knows every Excel trick and financial modeling template available), and it is used against us in job prospects and interviews.

- 307 -

It seems Black American people would rather take the easy way, relax and not take the time to study in detail or take an extracurricular class to stay on top of the latest greatest inventions and tactics which provides an advantage in life as far as employment opportunity goes. To no fault of our own could be the lesser pay we receive which does not allow us to attend conventions, subscribe to a $200.00/Yr trade magazine or newspaper, nor to take an extra-curricular class costing $349.00-$1,000.00

Variable prepaid forward contracts provide financial advisement clients with virtually – if not completely - tax free income. Flash website production (though currently outdated) provides clients with moving and engaging website experiences for their existing customers and to attract new customers.

In essence, while they can't take education away from you, if you do not make an effort toward a protracted education within your chosen profession or self-interest, every time a new technique comes along which you have no knowledge of, your education is being taken away.

From my personal experience, it seemed employers did not want to present me with much challenging work and promulgate my growth on the job and in my field of expertise. If a person is not allowed to practice on the job, and given remedial task, that downgrades ones' experience level. I passed the CPA exam and was presented with no

MICHAEL IRVIN WALKER

opportunity for advancement in my field; IN FACT, AFTER I PASSED THE EXAM IS WHEN I HAD THE MOST DIFFICULT TIME FINDING EMPLOYMENT!

#blackpeople any grown ass man or woman who lets their daughter have a child at age 13-17 is a fucking idiot ghetto bastard

I was working at a local community center for summer employment. There was a cute young 13 to 14 year old girl who used to come by; It was widely known that she had a child of her own. This was not the first time such a situation had taken place to my knowledge; when I was 8 years old, a guy from my neighborhood was 13 years old and his first child had just been born. A good friend of mine, his and his girlfriend's first child was born when they were both age 14. My cousin had her first child at age 15. It all seemed normal back then, liberal/non-judgmental; have a child, provide a roof over its head, get on welfare and live happily ever after.

In my 20s, I can recall saying a few times in conversation, "just because a woman is not married does not mean she should not have a child" or "just because a woman becomes pregnant, doesn't mean she and the guy should be married instantly." It wasn't until recent years, in the new millennium; around the time I started trying to speak English more clearly and properly enunciate my words; around the time I

- 309 -

started picking up magazines and writing definitions of words to improve my vocabulary; around the time I started to look at Black American people's lives in New York City and the desolate situation many of us lived in; I began to rethink this liberalism in thought.

Black American people have the highest number (or highest percentage as a total population) of babies born out of wedlock; Black American people are the highest number incarcerated in prisons (despite racial targeting, many convictions are legitimate); Black American men are the least enumerated college education and graduation category; Black American women are the largest non-married population; Black American people are the highest unemployed in this nation. Taking into consideration those facts, it seems at the impetus of them all; children without proper family planning.

Within the teen years, adults are in control or can heavily influence the decisions made by their children. At age 15, it does not make logical sense to let your child saddle themselves with the type of responsibility to be brought about with child birth, which hinders education prospects, employment commitments; thus, curtailing or ceasing long term wealth building and a comfortable life.

My first and only child was born 6 months after I graduated from college. I was an adult and was quite irresponsible in the act which led to child birth. I was immediately handed a $389 a month child support bill; give or take a few years and throw in added gifts,

MICHAEL IRVIN WALKER

visitation and transportation, by time the child is 18 years old, I would have spent $85,000. For a man who doesn't own a home, has never traveled out of the country (have been to Paris and London 2019), who has a hunger for learning yet no master's degree, that figure speaks volumes as to what could have been done with that sum of money belonging solely to me or married to my child's mother in a proper family.

I've told my child, if you are going to have a child without a spouse, graduate from college first, get a master's degree, work hard and play hard; by age 33 with hopefully a nest egg in the bank or some other investments, start to properly plan to have a child alone. A child hinders the futures of both the man and woman involved. At age 13, 14, 15, 16, WHY WOULD YOU ALLOW YOUR CHILD TO HINDER THEMSELVES in what could be potentially a greater childless life?

As for the polemics; for all of the situations where wed-lock child birth at an early age has turned out great, there are more examples where the situation has turned out greater in having a child properly with a spouse and/or at a maturity and education level which allows one to properly plan and handle the circumstances making sound, well thought out decisions for themselves and the child at hand.

black people notice when u want 2 try something new, others think of all the obstacles. If u listen, that's anathema 2 ultimate success

Have you ever spoken your dream aloud in a circle of Black American friends or family: "I'm going to build a nationally branded CPA firm which will be the main hub for Black American tax preparation and Black American sports and entertainment tax and wealth management."

Once you stated the dream, did you notice the obstacles being drawn up out of thin air as to why it would be virtually impossible to do so: "easier said than done; how are you going to do that; White American people are not going to let you control an enterprise like that; where are you going to find the money to start it; that's gonna take a lot of hard long work hours; I don't want to work that hard, let someone else be bothered with all of that as long as my bills are paid I'm good." This attitude is anathema to any type of success, even the success of professional NBA/NFL players, musicians or actors.

I can recall mentioning to a past girlfriend of mine since we like to drink merlot and a particular brand of vodka often, why not we start a liquor store? She went into a tirade of, "you have to fill out mountains of paper work; the liquor store can't be near a school; there isn't any funding to be granted to start such a business.' THE OBSTACLES!

- 312 -

MICHAEL IRVIN WALKER

While there are obstacles to be considered and overcome, the conversation doesn't seem to come from a place of, "lets hold a planning and strategy session to see how we'd plan to conquer the obstacles." Instead, it seems to come from a place of, "the obstacles are too great, we'll or you'll never be able to take on and succeed at such a venture.

I've been told or maybe even spoken to the effect myself that this is a result of slavery and Black Americans' inferiority complex, which no one wants to admit we obviously have. Psychologist at NYU have done research and found, "lower power groups tend to develop and perpetuate attitudes and justify their own inferior status." Black American people are the main culprits of this.

Jewish people took their inferior status and somehow made it a virtue; worked and outworked others to become a dominant force within American culture and politics. In that light, the main obstacle for Black American people to overcome is hard, prodigiously long work hours at whatever it is we'd like to do for an employer, our own business or in society; hard work seems to overcome racism, prejudice and discrimination.

Instead of saying "how are you going to do that" when someone mentions their dreams, say, "let's have a planning and strategy meeting to map out steps to be taken in order for you to do that." WORK HARD AND LONG UNTIL IT GETS DONE!

#blackpeople, a movie like "there will b blood'" boring as shit. then realize its actual story of how white men became billionaires n oil biz

The movie "There Will Be Blood"; BORING AS HELL, A DEFINITE SLEEPER! That is until you dig deep into your conscious and realize what the humdrum story is laying before your eyes. The ultimate story/ending is the completion of a road to multi-millionaire or billionaire status; even that is boring within itself. But think, what does it take to actually make $1,000,000, not from a sports or modeling contract, but from work to extrapolate, create and/or sell your own creation?

There Will Be Blood starts with a lone man down in a well hammering away in an attempt to find oil, breaking a leg and almost getting himself crushed in the process; it shows him journalizing his oil findings and sales revenue. He then proselytizes a crew of men (not documented in the film); he sketches and builds an oil drilling rig. In the process of drilling for oil, a baby appears out of nowhere.

He and the baby, at approximately age 10, go on the road to enter into contracts to drill for oil on person's land; contracts, of course most beneficial in royalty payments to himself, the oil driller. He tries to do similar contract deals with entire towns in town hall meetings. A young man then comes to him and sells - not gives him for free - but sells him information there is oil underneath his fathers' land that seeps from

- 314 -

MICHAEL IRVIN WALKER

underground naturally or when shot by a rifle or a shallow dig with hammer and stake. The oil prospector goes and finds this family under the pretense he's camping and hunting; shoots the ground and sees the oil seepage; offers the family a jerk contract to drill on their land; proceeds to the county commissioner's office and buys all of the land surrounding the area. He brings in his team of oil drillers and HE STRIKES A HUGE OIL WELL!

Upon striking the huge oil well, Standard Oil, the company started by John D. Rockerfeller offers him $1,000,000 to buy the property and oil wells. He turns Standard Oils' takeover acquisition down, makes a shared deal with Union Oil to build an oil pipeline across the land and to collect company ownership share of oil sales royalties into perpetuity.

Instead of Jim Crow "You were a Slave and Nigger" movies and/or comedies (which there is nothing wrong with acquiring a good laugh to ease stress), you should, or should I say, I do, try and take something learned and gain from a movie such as: "There Will Be Blood" which shows the hard work and dedication of one man to become a millionaire over a 20 year time period; "The Social Network" how Mark Zuckerberg took his education, combined it with the education of others in his dorm room, writing program code on windows and sparked to fruition a billion dollar idea. Mr. Zuckerberg didn't just wait to graduate and get in line for a great job, he created a job from his direct and learned education; Wall Street 2 "Money Never Sleeps" how the guys on Wall Street make millions of dollars together as a tight knit group, can have meetings with one another and in a few weeks make the economic world market rise or make the market fall.

In the book "Too Big To Fail" by Andrew Ross Sorkin, which the movie Wall Street 2 was loosely based upon, hundreds of White American men and women and a few Black Americans as well, would call upon one another and speak about a billion dollar deal in seconds; within days have teams of people gathered together in conference rooms and offices doing due diligence; flying back and forth to Japan and/or across the United States with little notice, to hold meetings with each other to discuss a deal or work together on one another's behalf; one phone call from a particular person, a telephone meeting between Warren Buffet and Lloyd Blankfein or Jamie Dimon and Richard Fuld or other powerful persons, CEOs and/or CFOs would take place.

These guys would work hours on in through the weekend till 1AM only getting home to get four hours of sleep a night. Tim Geithner slept at the New York Federal Bank office which provided a comfortable bunk I'm sure. But when is the last time you, as a Black American person knew or heard of anyone spending the night at their job site. It wasn't until 2008 that I found out CEOs have showers within their offices; often times staying in the office over-night, with a change of clothes in place to start work fresh early the next morning.

MICHAEL IRVIN WALKER

One aspect also taken from films and reading is that, though it may not be as easy it looks, White American men in particular will lend an ear to their White American brothers in a matter of minutes if the person has something smart and/or ingenious to say; not only that, they give their White American brother the time of day to make a sales pitch and help one another make and move dollars and/or solve problems; this being the impetus of how Mark Zuckerberg took his direct learned education and turned it into billions of dollars of value (granted meetings with the millionaire creator of Napster, Sean Parker).

I do not know how many Black American men CPAs are in the face of Russell Simmons and Andre Harrell at an "Art For Life" event trying to get advice of how to gain celebrity clients or obtaining Russell and Andre as clients, but when I spoke to them on the subject, I was blown off and not given an appropriate time to set up a meeting for a 10 minute chat; I was not given the chance to request a meeting. Yes, I know they are busy, but given Black American's economic status, more time should be allotted by persons of color to persons of color who seek you out as a professional for advice, especially if they've paid $1,500.00 to attend your annual event. And maybe they do; I just wasn't one of the lucky outliers.

I've called and went to the office (unannounced) to meet with a CPA who is known to work with many past music industry clients; handed him my CPA exam credentials. To his credit, he did have a meeting with me, imparted some advice upon me and ultimately decided not to hire me and did not respond to my e-mails afterwards. I can respect that. He gave me an opportunity; maybe there was nothing he could do for me or maybe I BLEW IT! A meeting or even a brief telephone call; I cannot ask for much more than that. I called Jay Brown's RocNation office in California every week or two weeks from June 2014 to February 2015 and was unable to get him on the phone.

#blackpeople I'll say pres obama running/winning has galvanized us politically, which is great. people n bars yelling @ the tv screen iluvit

During the presidential election of 2012, the re-election of President Barack Obama, who was campaigning against Mitt Romney, I watched the 2nd or 3rd televised debate between the two candidates at Voudou Bar in Brooklyn, NY on Nostrand Ave and Halsey Street. The bar was surprisingly packed with people, mostly Black Americans drinking, watching the debate and yelling politically ardent at the television screen regarding answers given by the respective candidates to the issues plaguing America at the time.

I could never recall, in all my lifetime, Black Americans gathering like that politically for a debate, election voting day, town hall meeting, etc. Though it

- 318 -

MICHAEL IRVIN WALKER

was not a surprise that Black American people had really gotten behind the political process in support of Barack Obama, there were a few people who had to make a condescending pithy statement to the crowd, "we are not Obama band wagon political supporters, WE'VE BEEN DOING THIS FOR YEARS"; just how for example, when I mention tennis, I start my conversation of interest with Pete Sampras, Michael Chang and Monica Celes, not the Williams sisters, though I try to do this in a non-condescending manner.

Hopefully political excitement, voting and donating to political campaigns is not a fad for Black Americans to pass with the passing of the two terms of presidency for President Barack Obama. Being involved in the political process is a great thing, whether that involvement is sparked by a candidate who belongs to your particular culture or race, is a part of your chosen political party or is a family member.

One of the problems of Black Americans is that we are not coalesced politically as a force to bring about strong change as was brought about by the civil rights movement or for the purpose of personal gain and political favors granted. Though political favors take lobbying and monetary resources, the process has its core in numbers and votes guaranteed to be delivered or guaranteed to be taken away.

The process needs exercising particularly in local political elections of judges and state prosecutors who are the persons "not" pursuing cases against and/or setting known murderers of Black Americans free and have done so for years as in the following cases: Martin Luther King, Huey Newton, Emmet Till, Medgar Evers, Usef Hawkins, Amadou Diallo, Sean Bell, Oscar Grant, Treyvon Martin, Philando Castile and the list goes on and on; no one has ever served a day of a prison sentence in the murder of those Black American men.

Judges and prosecutors sooner or later get appointed to the Supreme Court of The United States of America; the highest court in the land which could technically mandate that Black Americans be stripped of their freedom and become slaves and property once again. Therefore, it is important to know if a judge or prosecutor sees a Black American face, particularly dark skinned, and per Malcolm Gladwell, in a "BLINK" instantly sees an innate criminal, instantly guilty, who deserves to be unjustly locked up for many years.

Political power will get Black Americans justice when police or civilian White American men and women murder unarmed Black American men, women and children. Political power can get Black Americans CEO post of fortune 500 companies. Political power can build self-made Black American Fortune 500 companies. Political power can ensure Black American children are properly educated with a critical thinking and analytical mind, within a public

MICHAEL IRVIN WALKER

school system no less. Political power and influence can gain a particular group of people rights, which the written law of the land says they should not have, i.e. illegal Latino/Hispanic immigrants being granted amnesty and indemnity from ever being deported back to their homeland; demands met by immigrants that services be granted in their native homeland language to make life easier for them in their illegal homeland; there is even political power in an illegal immigrant population.

Iluvit @MinxMalone @berealblack4me @theroot247 black women as oversexed, yeah right. a black woman never sucked my dick w/o a 2 hr discussion

@MinxMalone @berealblack4me @theroot247 black women as mindless nincompoops u complain. black women as beautiful intellects u complain

@MinxMalone @berealblack4me @theroot247 article was complete bullshit. how is a beautiful intelligent sexy black woman an anesthetization

SCANDAL! While everyone loves the television show starring Kerry Washington, every Black American female seems to be caught up in the conundrum "I love the show, BUT WHY DOES SHE HAVE TO BE HAVING AN AFFAIR WITH A

MARRIED MAN?" One young woman, per the tweet above says the character of Olivia Pope is just an anesthetization of Black American slave girl, mammie, oversexed Black American woman of old.

Let us address the over-sexed issue first and foremost. Black American women are the least sexed; hence why 90% or more of the Black American NBA/NFL stars schtup and/or marry anything other than a beautiful dark skinned Black American woman. The mammie characters of old and/or the slave characters who were being raped by their slave masters, were in no way a desirable image and I've never seen a movie (though I'm sure there is one) where the Black American woman admired or liked and eagerly awaited her status of being awoken in the middle of the night to a penis shoved in her ass or mouth by massa; but rather I saw someone who fell into her forced roll, which she had no power to repudiate.

Olivia Pope of the television show "Scandal", a beautiful, educated, articulate Black American woman with power to move mountains, even the two mountains hanging below the President of the United States waist, how can she ever be compared to Kizzy of the television movie "Roots"?

Black American women are looking at the television show "Scandal" situation from a totally blind-sided perspective. Think about this: how intelligent of a paragon must one be to get into the sphere of the President; how sexy and alluring does a

MICHAEL IRVIN WALKER

woman have to be to get noticed by the President; even after getting noticed, how adroit, daring and self-assured does a Black American woman have to be to get her hands, mouth or her vagina onto the President's penis; a married president at that? (YES, GIVE MONICA LEWINSKY HER PROPER RESPECT!)

When you answer those questions, Olivia Pope is not some worthless piece of trash quietly sleeping in her slave quarters, suddenly stunned by her powerful master who comes in and takes her virginity away from her. Olivia had/has the power to get what she wants out of the President or deny his advances. Olivia Pope is the Black American woman that Black American men desire to marry: beautiful, ambitious, a go-getter, sexy, has educational and monetary paper (meaning paper college degree and paper money respectively) and commands attention when she walks into a room, particularly, the White House Oval Office!

A fact which many people, but I'm particularly speaking of Black American people, may not know (though I'm sure as of 2022, it is widely known); Olivia Pope was created and financed by a Black American woman, Shonda Rhimes, the executive producer of the show.

The executive producer green lights every detail of a show; the writing, the clothing, the hair, the make-up, the salacious scenes; if the executive producer doesn't agree, best believe things will get changed and in a hurry. Not only is the star of the show a non-half White American woman, Kerry Washington; the person in charge of the writing and financial responsibility for the shows continued success, Shonda Rhimes, is also A BLACK AMERICAN WOMAN!

Some young girls of my generation wanted to be Wonder Woman (a White American woman), Dolly Parton (a White American woman), Bo Derrick (a White American woman), Daisy Duke (even little Black American boys such as myself wanted a piece of Daisy Duke, a White American woman), Alex Carrington of Dynasty (a White American woman), Nikki Newman of the Young And The Restless (a White American woman); something they all could never be, A WHITE AMERICAN WOMAN!

Now, in this day in age, Olivia Pope, a regular Black American woman, no White American mixed in, educated with an ambitious nature; would it be so bad if a little Black American girl said to her mommy, "Mom, when I grow up, I WANT TO BE LIKE OLIVIA POPE! EDUCATED, BEAUTIFUL, SEXY, GREAT CAREER; even though in relations with a married man, just so happens he's the most POWERFUL MAN IN THE ENTIRE FREE WORLD! As we all know, love is not perfect. If Olivia Pope was with some married corner store Joe or someone on her own level career wise and financially, I may also have reservations. But the President of The United States ..

MICHAEL IRVIN WALKER

#blackpeople notice affirmative action n corporation has benefitted white women more than any other minority. white men promote white women

#blackpeople. moderators of debates: white man, white woman & white. my testament 2 fact white women gained affirmative action advantage

#blackpeople could some1 please tell me the U.S. problem with black men. every construction site, home reno, bridge, no black men working

#blackpeople Obama administration has achievement cards 4 groups: women, Jews, gays & lesbians. @ there was no card for African-Americans

In addition to things that Black American people should notice amongst ourselves, we should also notice other things that go on around us. For example, there has been a movement in the last 10 to 15 years to promote women in corporate America and Fortune 500 companies. Since I've been working in Corporate White America, a woman has either hired me directly, had significant input on the hiring decision or once I received an offer and was on the job, women had been in equal or higher positions than I.

It seems to my eyes view that no other movement in American history has moved as fast as the movement to give women, but particularly White American women, equal pay, place them among the ilk of high-status management CEO, COO, CFO and board of director positions. I recently read Dec 5, 2013, after Twitter appointed Marjorie Scardino, a White American woman, as its first woman board member, that companies are succumbing to outside/media pressure and criticism of a boy's club of executives. Major companies are responding swiftly and precipitously.

Sheryl Sandberg who was the COO of Facebook in 2014 (may still be) has been given a prominent face among women as a proponent of equality for women in corporate America. I read her book "Lean-In" and everything which she said regarding women - with the exception of the men in high profile business meetings not knowing where the women's bathroom was - could be attributed to Black American people, both men and women.

Yes, there was the civil rights movement and affirmative action, but yet, how many Black American CEO men of major Fortune 500 companies can you count since that enactment of law? The first Black American CEO I've known of a Fortune 500 Company was of AOL/TimeWarner in 2001. Currently as of this writing, there are only 6 Black American CEOs of Fortune 500 companies: Kenneth Chenault of American Express (a very light/half White American man), Ursula Burns of Xerox (a real brown to dark

- 326 -

MICHAEL IRVIN WALKER

skinned Black American woman with a low cut afro to boot), Clarence Otis of Darden Restaurants (never heard of him nor Darden), Roger Ferguson of TIAA-CREF (dark skinned Black American male) and Don Thompson (brown to dark skinned Black American male) of McDonalds; 6 out of 500, that's 1.2%, compared with 18 (including Ursula Burns) out of 500 CEOs who are women, that's 3.4% with the Burns exclusion; double that of Black American men.

Excluding CEO post, there have been many more women invited to the executive ranks of Fortune 500 and prominent upcoming powerful companies who will be stars in the future of our coming generations; the number of women is out pacing the number of Black American men gaining ranks to management positions or even being given the opportunity to step foot in the companies to prove themselves worthy.

Though a Black American, half White American man has become President of the United States of America before any woman - White American, Black American or half White American - a White American woman is in line right behind him in the form of Hillary Clinton (she blew that with "I Carry Hot Sause In My Bag"; pandering a lot too much.)

It took Black American people forty to fifty years to gain a slither of parity in access to corporate job opportunity, political office, college admissions, etc. In what I can see as fifteen years at the most, with a lot of noise particularly in the last 5 years, women have gained access and equal rights, equal job positions, equal pay (my last job, a woman two years my senior was being paid $165,000 more than I), relegating some men to the status of "stay at home dads", FASTER THAN ANY OTHER DISADVANTAGED RACE OF PEOPLE, MOST OF ALL, LIGHT YEARS FASTER THAN BLACK AMERICAN PEOPLE!

After President Obama's re-election to the presidency in 2012, I recall hearing about a forum he held in Washington. The topic of discussion was achievement cards of: gays and lesbians, women, Jews. Here it was, a Black American man (though half White American) was having a forum for disadvantaged groups of persons seeking equal treatment in the world, in the work force to receive equal pay, etc. And yet, BLACK AMERICAN MEN WERE NOT INCLUDED and up FOR DISCUSSION!

Everyone knows the statistics: near non-existent enrollment into colleges and universities, highest jail and prison population, also (along with Black American women) precluded from the good-ole-boys clubs and opportunity when allowed into corporate America.

Who is looking at our achievement progress and trying to increase our Black American numbers of participation? If not the Black (though Half White American) President of the United States, WE AS BLACK PEOPLE, ESPECIALLY MEN, ARE FUCKED!

MICHAEL IRVIN WALKER

The gay and lesbian movement is also running at a high speed: gay couples on almost every television show appearing in explicit sex scenes on primetime television; appearing on day time soap operas. A gay woman ran for mayor of New York City in 2013. Gay celebrities and television show host are coming out of the closet in droves; an NBA player came out and admitted he was gay in 2013; a college football player came out as gay before the 2014 NFL draft combine; a famous Hip Hop DJ in New York City came out and admitted he liked to participate in receiving fellatio from transgender dressed male prostitutes.

There is a wide level of acceptance for the gay and lesbian movement. Yet again, I have to look askance at this level of acceptance when Black American men have been crying for justice in employment opportunity (still the highest unemployed of any group), justice in the courts (still receiving the highest sentences for crimes than persons of other races who commit equal crimes or worse), justice in media and celebrity status (just ask Kanye West; though he has received his just do; but once again, ONLY A BLACK CELEBIRITY CAN).

BLACK AMERICAN MEN ARE STILL SUFFERING and there is not, has not been and seemingly never will be a great shift in the paradigm of a show toward equality, justice and freedom as there is for women, gays and lesbians.

While I'm not complaining about women, gays and lesbians having equal rights, I am complaining about the speed and rapacious nature at which women's, gays and lesbians concerns are being heard and quickly addressed; the equality is not being proportionately distributed. And, it seems no one is hiding the fact, no one is bringing it up to the forefront and/or NO ONE, NOT EVEN PRESIDENT BARACK OBAMA, GIVES A DAMN!

against the gay special movement when as a black man I still get discriminated against n the job hunt. I CAN'T TAKE OFF MY BLACK! #thetalk

against the gay special movement, & no, it is not the same as civil rights movement, hell, black people can barely get on tv shows

It has been said, "The gay and lesbian legal marriage movement is akin to the Black American Civil Rights Movement of the 60s." How so? Black American people were human beings just like we all are, law abiding citizens just like the majority of other Americans and participating in normal everyday activities just like the majority of other Americans: eating, drinking, going to the restroom, producing children for the extension and betterment of the future world and working jobs to support the maintenance of life and freedom. Gay and lesbian people do all of those same things also.

- 330 -

MICHAEL IRVIN WALKER

Where do I draw the line? The line gets drawn where you want the law to consider an alternative that the majority of persons in the nation do not participate in. I've come up with another analogy as I see fit to the gay marriage rights fight. A group of people suddenly decide they do not want to wear clothing anymore or to rather expose their genitals as a right of freedom and expression. They are not hurting anyone right? If you do not like it, don't look at the exposed genitalia; as long as they abide by the law, cause no harm to other citizens and are respectful productive citizens themselves, its fine right? We'll just make it law for them to not wear clothing; for no American shall be forced to or denied the right to live as he freely sees fit right? WRONG!

Gay and lesbianism though persons may be born or predisposed naturally to be that way, it is not the normal behavior of the majority of human beings. It is not natural and if it was the sole natural way (only homosexuals with absolutely no cross categorization of male and females) of human beings, the human race would surcease; even though the gay and lesbian argument is, they can and do produce children.

In tandem with their child bearing argument could be an argument for the legalization of drugs; drugs cause you to act weird, but it should be a person's choice to take them with their weird conscious altering effects or not to take them; the option of not taking them (just as the option of gay and lesbian people to produce children) and the

- 331 -

choice to live drug free is what leaves the gate open for the possibility that not everyone will take drugs, endanger their lives and the lives of others and profligately destroy human society.

Gay people love each other, do no harm to others, work and function like other human beings, but the gay life style is still an alternative. Laws should not be created to foster alternatives, which could potentially (though highly unlikely) destroy the human race; therefore, marriage should not be legalized.

Marriage is between a man and woman to produce offspring for the population, growth and continuity of human society. With no man and woman bonding to produce offspring, there should not be marriage and lawful privileges which are existent for the promulgation of marriage and family life; no tax breaks for gay couples.

You may choose a person, whomever you wish (gay, straight, boyfriend, girlfriend, child) as a dependent or family member to provide employee health insurance under the family plan. Estates should have a one-time tax exclusion to immediate blood family members only: husband and wife who intended to marry for the reproduction and maintenance of family legacy and human life, and their birth children only. One step further, the estate tax should be lower for a one-time pass down to anyone the grantor sees fit (gay, straight, boyfriend, girlfriend) NO SPECIAL CAVEATS AND/OR RIDERS FOR GAYS AND LESBIANS! PERIOD!

MICHAEL IRVIN WALKER

As the gay and lesbian rights movement pertains to the Civil Rights Movement, it does not compare: Black American people were not an alternative species of human being, Black American people (with the exception of a minority few who could pass for White American) could not hide their skin color; choose to stay quiet about their race and private home life and go about in the world usurping normal advantageous opportunities, legally and/or successfully run their own companies/industries in the economic, art and political world.

To recapitulate the point once again, Ruth Bader Ginsburg stated in a New York Times article titled "The Unsinkable R.B.G. ". "The speed with which the country has already accepted gay rights was, just a matter of gay people coming out, and the rest of the country realizing that "we all knew and liked and loved people who were gay." Yeah, that sounds nice from a well-respected female legal mind and member of The Supreme Court of the United States of America.

My immediate instantaneous thought, and I quote, "The thing that DOES NOT make the Gay and Lesbian Rights Movement akin to the Civil Rights Movement, is that with the exception of a few creole, light-skinned and half White/Black Americans, **MOST OF US COULD NEVER TAKE OFF OR PUT OUR BLACKNESS IN THE CLOSET FOR AMERICA TO REALIZE THEY LOVED US FIRST, AND THAT WE WERE BLACK SECOND!!!**

- 333 -

However, gay people, particularly gay White American males, in the closet or not, have made tremendous strides, held the reigns of success and shared that success with their White American brothers, gay or not. Black American people could not make such power moves by hiding or naturally being a part of the power structure of the land.

Sure, Black American people could not legally marry White American people, but that is a small hick-up compared to what gay people could do just by the mere fact of hiding under a veil. And even in the denying of miscegenation, those marriages were still in line with the majority of other Americans or human beings; between men and women with the intent to naturally procreate for the succession of society and the human race.

I do not condone discrimination, denial of entry, loss of job or the loss of basic societal liberty of gay and lesbian people, but the creation of laws for the special purpose of LGBTQ, I say NO!

MICHAEL IRVIN WALKER

EPILOGUE:

I started writing this book in 2012, have equivocated on rather to release my name and identity with it, as it contains very controversial topics, particularly Gay and Lesbian marriage rights, for which I hope I will not be cancelled before I even get started.

Many things have changed since the first draft; most notably, Brian Grazier, Ron Howard and Joel Cohen executive producing / directing television shows and movies starring Black Americans. As of Dec 2021 / Jan 2022 there is even another television show on NBC starring regular Non half White/Black American people, "Grand Crew".

LGBTQ have marriage rights and other rights as well, and I am not up in arms / ire about that.

My dreams of building a successful Black American CPA Firm have been palliated and made moribund.

There is no intended disrespect to those mentioned in the book who have since passed in life: Andre Harrell, Sidney Poitier (he was married to a Black American woman), Ruth Bader Ginsburg or any others since deceased that I have not mentioned here.

Upon moving to Los Angles, I discovered that all people are brand-washed by NIKE; particularly Air Force I, Dunk Lo Pro, Jordans, & still Air Max.

I have given up on criticizing Black American women for their hairstyle (weave/braid) choices. Their hair is the most difficult to maintain; for even the wearing to bonnets (though I do not approve) I understand; the covering and protection of Black American women's hair from sun and dryness is important to its growth, moisturization and greater presentation when the time comes: date, lady's night, church, wedding, etc.

In 2022, a real Black American (Non-Mixed with White) woman, Ketanji Brown Jackson, has been nominated to the Supreme Court of the United States; a historic first, yet, as seemingly with all Black American historic first, there is White American mixed in somehow (husband White; children Mixed Black/White American).

Some things have not changed, such as I still cannot gain any footing in Corporate America with a CPA License; White American women, Asian American and White American men are still being paid double to triple what I am; see the payroll journal (mentioned prior) attached; particularly, White American woman, paid $185,000, Asian American woman paid $250,000, White American man (non-college degree) paid $300,000 (take earnings/salary column, multiply by 24). As it seems, I am not a good enough accountant, even with a CPA License - and it seems the only form of generational wealth for Black American people - I am focusing on creativity and entertainment as my sole subsistence until death do I part!

MICHAEL IRVIN WALKER

The journey of:

NEVER AGAIN APPLYING FOR AN ACCOUNTING JOB, SURVIVING IN THE MOMENTS AND BEING A FULL-TIME ENTERTAINER BEGINS JANUARY 2, 2022.

Follow me on instagram:

@michael_irvin_walker

@blk_peepstop (I.G. DISABLED THIS ACCOUNT)

YOU ARE NOT HUNGRY

NOR PARCHED!

YOU ARE WARM!

YOU ARE RESTED!

LIVE IN THE MOMENT!

DON'T STRESS IT!

- 338 -

MICHAEL IRVIN WALKER

Biography:

Michael Irvin Walker, CPA graduated from Youngstown State University – Major Accounting; obtained his Certified Public Accountant License in December 2013; has been fired from eight corporate employers: The Strober Organization, Draft WorldWide Advertising Agency, Titan Outdoor Advertising, Sforza & Walker CPAs (not a partner), Livewell Care Inc, Verifi Inc, Green Lots Inc, and one non-disclosed.

Michael has always had a penchant for writing, as started by his 12th Grade literature teacher who started her students writing daily journals; see his personal journals which he started chronicling around 1999 and have placed on Wordpress: The Only Child 1988 Coming of Age in the New Millennium.

After living in New York City for 16 years, Michael moved in 2015 back to Warren, OH the hometown in which he was born; subsequently 6 months later, moved to Los Angeles, CA June 19, 2016. He has since been passively pursuing an acting career, attending acting classes in: dramatic improv, on-camera audition technique and scene study. As of November 19, 2021 after being fired from his 8th corporate accounting job - 6th as a CPA - he has officially declared himself: ACTOR, VOICE-OVER ACTOR, WRITER, RAPPER AND POD-CAST PRODUCER!

PAYROLL JOURNAL

EMPLOYEE NAME ID	HOURS, EARNINGS, REIMBURSEMENTS & OTHER PAYMENTS					WITHHOLDINGS		DEDUCTIONS	NET PAY ALLOCATIONS
	DESCRIPTION	RATE	HOURS	EARNINGS	REIMB & OTHER PAYMENTS				
▉	Salary			3,900.00		Social Security	243.81	OPS	Direct Deposit # 115529
	Reimb Txble			32.50		Medicare	57.02		Net Pay 3,301.85
						Fed Income Tax	329.82		Check Amt 0.00
	EMPLOYEE TOTAL			3,932.50			630.65		Chkg 100 2,314.31
									2,314.31
▉	Salary			3,125.00		Social Security	196.85	Exec Asst	Net Pay 2,314.11
	Reimb Txble			50.00		Medicare	46.04		2,314.11
						Fed Income Tax	406.31		
						CA Income Tax	173.59		
	EMPLOYEE TOTAL			3,175.00		CA Disability	38.10		
▉	Salary	96.67		2,708.33		Social Security	167.91	OPS	Net Pay 1,851.49
						Medicare	39.27		617.16
	EMPLOYEE TOTAL			2,708.33		CA Disability	32.50		617.16
							660.89	Garnishment 3	
▉	Salary			4,583.33		Social Security	289.89	POP EE Pretax	Net Pay 3,067.23
						Medicare	65.69	OP	52.93
						Fed Income Tax	755.67		52.93
	EMPLOYEE TOTAL			4,583.33		CA Income Tax	306.56		
						CA Disability	54.36		
▉	Salary	96.67		6,041.67		Social Security	1,463.17	POP EE Post Tax	Net Pay 4,322.66
						Medicare	87.61	OPS	208.13
						Fed Income Tax	1,032.38		208.13
						WA PML	7.25		
	EMPLOYEE TOTAL			6,041.67		WA PFL	8.05		
▉	Salary	96.67		10,416.67		Social Security	645.83	MRKTG	Net Pay 6,881.38
						Medicare	151.04		
						Fed Income Tax	2,402.16		
	EMPLOYEE TOTAL			10,416.67		IN Income Tax	336.46		
							3,535.49		
▉	Salary			10,416.67		Social Security	151.52	CFO $250k	Net Pay 6,522.57
	Reimb Txble			32.50		Medicare	2,178.67		6,522.57
						Fed Income Tax	823.17		
	EMPLOYEE TOTAL			10,449.17		CA Income Tax	125.39		
						CA Disability	3,925.60		

0087 1906-6233 ▮

EMPLOYEE NAME / ID

HOURS, EARNINGS, REIMBURSEMENTS & OTHER PAYMENTS

Period Start - End Date 11/01/21 - 11/15/21
Check Date 11/15/21

ID (Employee)	DESCRIPTION	RATE	HOURS	EARNINGS	REIMB & OTHER PAYMENTS	WITHHOLDINGS	DEDUCTIONS	NET PAY ALLOCATIONS
▮	Salary			4,375.00		Social Security 273.27		
	Reimb Txble			32.50		Medicare 63.91		
	EMPLOYEE TOTAL			4,407.50		Fed Income Tax 726.17		
						CA Income Tax 285.41		
						CA Disability 52.89		
						1,411.65	Chkg 2.89 — MERCH OPS	Net Pay 2,995.85
▮	Salary			5,000.00		Social Security 310.00		
	EMPLOYEE TOTAL			5,000.00		Medicare 72.50		
						Fed Income Tax 825.38		
						CA Income Tax 398.28		
						CA Disability 60.00		
						1,628.16	POP EE Post Tax 59.99 — DESIGN ENG	Net Pay 3,371.84
▮	Salary			5,000.00		Social Security 310.00		
	EMPLOYEE TOTAL			5,000.00		Medicare 72.50		
						Fed Income Tax 658.71		
						IN Income Tax 161.50		
						1,202.71	POP EE Post Tax 59.99 — OPS	Net Pay 3,737.30
▮	Salary			7,708.33		Social Security 479.93		
	Reimb Txble			32.50		Medicare 112.24		
	EMPLOYEE TOTAL			7,740.83		Fed Income Tax 896.61		
						CA Income Tax 646.67		
						CA Disability 92.89		
						2,194.34	POP EE Post Tax 263.92 — LWYR $185k	Net Pay 5,282.57
▮	Salary			3,937.50		Social Security 246.14		
	Reimb Txble			32.50		Medicare 57.57		
	EMPLOYEE TOTAL			3,970.00		Fed Income Tax 581.21		
						IL Income Tax 195.52		
						1,081.44	OPS	Net Pay 2,888.56
▮	Salary			4,583.33		Social Security 286.18		
	Reimb Txble			32.50		Medicare 66.93		
	EMPLOYEE TOTAL			4,615.83		Fed Income Tax 819.17		
						CA Income Tax 320.98		
						CA Disability 55.39		
						1,548.65	MRKTG OPS	Net Pay 3,067.18
▮ (cont.)	Salary			5,208.33		Social Security 324.93		
	Reimb Txble			32.50		Medicare 75.99		
						Fed Income Tax 840.17		
						CA Income Tax 307.87		
						CA Disability 62.89		
							POP EE Post Tax 244.59 — OPS	Net Pay ▮

PAYROLL JOURNAL

EMPLOYEE NAME / ID	DESCRIPTION	RATE	HOURS	EARNINGS	REIMB & OTHER PAYMENTS	WITHHOLDINGS		DEDUCTIONS		NET PAY ALLOCATIONS	
(cont.)											
■■■■ (cont.)	EMPLOYEE TOTAL			5,240.83		Medicare	1,671.85	POP EE Post Tax	244.59	Net Pay	3,324.39
19	Salary			12,500.00		Fed Income Tax	3,268.11	COO $300K			
	Reimb Txble			32.50		CA Income Tax	1,035.29				
	EMPLOYEE TOTAL			12,525.50		Medicare	4,598.91		2.78	Net Pay	7,930.81
	Salary			8,333.33		Fed Income Tax	1,170.13	POP EE Post Tax	473.41	Net Pay	
	EMPLOYEE TOTAL			8,333.33		Medicare	120.83	ENGNR CODE			
	Salary			8,333.33		Social Security	1,293.96	$200K			
	Reimb Txble	M686.67		32.50		Medicare	247.44	POP EE Post Tax	473.41	Net Pay	6,568.96
	EMPLOYEE TOTAL			8,333.33		Fed Income Tax		BLK ACCTNT	51.50		
	Salary			3,125.00		CA Income Tax	47.89	$95K			
■■■■ Ahmadi	EMPLOYEE TOTAL	98.67		3,125.00		CA Disability					
38						Social Security	193.75	HR	51.50	Net Pay	
						Medicare	45.31				
						Fed Income Tax	395.31				
						CA Income Tax	168.47	OPS	123.02	Net Pay	2,284.86
	Salary			3,125.00		CA Disability	37.50				
	Reimb Txble			32.50		Social Security	840.34	POP EE Post Tax	123.02	Net Pay	
	EMPLOYEE TOTAL			5,971.88		Medicare	87.07	OPS			
	Salary			6,004.38		Fed Income Tax	778.01				
	Reimb Txble			32.50		CO Income Tax	235.00	OPS	123.02	Net Pay	4,411.01
	EMPLOYEE TOTAL			3,958.33		Social Security	1,470.35	POP EE Post Tax	25.78		
	Salary			3,958.33		Medicare	247.43				
	Reimb Txble			32.50		Fed Income Tax	57.87				
	EMPLOYEE TOTAL			3,990.83		Medicare	565.80			Net Pay	3,073.85
	Salary	260.01				Fed Income Tax	891.10		25.78		
	Reimb Txble					Social Security				Check Amt	0.00
						Medicare				Dir Dep	80,096.59
						Fed Income Tax					

PAYROLL JOURNAL

0087 1906-6233

EMPLOYEE NAME	ID	HOURS, EARNINGS, REIMBURSEMENTS & OTHER PAYMENTS					WITHHOLDINGS	DEDUCTIONS	NET PAY ALLOCATIONS
		DESCRIPTION	RATE	HOURS	EARNINGS	REIMB & OTHER PAYMENTS			

WITHHOLDINGS

CA Income Tax	4,716.24
CA Disability	656.80
CO Income Tax	226.00
IL Income Tax	196.52
IN Income Tax	487.96
WA EE PFL	8.05
WA EE PML	7.25
	33,037.73

Employer Liabilities

Social Security	5,845.06
Medicare	1,670.47
Fed Unemploy	14.30
CA Unemploy	116.75
CA Emp Train	2.38

(IC) = Independent Contractor

Period Start - End Date   11/01/21 - 11/15/21
Check Date   11/15/21

www.ingramcontent.com/pod-product-compliance
Lightning Source LLC
Chambersburg PA
CBHW022044020426
42335CB00012B/531